The Essential Guide to Becoming a Master Student

Custom Edition

2/28

read Ch. 8
"Creating Relationships"
Journal entry 19 + 20

Self assessment
essay

Dave Ellis

CENGAGE
Learning·

Australia • Brazil • Japan • Korea • Mexico • Singapore • Spain • United Kingdom • United States

CENGAGE
Learning·

The Essential Guide to Becoming a Master Student:Custom Edition

The Essential Guide to Becoming a Master Student, Third Edition
Dave Ellis

© 2013, 2011, 2009 Cengage Learning. All rights reserved.

Becoming a Master Student: Concise
Dave Ellis

© 2013 Cengage Learning. All rights reserved.

On Course: Strategies for Creating Success in College and in Life
Skip Downing

© 2014, 2011 Cengage Learning. All rights reserved.

Senior Manager, Student Engagement:

Linda deStefano

Manager, Student Engagement:

Julie Dierig

Marketing Manager:

Rachael Kloos

Manager, Premedia:

Kim Fry

Manager, Intellectual Property Project Manager:

Brian Methe

Senior Manager, Production:

Donna M. Brown

Manager, Production:

Terri Daley

For product information and technology assistance, contact us at
Cengage Learning Customer & Sales Support, 1-800-354-9706

For permission to use material from this text or product,
submit all requests online at **cengage.com/permissions**
Further permissions questions can be emailed to
permissionrequest@cengage.com

This book contains select works from existing Cengage Learning resources and was produced by Cengage Learning Custom Solutions for collegiate use. As such, those adopting and/or contributing to this work are responsible for editorial content accuracy, continuity and completeness.

Compilation © 2014 Cengage Learning

ISBN: 9781305280953

WCN: 01-100-101

Cengage Learning
20 Channel Center Street
Boston, MA 02210
USA

Cengage Learning is a leading provider of customized learning solutions with office locations around the globe, including Singapore, the United Kingdom, Australia, Mexico, Brazil, and Japan. Locate your local office at:
www.international.cengage.com/region.

Cengage Learning products are represented in Canada by Nelson Education, Ltd.

For your lifelong learning solutions, visit **www.cengage.com/custom.**

Visit our corporate website at **www.cengage.com.**

Brief Contents

Images: Oliver Cleve/Getty Images

Contents

CHAPTER 4 Participating in Class & Taking Notes 51

CHAPTER 5 Maximizing Your Memory & Mastering Tests 67

CHAPTER 6 Using Technology to Succeed 81

CHAPTER 7 Thinking Clearly & Communicating Your Ideas 93

CHAPTER 8 **Creating Positive Relationships**   **107**

CHAPTER 9 **Choosing Greater Health**   **123**

CHAPTER 10 **Choosing Your Major & Planning Your Career**   **135**

Getting Involved

Use this **Master Student Map** to ask yourself

WHY THE INTRODUCTION MATTERS . . .

- You can ease your transition to higher education and set up a lifelong pattern of success by starting with some key strategies.

WHAT IS INCLUDED . . .

HOW YOU CAN USE THIS INTRODUCTION . . .

- Connect with the natural learner within me.
- Discover ways to interact with this book that multiply its value.
- Use a journal to translate personal discoveries into powerful new behaviors.

WHAT IF . . .

- I could use the ideas in this book to get what I want in my life more consistently?

© Ruslan Ivantsov/Shutterstock.com

JOURNAL ENTRY 1

Discover what you want from this book

Start becoming a master student this moment by doing a 5-minute chapter preview. The goal is for you to get the big picture of what this chapter includes in order to help you understand and recall the details later.

Here's how to do the preview: Look at every page in this chapter. Move quickly. Scan headlines. Look at pictures. Notice any forms, charts, and diagrams. Then complete the following sentences.

Three things that I can do right away to promote my success in school are …

_____

_____

_____

What I want most from this book and this course is …

_____

_____

_____

_____

_____

POWER process

Discover what you want

Imagine a person who walks up to a counter at the airport to buy a plane ticket for his next vacation. "Just give me a ticket," he says to the reservation agent. "Anywhere will do."

The agent stares back at him in disbelief. "I'm sorry, sir," she replies. "I'll need some more details. Just minor things—such as the name of your destination city and your arrival and departure dates."

"Oh, I'm not fussy," says the would-be vacationer. "I just want to get away. You choose for me."

Compare this person to another traveler who walks up to the counter and says, "I'd like a ticket to Ixtapa, Mexico, departing on Saturday, March 23, and returning Sunday, April 7. Please give me a window seat, first class, with vegetarian meals."

Now, ask yourself which traveler is more likely to end up with a vacation that he'll enjoy.

The same principle applies in any area of life. Knowing where we want to go increases the probability that we will arrive at our destination. Discovering what we want makes it more likely that we'll attain it.

Okay, so the example about the traveler with no destination is far-fetched. Before you dismiss it, though, do an informal experiment: Ask three other students what they want to get out of their education. Be prepared for hemming and hawing, vague generalities, and maybe even a helping of pie in the sky à la mode.

This is amazing, considering the stakes involved. Students routinely invest years of their lives and thousands of dollars, with only a hazy idea of their destination in life.

Now suppose that you asked someone what she wanted from her education and you got this answer: "I plan to get a degree in journalism with double minors in earth science and Portuguese so that I can work as a reporter covering the environment in Brazil." The details of a person's vision offer clues to their skills and sense of purpose.

Another clue is the presence of "stretch goals"—those that are big *and* achievable. A 40-year-old might spend years talking about his desire to be a professional athlete some day. Chances are, that's no longer achievable. However, setting a goal to lose 10 pounds by playing basketball at the gym 3 days a week is another matter. That's a stretch—a challenge. It's also doable.

Discovering what you want helps you succeed in higher education. Many students quit school simply because they are unsure about what they want from it. With well-defined goals in mind, you can look for connections between what you want and what you study. The more connections, the more likely you'll stay in school—and get what you want in every area of life.[1]

You're One Click Away …
from accessing Power Process media online and finding out more about "Discovering what you want."

Making the transition to higher education: *Five things you can do now*

© razihusin/Shutterstock.com

1. Plug into resources. A supercharger increases the air supply to an internal combustion engine. The resulting difference in power can be dramatic. You can make just as powerful a difference in your education if you supercharge it by using all of the resources available to students. In this case, your "air supply" includes people, campus clubs and organizations, and school and community services.

Of all resources, people are the most important. You can isolate yourself, study hard, and get a good education. However, doing this is not the most powerful use of your tuition money. When you establish relationships with teachers, staff members, fellow students, and potential employers, you can get a *great* education. Build a network of people who will personally support your success in school.

Accessing resources is especially important if you are the first person in your family to enter higher education. As a first-generation student, you are having experiences that people in your family may not understand. Talk to your relatives about your activities at school. If they ask how they can help you, give specific answers. Also ask your instructors about programs for first-generation students on your campus.

2. Meet with your academic advisor. One person in particular—your academic advisor—can help you access resources and make the transition to higher education. Meet with this person regularly. Advisors generally know about course requirements, options for declaring majors, and the resources available at your school. Peer advisors might also be available.

When you work with an advisor, remember that you're a paying customer and have a right to be satisfied with the service you get. Change advisors if that seems appropriate.

3. Show up for class. The amount that you pay in tuition and fees makes a powerful argument for going to classes regularly. In large part, the material that you're tested on comes from events that take place in class.

Showing up for class occurs on two levels. The most visible level is being physically present in the classroom. Even more important, though, is showing up mentally. This kind of attendance includes taking detailed notes, asking questions, and contributing to class discussions.

Succeeding in school can help you get almost anything you want, including the career, income, and relationships you desire. Attending class is an investment in yourself.

4. Take the initiative in meeting new people. Realize that most of the people in this new world of higher education are waiting to be welcomed. You can help them and help yourself at the same time. Introduce yourself to classmates and instructors. Just before or after class is a good time.

Perhaps you imagined that higher education would be a hotbed of social activity—and now find yourself feeling lonely and disconnected. Your feelings are common. Remember that plugging into the social networks at any school takes time—and it's worth the effort. Connecting to school socially as well as academically promotes your success and your enjoyment.

5. Admit your feelings—whatever they are. School can be an intimidating experience for new students. People of diverse cultures, adult learners, commuters, and people with disabilities may feel excluded. Feelings of anxiety, isolation, and homesickness are common among students.

Those emotions are common among new students, and there's nothing wrong with them. Simply admitting the truth about how you feel—to yourself and to someone else—can help you cope. And you can almost always do something constructive in the present moment, no matter how you feel.

If your feelings about the transition to higher education make it hard for you to carry out the activities of daily life—going to class, working, studying, and relating to people—then get professional help. Start with a counselor at the student health service on your campus. The mere act of seeking help can make a difference. ◼

You're One Click Away …
from more strategies for mastering the art of transition.

Master student *qualities*

This book is about something that cannot be taught. It's about becoming a master student.

Mastery means attaining a level of skill that goes beyond technique. For a master, work is effortless; struggle evaporates. The master carpenter is so familiar with her tools that they are part of her. To a master chef, utensils are old friends. Because these masters don't have to think about the details of the process, they bring more of themselves to their work.

Mastery can lead to flashy results: an incredible painting, for example, or a gem of a short story. In basketball, mastery might result in an unbelievable shot at the buzzer. For a musician, it might be the performance of a lifetime, the moment when everything comes together. You could describe these experiences as "flow" or being "in the zone."

Often, the result of mastery is a sense of profound satisfaction, well-being, and timelessness. Distractions fade. Time stops. Work becomes

© Oliver Cleve/Getty Images

play. After hours of patient practice, after setting clear goals and getting precise feedback, the master has learned to be fully in control.

At the same time, he lets go of control. Results happen without effort, struggle, or worry. Work seems self-propelled. The master is in control by being out of control. He lets go and allows the creative process to take over. That's why after a spectacular performance by an athlete or artist, observers often say, "He played full out—and made it look like he wasn't even trying."

Likewise, the master student is one who makes learning look easy. She works hard without seeming to make any effort. She's relaxed *and* alert, disciplined *and* spontaneous, focused *and* fun-loving.

You might say that those statements don't make sense. Actually, mastery does *not* make sense. It cannot be captured with words. It defies analysis. Mastery cannot be taught. It can only be learned and experienced.

By design, you are a learning machine. As an infant, you learned to walk. As a toddler, you learned to talk. By the time you reached age 5, you'd mastered many skills needed to thrive in the world. And you learned all these things without formal instruction, without lectures, without books, without conscious effort, and without fear.

Shortly after we start school, however, something happens to us. Somehow we start forgetting about the master student inside us. Even under the best teachers, we experience the discomfort that sometimes accompanies learning. We start avoiding situations that might lead to embarrassment. We turn away from experiences that could lead to mistakes. We accumulate a growing list of ideas to defend, a catalog of familiar experiences that discourages us from learning anything new. Slowly we restrict our possibilities and potentials.

However, the story doesn't end there. You can open a new chapter in your life, starting today. You can rediscover the natural learner within you. Each chapter of this book is about a step you can take on this path.

Master students share certain qualities. Though they imply various strategies for learning, they ultimately go beyond what people *do*. Master student qualities are values. They are ways of *being* exceptional.

Following is a list of master student qualities. Remember that the list is not complete. It merely points in a direction.

As you read the following list, look to yourself. Put a check mark next to each quality that you've already demonstrated. Put another mark, say an exclamation point, next to each quality you want to actively work on possessing. This is not a test. It is simply a chance to celebrate what you've accomplished so far—and start thinking about what's possible for your future.

☐ **Inquisitive.** The master student is curious about everything. By posing questions, she can generate interest in the most mundane, humdrum situations.

Able to focus attention. Watch a 2-year-old at play. Pay attention to his eyes. The wide-eyed look reveals an energy and a capacity for amazement that keep his attention absolutely focused in the here and now. The master student's focused attention has this kind of childlike quality. The world, to a master student, is always new.

Willing to change. The unknown does not frighten the master student. In fact, she welcomes it—even the unknown in herself.

Competent. Mastery of skills is important to the master student. When he learns mathematical formulas, he studies them until they become second nature. He practices until he knows them cold, then puts in a few extra minutes. He also is able to apply what she learns to new and different situations.

Joyful. More often than not, the master student is seen with a smile on her face—sometimes a smile at nothing in particular other than amazement at the world and her experience of it.

Energetic. Notice the student with a spring in his step, the one who is enthusiastic and involved in class. When he reads, he often sits on the very edge of his chair, and he plays with the same intensity.

Self-aware. The master student is willing to evaluate herself and her behavior. She regularly tells the truth about his strengths and those aspects that could be improved.

Responsible. There is a difference between responsibility and blame, and the master student knows it well. He is willing to take responsibility for everything in his life—even for events that most people would blame on others. For example, if a master student takes a required class that most students consider boring, he chooses to take responsibility for his interest level. He looks for ways to link the class to one of his goals. He sees the class as an opportunity to experiment with new study techniques that will enhance his performance in any course. He remembers that by choosing his thoughts and behaviors, he can create interesting classes, enjoyable relationships, fulfilling work experiences, or just about anything else he wants.

Willing to take risks. The master student often takes on projects with no guarantee of success. She participates in class dialogues at the risk of looking foolish. She tackles difficult subjects in term papers. She welcomes the risk of a challenging course.

Willing to participate. Don't look for the master student on the sidelines. He's in the game. He is a team player who can be counted on. He is engaged at school, at work, and with friends and family. He is willing to make a commitment and to follow through on it.

Courageous. The master student admits her fear and fully experiences it. For example, she will approach a tough exam as an opportunity to explore feelings of anxiety and tension related to the pressure to perform. She does not deny fear; she embraces it. If she doesn't understand something or if she makes a mistake, she admits it. When she faces a challenge and bumps into her limits, she asks for help. And, she's just as willing to give help as to receive it.

Self-directed. Rewards or punishments provided by others do not motivate the master student. His desire to learn comes from within, and his goals come from himself. He competes like a star athlete—not to defeat other people but to push himself to the next level of excellence.

Spontaneous. The master student is truly in the here and now. She is able to respond to the moment in fresh, surprising, and unplanned ways.

Relaxed about grades. Grades make the master student neither depressed nor euphoric. He recognizes that sometimes grades are important. At the same time, grades are not the only reason he studies. He does not measure his worth as a human being by the grades he receives.

Intuitive. The master student has an inner sense that cannot be explained by logic alone. She trusts her "gut instincts" as well as her mind.

Creative. Where others see dull details and trivia, the master student sees opportunities to create. He can gather pieces of knowledge from a wide range of subjects and put them together in new ways. The master student is creative in every aspect of his life.

Willing to be uncomfortable. The master student does not place comfort first. When discomfort is necessary to reach a goal, she is willing to experience it. She can endure personal hardships and can look at unpleasant things with detachment.

Optimistic. The master student sees setbacks as temporary and isolated, knowing that he can choose his response to any circumstance.

Willing to laugh. The master student might laugh at any moment, and her sense of humor includes the ability to laugh at herself.

Hungry. Human beings begin life with a natural appetite for knowledge. The master student taps that hunger, and it gives him a desire to learn for the sake of learning.

Willing to work. Once inspired, the master student is willing to follow through with sweat. She knows that genius and creativity are the result of persistence and work. When in high gear, the master student works with the intensity of a child at play.

Caring. A master student cares about knowledge and has a passion for ideas. He also cares about people and appreciates learning from others. He collaborates on projects and thrives on teams. He flourishes in a community that values win–win outcomes, cooperation, and love. ■

Get the **most** out of *this book*

The purpose of this book is to help you make a successful transition to higher education by setting up a path to mastery that will last the rest of your life. And this book is worthless—*if reading it is all you do.* You'll get your money's worth only if you actively use the ideas that are presented in these pages.

The author of *Becoming a Master Student* didn't like traditional textbooks. They put him to sleep. So, he chose to create a different kind of book. You're holding the result in your hands.

Nothing in this book appears by accident. Every element on every page serves as a prompt to take ideas and put them into action.

Articles are the backbone of this book. You're reading one right now. Articles are important because *The Essential Guide to Becoming a Master Student* is designed to look like a magazine rather than a textbook.

Most magazines are filled with advertisements. So is this book. The difference is that you won't find any glossy photos of celebrities or consumer products. Instead, the articles are self-contained "advertisements" for tips, tools, strategies, and techniques that you can use immediately. You can read any article from any chapter in any order at any time. If you read each chapter from start to finish, you'll gain the advantage of seeing how the key concepts fit together.

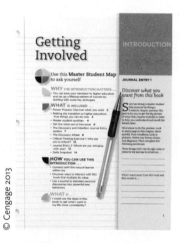

A **Master Student Map** begins each chapter. Think of it as a GPS device for ideas. Each chapter in this book takes you on a journey, and the Master Student Map is your guide. You can orient yourself for maximum learning every time you open this book by asking the four questions listed in the Map: *Why? What? How?* and *What if?* And as you'll discover in Chapter 1, those four questions are keys to learning anything at all.

There's a **Power Process** on the second page of each chapter. These are suggestions to play with your perspective on the world so that it becomes easier to use the ideas suggested in articles.

Students often refer to the Power Processes as their favorite part of the book. Approach them with a sense of possibility.

Journal Entries are just as essential. These are invitations for you to discover what you want in life and how you intend to get it. For more details, see "The Discovery and Intention Journal Entry system" on page 7.

There's a **Critical Thinking Exercise** in each chapter as well. They're here because Master Students love good questions. Each Critical Thinking Exercise serves up a specific question and guides you to reflect on it in a sustained way. Once you know what it's like to dive deeply into an idea, you'll never be satisfied with superficial answers again.

A **Skills Snapshot** ends each chapter. These connect with the **Discovery Wheel** included later in this chapter. Like the Discovery Wheel, the Skills Snapshots invite you to tell the truth in a nonjudgmental way about where you stand today in your path to becoming a Master Student.

Another element of this book takes you well beyond its pages. When you see **You're One Click Away . . .**, remember to go online to this book's **You're One Click Away . . .**
College Success CourseMate for additional content. (Your instructor will explain how to do this.) Think of the College Success CourseMate as your book in the "cloud"—a resource that you can access any time with any Internet-connected device.

P.S. The pages of *The Essential Guide to Becoming a Master Student* are perforated because some of the information here is too important to leave in the book. You can rip out pages and then reinsert them later by sticking them into the spine of the book. A piece of tape will hold them in place. ■

The Discovery and Intention Journal Entry system

Success is no mystery. Successful people have left clues—*many* clues, in fact. There are thousands of articles and books that give tools, tips, techniques, and strategies for success. Do an Internet search on *success* and you'll get over 300 million results.

If that sounds overwhelming, don't worry. Success is simply the process of setting and achieving goals. And the essentials of that process can be described in three words: *Discovery. Intention. Action.* Success is really that simple. It's not always easy, but there are no secrets about the process.

Throughout this book are Journal Entries. These are invitations to reflect and write. They are also your chance to personally experience success through the cycle of discovery, intention, and action.

WRITE DISCOVERY STATEMENTS

The first stage is a Discovery Statement. These often begin with a prompt, such as "I discovered that..." Here is an opportunity to reflect on "where you are." Discovery Statements describe your current strengths and areas for improvement. Discovery Statements can also be descriptions of your feelings, thoughts, and behavior. Whenever you get an "aha!" moment—a flash of insight or a sudden solution to a problem--put it in a Discovery Statement. To write effective Discovery Statements, remember the following.

Record the specifics about your thoughts, feelings, and behavior. Notice your thoughts, observe your actions, and record them accurately. Get the facts. If you spent 30 minutes surfing the Internet instead of reading your anatomy text, write about it. Include the details.

Use discomfort as a signal. When you approach a daunting task such as a difficult math problem, notice your physical sensations. Feeling uncomfortable, bored, or tired might be a signal that you're about to do valuable work. Stick with it. Write about it. Tell yourself you can handle the discomfort just a little bit longer. You will be rewarded with a new insight.

Suspend judgment. When you are discovering yourself, be gentle. Suspend self-judgment. If you continually judge your behaviors as "bad" or "stupid," your mind will quit making discoveries. For your own benefit, be kind to yourself.

Tell the truth. Suspending judgment helps you tell the truth about yourself. "The truth will set you free" is a saying that endures for a reason. The closer you get to the truth, the more powerful your Discovery Statements. And if you notice that you are avoiding the truth, don't blame yourself. Just tell the truth about it.

WRITE INTENTION STATEMENTS

Intention Statements can be used to alter your course. They are statements of your commitment to do a specific task or achieve a goal. Whereas Discovery Statements promote awareness, Intention Statements are blueprints for action. The two processes reinforce each other.

Make intentions positive. The purpose of writing Intention Statements is to focus on what you *do* want rather than what you *don't* want. Instead of writing "I will not fall asleep while studying chemistry," write, "I intend to stay awake when studying chemistry." Also avoid the word *try.* Trying is not doing. When we hedge our bets with *try,* we can always tell ourselves, "Well, I *tried* to stay awake."

Make intentions observable. Rather than writing "I intend to work harder on my history assignments," write, "I intend to review my class notes daily and make summary sheets of my reading."

Make intentions small and achievable. Break large goals into small, specific tasks that can be accomplished quickly. Small and simple changes in behavior—when practiced consistently over time—can have large and lasting effects.

When setting your goals, anticipate self-sabotage. Be aware of what you might do, consciously or unconsciously, to undermine your best intentions. Also be careful about intentions that depend on other people. If you intend for your study group to complete an assignment by Monday, then your success depends on the students in the group. Likewise, you can support your group's success by following through on your own stated intentions.

Set time lines. For example, if you are assigned a paper to write, break the assignment into small tasks and set a precise due date for each one: "I intend to select a topic for my paper by 9 A.M. Wednesday."

ACT NOW!

Carefully crafted Discovery Statements are a beauty to behold. Precise Intention Statements can inspire awe. But neither will be of much use until you put them into action.

Life responds to what you *do*. Successful people are those who consistently produce the results that they want. And results follow from specific, consistent behaviors. If you want new results in your life, then take new actions.

When it comes to taking action, remember that even simple changes in behavior can produce results. If you feel like procrastinating, then tackle just one small, specific task related to your intention. Find something you can complete in 5 minutes or less, and do it *now*. For example, access just one Web site related to the topic of your next assigned paper. Or spend just 3 minutes previewing a reading assignment. Taking "baby steps" like these can move you into action with grace and ease.

Changing your behavior might lead to feelings of discomfort. Instead of reverting back to your old behaviors, befriend the yucky feelings. Taking action has a way of dissolving discomfort.

· ·

That's the system in a nutshell. Discovery leads to awareness. Intention leads to commitment, which naturally leads to focused action.

· ·

REPEAT THE CYCLE

Using the Discovery and Intention Journal Entry system is a little like flying a plane. Airplanes are seldom exactly on course. Human and automatic pilots are always checking an airplane's positions and making corrections. The resulting flight path looks like a zig-zag. The plane is almost always flying in the wrong direction. The cycle of constant observation and course correction enables it to arrive at the planned destination.

The process of discovery, intention, and action works in a similar way. First, you write Discovery Statements about where you are now. Next, you write Intention Statements about where you want to be and the specific steps you will take to get there. Follow up with action—the sooner, the better.

Then start the cycle again. Write Discovery Statements about whether you act on your Intention Statements—and what you learn in the process. Follow up with more Intention Statements about what you will do differently in the future. Then move into action and describe what happens next.

Sometimes a Discovery or Intention Statement will be long and detailed. Usually, it will be short—maybe just a line or two. With practice, the cycle will become automatic.

By the way, don't panic when you fail to complete an intended task. Straying off course is normal. Simply recall your intention and act accordingly. Miraculous progress might not come immediately. Do not be concerned. Stay with the cycle. Give it time.

Also remember that this process never ends. Each time you repeat the cycle, you get new results. Your actions become a little more aligned with your intentions, and your intentions more accurately reflect your discoveries. Over time, these small course corrections add up. Your life shifts in significant ways as you move in the direction of your dreams.

The following statement might strike you as improbable, but it is true: It can take the same amount of energy to get what you *don't* want in school as it takes to get what you *do* want. Sometimes getting what you don't want takes even more effort. An airplane burns the same amount of fuel flying away from its destination as it does flying toward it. It pays to stay on course.

You can use the Discovery and Intention Journal Entry system to stay on your own course and get what you want out of school. Start with the Journal Entries included in the text. Then go beyond them. Write Journal Entries of your own at any time, for any purpose. Create new strategies whenever you need them, based on your current situation.

It's all about getting what you want and becoming more effective in everything you do. This is the path of mastery, a path that you can travel for the rest of your life.

Once you get the hang of it, you might discover you can fly. ▪

 You're One Click Away...
from more suggestions for Discovery, Intention, and Action Statements.

THE DISCOVERY WHEEL

The Discovery Wheel is an opportunity to tell the truth about the kind of person you are—and the kind of person you want to become.

This tool is based on a fundamental idea: Success in any area of life starts with telling the truth about what is working—and what *isn't*—in our lives right now. When we acknowledge our strengths, we gain an accurate picture of what we can accomplish. When we admit that we have a problem, we free up energy to find a solution. It's that simple.

The Discovery Wheel gives you an opportunity to sit back for a few minutes and think about yourself. This is not a test. There are no trick questions. There are no grades. The answers you provide will have meaning only for you.

HOW THE DISCOVERY WHEEL WORKS

By doing the Discovery Wheel, you can gain awareness of your current behaviors—especially the kind of behaviors that affect your success in school. With this knowledge, you can choose new behaviors and start to enjoy new results in your life.

During this exercise, you fill in a circle similar to the one on this page. The closer the shading comes to the outer edge of the circle, the higher your evaluation of a specific skill. In the example below, the student has rated her reading skills low and her note-taking skills high.

The terms *high* and *low* are not positive or negative judgments. When doing the Discovery Wheel, you are just making observations about yourself. You're like a scientist running an experiment. You are just collecting data and recording the facts. You're not evaluating yourself as good or bad.

Also remember that the Discovery Wheel is not a permanent picture of who you are. It is a picture of what you're doing right now. You'll do this exercise again, near the end of this book. Also, the Skills Snapshot at the end of each chapter is like a mini–Discovery Wheel that allows you to update your self-evaluations.

In short, you will have many chances to measure your progress. So be honest about where you are right now.

To succeed at this exercise, tell the truth about your strengths. This is no time for modesty! Also, lighten up and be willing to laugh at yourself. A little humor can make it easier to tell the truth about your areas for improvement.

To begin this exercise, read the following statements and give yourself points for each one. Use the point system described below. Then add up your point total for each category and shade the Discovery Wheel on page 11 to the appropriate level.

5 points: This statement is always or almost always true of me.

4 points: This statement is often true of me.

3 points: This statement is true of me about half the time.

2 points: This statement is seldom true of me.

1 point: This statement is never or almost never true of me.

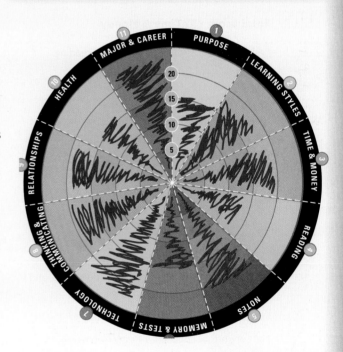

1. _2_/_5_   I can clearly state my overall purpose in life.

2. _5_   I can explain how school relates to what I plan to do after I graduate.

3. _3_   I capture key insights in writing and clarify exactly how I intend to act on them.

4. _2_   I am skilled at making transitions.

5. _3_   I seek out and use resources to support my success.

_15_   **Total score (1) Purpose**

1. __4__ I enjoy learning.

2. __3__ I make a habit of assessing my personal strengths and areas for improvement.

3. __3__ I monitor my understanding of a topic and change learning strategies if I get confused.

4. __2__ I use my knowledge of various learning styles to support my success in school.

5. __4__ I am open to different points of view on almost any topic.

__16__ **Total score (2) Learning Styles**

1. __3__ I can clearly describe what I want to experience in major areas of my life, including career, relationships, financial well-being, and health.

2. __1__ I set goals and periodically review them.

3. __2__ I plan each day and often accomplish what I plan.

4. __3__ I will have enough money to complete my education.

5. __3__ I monitor my income, keep track of my expenses, and live within my means.

__12__ **Total score (3) Time & Money**

1. __2__ I ask myself questions about what I'm reading.

2. __3__ I preview and review reading assignments.

3. __3__ I relate what I read to my life.

4. __2__ I select strategies to fit the type of material I'm reading.

5. __2__ When I don't understand what I'm reading, I note my questions and find answers.

__12__ **Total score (4) Reading**

1. __4__ When I am in class, I focus my attention.

2. __4__ I take notes in class.

3. __2__ I can explain various methods for taking notes, and I choose those that work best for me.

4. __3__ I distinguish key points from supporting examples.

5. __3__ I put important concepts into my own words.

__16__ **Total score (5) Notes**

1. __3__ The way that I talk about my value as a person is independent of my grades.

2. __3__ I often succeed at predicting test questions.

3. __2__ I review for tests throughout the term.

4. __4__ I manage my time during tests.

5. __2__ I use techniques to remember key facts and ideas.

__14__ **Total score (6) Memory & Tests**

1. __2__ I am in charge of how I manage my time and attention when I use technology.

2. __4__ I use technology in ways that directly support my success in school.

3. __3__ I think critically about information that I find online.

4. __1__ I use social networks to build constructive relationships with people.

5. __3__ I use technology to collaborate effectively with other people on projects.

__13__ **Total score (7) Technology**

1. __3__ I use brainstorming to generate solutions to problems.

2. __4__ I can detect common errors in logic and gaps in evidence.

3. __4__ When researching, I find relevant facts and properly credit their sources.

4. __4__ I edit my writing for clarity, accuracy, and coherence.

5. __3__ I prepare and deliver effective presentations.

__18__ **Total score (8) Thinking & Communicating**

1. __2__ Other people tell me that I am a good listener.

2. __3__ I communicate my upsets without blaming others.

3. __3__ I build rewarding relationships with people from other backgrounds.

4. __3__ I effectively resolve conflict.

5. __3__ I participate effectively in teams and take on leadership roles.

__14__ **Total score (9) Relationships**

1. __4__ I have enough energy to study, attend classes, and enjoy other areas of my life.

2. __2__ The way I eat supports my long-term health.

3. __2__ I exercise regularly.

4. __X 5__ I can cope effectively with stress.

5. __3__ I'm in control of alcohol or other drugs I put in my body.

__16__ **Total score (10) Health**

1. __3__ I have a detailed list of my skills.

2. __1__ I have a written career plan and update it regularly.

3. __1__ I use the career-planning services at my school.

4. __2__ I participate in internships, extracurricular activities, information interviews, and on-the-job experiences to test and refine my career plan.

5. __4__ I have declared a major related to my interests, skills, and core values.

__11__ **Total score (11) Major & Career**

Using the total score from each category above, shade in each section of the blank Discovery Wheel below. If you want, use different colors. For example, you could use green for areas you want to work on.

REFLECT ON YOUR DISCOVERY WHEEL

Now that you have completed your Discovery Wheel, spend a few minutes with it. Get a sense of its weight, shape, and balance. How would it sound if it rolled down a hill?

Next, complete the following sentences in the space below. Just write down whatever comes to mind. Remember, this is not a test.

The two areas in which I am strongest are . . .

(8) and (2) Though I feel my test taking is probably stronger then my note taking

The two areas in which I most want to improve are . . .

Purpose and Time management

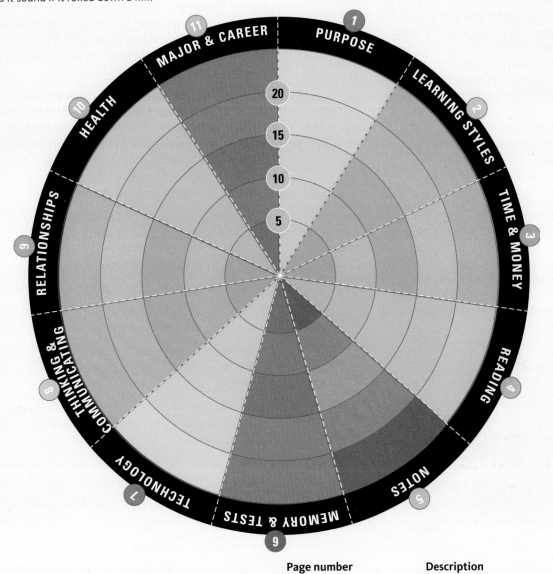

<table>
<thead>
<tr><th>Page number</th><th>Description</th></tr>
</thead>
<tbody>
<tr><td></td><td></td></tr>
<tr><td></td><td></td></tr>
<tr><td></td><td></td></tr>
<tr><td></td><td></td></tr>
<tr><td></td><td></td></tr>
</tbody>
</table>

Finally, take about 15 minutes to do a "textbook reconnaissance," much like the preview you did for this chapter. First, scan the Table of Contents for the entire book. Next, look at every page in the book. Move quickly. Skim the words in bold print. Glance at pictures. Look for suggestions that can help with behaviors you want to change. Find five such suggestions that look especially interesting to you. Then write the page number and a short description of each idea.

You're One Click Away...
from doing this exercise online.

CRITICAL THINKING EXERCISE 1

Why are you in school?

In each chapter of this book is at least one Critical Thinking Exercise. These exercises offer you a chance to apply a model for thinking that's explained more thoroughly in Chapter 7. This model has two basic parts. The first part is creative thinking, which opens up many possible ideas about any topic and many possible solutions to any problem. The second part is critical thinking, which narrows down your initial ideas and solutions to those that are most workable and supported by logic and evidence.

This first exercise asks you to do both kinds of thinking. You will begin by creating ideas and then follow up by refining them.

Part 1

Select a time and place when you know you will not be disturbed for at least 20 minutes. Relax for two or three minutes, clearing your mind. Then complete the following sentences with any ideas that enter your mind. Continue on additional paper as needed.

What I want from my education is . . .

A much stronger understanding of all Maths. A degree that will get me a decent job.

When I complete my education, I want to be able to . . .

Teach high school level math (Calc + Trig)

I also want . . .

A stable job. A nice house. A beautiful wife. The ability to move up to college level teaching. A pizza. This is a very open ended question

Part 2

After completing Part 1, take a short break. Reward yourself by doing something that you enjoy. Then review the above list of things that you want from your education. See whether you can summarize them in a one-sentence, polished statement. This will become a statement of your purpose for taking part in higher education.

Write several drafts of this purpose statement, and review it periodically as you continue your education. With each draft, see whether you can capture the essence of what you want from higher education—and from your life. Craft a statement that you can easily memorize, one that sparks your enthusiasm and makes you want to get up in the morning.

You might find it difficult to express your purpose statement in one sentence. If so, write a paragraph or more. Then look for the sentence that seems most charged with energy for you.

Following are some sample purpose statements:

- My purpose for being in school is to gain skills that I can use to contribute to others.

- My purpose for being in school is to live an abundant life that is filled with happiness, health, love, and wealth.

- My purpose for being in school is to enjoy myself by making lasting friendships and following the lead of my interests.

Write at least one draft of your purpose statement below:

 **You're One Click Away . . .**
from more sample purpose statements.

JOURNAL ENTRY 2
Discovery/Intention Statement

Whom are you bringing with you?

You've succeeded in entering higher education. Congratulations. Behind you stand networks of people and services that support your success in school. Take some time now to discover the details about that network. Then commit to using it.

Discovery Statement

Reflect on all the people who helped you get this far in your educational journey. These people might include valued teachers, family members, fellow students, and friends. Think of those who helped you at a crucial point in your schooling and encouraged you to continue your education. These are the people who stand with you as you begin your freshman year. List their names in the space below, and use additional paper as needed.

I discovered that the people who've made a special contribution to my life so far include . . .

_____

_____

_____

_____

_____

_____

Intention Statement

Next, create an intention to use campus services. Examples include academic advising, counseling, tutoring, and services from the housing, financial aid, and health offices at your school. For ideas, see your school catalog and Web site. Use the space below to list specific services that interest you.

To support my success in school, I intend to . . .

_____

_____

_____

Action Statement

Finally, prepare to follow up with people on both of the lists that you've just created. List contact information (name, address, phone number, Web site address, and email address) for the people included in your Discovery Statement. Plan to thank them for supporting you. Keep them updated on how you're doing in school.

Also list contact information for the services included in your Intention Statement, and schedule a time to see someone from each office. Begin writing in the space below and continue on additional paper.

_____

_____

_____

_____

_____

_____

_____

_____

_____

_____

_____

_____

_____

_____

_____

_____

_____

_____

_____

_____

_____

SKILLS *Snapshot*

One of the most important skills you will ever develop is the ability to change a habit. Taking just a handful of the suggestions from this book and turning them into habits could transform your experience of higher education.

Start by reflecting on your current skill at changing habits. Complete the following sentences:

The last habit I tried to change was...

I would describe my success at changing that habit as...

In his book *The Power of Habit*,[2] Charles Duhigg explains that any habit has three elements. First is a *routine*. This is a behavior that we repeat, usually without thinking. Examples are taking a second helping at dinner, biting fingernails, or automatically hitting the "snooze" button when the alarm goes off in the morning.

The second element is a *cue*. This is an event that occurs just before we perform the routine. It might be an internal event, such as a change in mood. Or it could be an external event, such as seeing an advertisement that triggers food cravings.

Finally comes the *reward*. This is the "payoff" for the routine—usually a feeling of pleasure or a reduction in stress.

Taken together, the above elements form a *habit loop*: You perceive a *cue* and then perform a *routine* in order to get a *reward*. Armed with this information, you can greatly increase your skill at changing habits. Use the following four steps that Duhigg recommends:

Step 1: Identify the routine. In the space below, describe a specific habit that you want to change right now. Refer to a specific behavior that anyone could observe—preferably a physical, visible action that you perform every day.

_____

_____

_____

_____

Step 2: Identify the cue. Next, think about what takes place immediately before you perform the routine. For instance, drinking a cup of coffee (cue) might trigger the urge to eat a chocolate chip cookie (routine). Use the following space to describe the cue for the behavior you listed in Step 1.

_____

_____

_____

_____

Step 3: Identify the reward. Reflect on the reward you get from your routine. Do you gain a distraction from discomfort? A pleasant sensation in your body? A chance to socialize with friends or coworkers? Write about your reward below.

_____

_____

_____

_____

Step 4: Choose a new routine. Now your challenge is to choose a behavior that offers a similar reward with as few disadvantages as possible. Instead of eating a whole chocolate chip cookie, for example, you could break off just one small section, eat it slowly with full attention, and throw the rest away. This can allow you to experience a familiar pleasure with a fraction of the calories.

Describe your new routine here.

_____

_____

_____

Act on your intention every day for the next week, and keep track of the results. If you don't succeed at changing the habit, just tell the truth about it. Then experiment with different routines until you discover one that works.

Using Your Learning Styles

Use this **Master Student Map** to ask yourself

WHY THIS CHAPTER MATTERS . . .

- Discovering how you prefer to learn can help you leverage your strengths.

WHAT IS INCLUDED. . .

HOW YOU CAN USE THIS INTRODUCTION . . .

- Experience the power of telling the truth about my current skills.
- Discover my preferred learning styles.
- Experiment with new approaches to learning.

WHAT IF . . .

- I could consistently choose learning strategies that support my success in school and at work?

© Ruslan Ivantsov/Shutterstock.com

JOURNAL ENTRY 3

Discover what you want from this chapter

See whether you can recall a time when an instructor's approach to teaching a class did not work for you. Perhaps the instructor relied on lectures when you wanted hands-on activities. Or maybe the instructor presented a lot of abstract ideas without talking about how to apply them in the world outside the classroom. Describe your experience here.

I discovered that I ...

_____

_____

_____

Now scan this chapter for three suggestions that you can use if you ever encounter another mismatch between an instructor's style of teaching and your personal preferences for learning.

I intend to use ...

_____

_____

_____

Ideas are tools

There are many ideas in this book. When you first encounter them, don't believe any of them. Instead, think of the ideas as tools.

For example, you use a hammer for a purpose—to drive a nail. You don't try to figure out whether the hammer is "right." You just use it. If it works, you use it again. If it doesn't work, you get a different hammer.

People have plenty of room in their lives for different kinds of hammers, but they tend to limit their openness to different kinds of ideas. A new idea, at some level, is a threat to their very being—unlike a new hammer, which is simply a new hammer.

Most of us have a built-in desire to be right. Our ideas, we often think, represent ourselves.

Some ideas are worth dying for. But please note: This book does not contain any of those ideas. The ideas on these pages are strictly "hammers."

Imagine someone defending a hammer. Picture this person holding up a hammer and declaring, "I hold this hammer to be self-evident. Give me this hammer or give me death. Those other hammers are flawed. There are only two kinds of people in this world: people who believe in this hammer and people who don't."

That ridiculous picture makes a point. This book is not a manifesto. It's a toolbox, and tools are meant to be used.

If you read about a tool in this book that doesn't sound "right" or one that sounds a little goofy, remember that the ideas here are for using, not necessarily for believing. Suspend your judgment. Test the idea for yourself. If it works, use it. If it doesn't, don't use it.

Any tool—whether it's a hammer, a computer program, or a study technique based on your knowledge of learning styles—is designed to do a specific job. A master mechanic carries a variety of tools, because no single tool works for all jobs. If you throw a tool away because it doesn't work in one situation, you won't be able to pull it out later when it's just what you need. So if an idea doesn't work for you and you are satisfied that you gave it a fair chance, don't throw it away. File it away instead. The idea might come in handy soon.

And remember, this book is not about figuring out the "right" way. Even the "ideas are tools" approach is not "right."

It's a hammer . . . (or maybe a saw).

You're One Click Away . . .
*from accessing the Power Process Media online
and finding out more about how "ideas are tools."*

LEARNING STYLES:
Discovering how you learn

1

Right now, you are investing substantial amounts of time, money, and energy in your education. What you get in return for this investment depends on how well you understand the process of learning and use it to your advantage.

If you don't understand learning, you might feel bored or confused in class. After getting a low grade, you might have no idea how to respond. Over time, frustration can mount to the point where you question the value of being in school.

Some students answer that question by dropping out of school. These students lose a chance to create the life they want, and society loses the contributions of educated workers.

You can prevent that outcome. Gain strategies for going beyond boredom and confusion. Discover new options for achieving goals, solving problems, listening more fully, speaking more persuasively, and resolving conflicts between people. Start by understanding the different ways that people create meaning from their experience and change their behavior. In other words, learn about *how* we learn.

WE LEARN BY PERCEIVING AND PROCESSING

When we learn well, says psychologist David Kolb, two things happen.[1] First, we *perceive*. That is, we notice events and "take in" new experiences.

Second, we *process*. We respond to experiences in ways that help us make sense of them.

Some people especially prefer to perceive through *feeling* (also called *concrete experience*). They like to absorb information through their five senses. They learn by getting directly involved in new experiences. When solving problems, they rely on intuition as much as intellect.

Other people like to perceive by *thinking* (also called *abstract conceptualization*). They analyze, intellectualize, and create theories. Often these people take a scientific approach to problem solving and excel in traditional classrooms.

Some people prefer to process by *watching* (also called *reflective observation*). They prefer to stand back, watch what is going on, and reflect on it. They consider several points of view as they attempt to make sense of things and generate many ideas about how something happens.

Other people like to process by *doing* (also called *active experimentation*). They prefer to jump in and start doing things immediately. These people are willing to take risks as they attempt to make sense of things. They are results-oriented and look for practical ways to apply what they learn.

PERCEIVING AND PROCESSING—AN EXAMPLE

Suppose that you get a new cell phone. It has more features than any phone you've used before. You have many options for learning how to use it. For example:

- Just get your hands on the phone right away, press some buttons, and see whether you can dial a number or send a text message.
- Read the instruction manual and view help screens on the phone before you try to make a call.
- Recall experiences you've had with phones in the past and what you've learned by watching other people use their cell phones.
- Ask a friend who owns the same type of phone to coach you as you experiment with making calls and sending messages.

These actions illustrate the different approaches to learning:

- Getting your hands on the phone right away and seeing whether you can make it work is an example of learning through *feeling* (or *concrete experience*).
- Reading the manual and help screens before you use the phone is an example of learning through *thinking* (or *abstract conceptualization*).
- Recalling what you've experienced in the past is an example of learning through watching (or reflective observation).
- Asking a friend to coach you through a hands-on activity with the phone is an example of learning through *doing* (or *active experimentation*).

In summary, your learning style is the unique way that you blend thinking, feeling, watching, and doing. You tend to use this approach in learning anything—from cell phones to English composition or sky diving. Doing the recommended activities in this chapter will help you explore your learning style in more detail. ■

JOURNAL ENTRY 4
Discovery Statement

Prepare for the Learning Style Inventory (LSI)

As a "warm-up" for the Learning Style Inventory that follows, think about times when you felt successful at learning. Underline or highlight any of the following statements that describe those situations.

- I was in a structured setting, with a lot of directions about what to do.
- I was free to learn at my own pace and in my own way.
- I learned as part of a small group.
- I learned mainly by working alone in a quiet place.
- I learned in a place where there was a lot of activity going on.
- I formed pictures in my mind.
- I learned by *doing* something—moving around, touching something, or trying out a process for myself.
- I learned by talking to myself or explaining ideas to other people.
- I got the "big picture" before I tried to understand the details.
- I listened to a lecture and then thought about it after class.
- I read a book or article and then thought about it afterward.
- I used a variety of media—such as videos, films, audio recordings, or computers—to assist my learning.
- I was considering where to attend school and had to actually set foot on each campus before choosing.
- I was shopping for a car and paid more attention to how I felt about test-driving each one than to the sticker prices or mileage estimates.
- I was thinking about going to a movie and carefully read the reviews before choosing one.

Reviewing this list, do you see any patterns in the way you prefer to learn? If so, briefly describe them.

Directions for completing the Learning Style Inventory

To help you become more aware of learning styles, a psychologist named David Kolb developed the Learning Style Inventory (LSI). This inventory is included on the next page. Responding to the items in the LSI can help you discover a lot about the ways you learn. Following the LSI are suggestions for using your results to promote your success.

The LSI is not a test. There are no right or wrong answers. Your goal is simply to develop a profile of your current learning style. So, take the LSI quickly. You might find it useful to recall a recent time when you learned something new at school, home, or work. However, do not agonize over your responses.

Note that the LSI consists of 12 sentences, each with four different endings. You will read each sentence, and then write a "4" next to the ending that best describes the way you currently learn. Then you will continue ranking the other endings with a "3," "2," or "1," representing the ending that least describes you. This is a forced-choice inventory, so you must rank each ending. Do not leave any endings blank. Use each number only once for each question.

Following are more specific directions:

1. Before you write on page LSI–1, remove the sheet of paper following page LSI–2.
2. Read the instructions at the top of page LSI–1. When you understand example A, you are ready to begin.
3. While writing on page LSI–1, *press firmly* so that your answers will show up on page LSI–3.

Learning Style Inventory

Complete items 1–12 below. Use the following example as a guide:

A. When I learn: __2__ I am happy.   __3__ I am fast.   __4__ I am logical.   __1__ I am careful.

Do not leave any endings blank. Use each number only once for each question. Before completing the items, remove the sheet of paper following this page. While writing, press firmly.

1. When I learn:	__1__ I like to deal with my feelings.	__2__ I like to think about ideas.	__4__ I like to be doing things.	__3__ I like to watch and listen.
2. I learn best when:	__2__ I listen and watch carefully.	__4__ I rely on logical thinking.	__3__ I trust my hunches and feelings.	__1__ I work hard to get things done.
3. When I am learning:	__4__ I tend to reason things out.	__1__ I am responsible about things.	__3__ I am quiet and reserved.	__2__ I have strong feelings and reactions.
4. I learn by:	__1__ feeling.	__3__ doing.	__2__ watching.	__4__ thinking.
5. When I learn:	__1__ I am open to new experiences.	__2__ I look at all sides of issues.	__4__ I like to analyze things, break them down into their parts.	__3__ I like to try things out.
6. When I am learning:	__2__ I am an observing person.	__1__ I am an active person.	__3__ I am an intuitive person.	__4__ I am a logical person.
7. I learn best from:	__2__ observation.	__1__ personal relationships.	__4__ rational theories.	__3__ a chance to try out and practice.
8. When I learn:	__2__ I like to see results from my work.	__4__ I like ideas and theories.	__3__ I take my time before acting.	__1__ I feel personally involved in things.
9. I learn best when:	__3__ I rely on my observations.	__1__ I rely on my feelings.	__2__ I can try things out for myself.	__4__ I rely on my ideas.
10. When I am learning:	__3__ I am a reserved person.	__2__ I am an accepting person.	__1__ I am a responsible person.	__4__ I am a rational person.
11. When I learn:	__2__ I get involved.	__3__ I like to observe.	__4__ I evaluate things.	__1__ I like to be active.
12. I learn best when:	__4__ I analyze ideas.	__2__ I am receptive and open-minded.	__1__ I am careful.	__3__ I am practical.

Taking the next steps

Now that you've finished taking the Learning Style Inventory, you probably have some questions about what it means. You're about to discover some answers! In the following pages, you will find instructions for:

- Scoring your inventory (page LSI–3)

- Plotting your scores on to a Learning Style Graph that literally gives a "big picture" of your learning style (page LSI–5)

- Interpreting your Learning Style Graph by seeing how it relates to four distinct modes, or styles, of learning (page LSI–6)

- Developing all four modes of learning (page LSI–7)

- Balancing your learning preferences (page LSI–8)

Take your time to absorb all this material. Be willing to read through it several times and ask questions.

Your efforts will be rewarded. In addition to discovering more details about *how* you learn, you'll gain a set of strategies for applying this knowledge to your courses. With these strategies, you can use your knowledge of learning styles to actively promote your success in school.

Above all, aim to recover your natural gift for learning—the defining quality of a master student. Rediscover a world where the boundaries between learning and fun, between work and play, all disappear. While immersing yourself in new experiences, blend the sophistication of an adult with the wonder of a child. This path is one that you can travel for the rest of your life.

Scoring your Inventory

Now that you have taken the Learning Style Inventory, it's time to fill out the Learning Style Graph (page LSI-5) and interpret your results. To do this, follow these steps.

Next, add up all of the numbers for **"Teal W,"** **"Purple T,"** and **"Orange D,"** and also write down those totals in the box to the right.

STEP 2 Add the four totals to arrive at a GRAND TOTAL, and write down that figure in the box to the right. (**Note:** The grand total should equal 120. If you have a different amount, go back and re-add the colored letters; it was probably just an addition error.) Now remove this page and continue with Step 3 on page LSI-5.

STEP 1 First, add up all of the numbers you gave to the items marked with brown F letters. Then write down that total in the box to the right, next to **"Brown F."**

F	T	D	W
W	T	F	D
T	D	W	F
F	D	W	T
F	W	T	D
W	D	F	T
W	F	T	D
D	T	W	F
W	F	D	T
W	F	D	T
F	W	T	D
T	F	W	D

**Remove this page after you have completed Steps 1 and 2 on page LSI-3.
Then continue with Step 3 on page LSI-5.**

Learning Style Graph

Remove the sheet of paper that follows this page. Then transfer your totals from Step 2 on page LSI–3 to the lines on the Learning Style Graph below. On the brown (F) line, find the number that corresponds to your "Brown F" total from page LSI–3. Then write an X on this number. Do the same for your "Teal W," "Purple T," and "Orange D" totals. The graph on this page is for you to keep. The graph on page LSI–7 is for you to turn in to your instructor if required to do so.

Now, pressing firmly, draw four straight lines to connect the four X's, and shade in the area to form a "kite." This is your learning style profile. (For an example, see the illustration to the right.) Each X that you placed on these lines indicates your preference for a different aspect of learning:

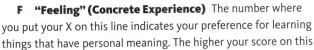

F "Feeling" (Concrete Experience) The number where you put your X on this line indicates your preference for learning things that have personal meaning. The higher your score on this line, the more you like to learn things that you feel are important and relevant to yourself.

W "Watching" (Reflective Observation) Your number on this line indicates how important it is for you to reflect on the things you are learning. If your score is high on this line, you probably find it important to watch others as they learn about an assignment and then report on it to the class. You probably like to plan things out and take the time to make sure that you fully understand a topic.

T "Thinking" (Abstract Conceptualization) Your number on this line indicates your preference for learning ideas, facts, and figures. If your score is high on this line, you probably like to absorb many concepts and gather lots of information on a new topic.

D "Doing" (Active Experimentation) Your number on this line indicates your preference for applying ideas, using trial and error, and practicing what you learn. If your score is high on this line, you probably enjoy hands-on activities that allow you to test out ideas to see what works.

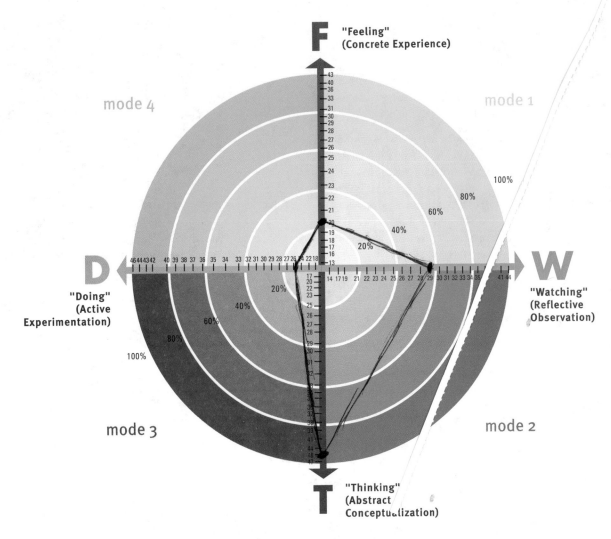

Interpreting your Learning Style Graph

When you examine your completed Learning Style Graph on page LSI–5, you will notice that your learning style profile (the "kite" that you drew) might be located primarily in one part of the graph. This will give you an idea of your preferred **mode** of learning—the kind of behaviors that feel most comfortable and familiar to you when you are learning something.

Using the descriptions below and the sample graphs, identify your preferred learning mode.

Mode 1 blends feeling and watching. If the majority of your learning style profile is in the upper right-hand corner of the Learning Style Graph, you probably prefer Mode 1 learning. You seek a purpose for new information and a personal connection with the content. You want to know why a course matters and how it challenges or fits in with what they already know. You embrace new ideas that relate directly to their current interests and goals.

Mode 2 blends watching and thinking. If your learning style profile is mostly in the lower right-hand corner of the Learning Style Graph, you probably prefer Mode 2 learning. You are interested in knowing what ideas or techniques are important. You seek a theory to explain events and are interested in what experts have to say. You enjoy learning lots of facts and then arranging these facts in a logical and concise manner. You break a subject down into its key elements or steps and master each one in a systematic way.

Mode 3 blends thinking and doing. If most of your learning style profile is in the lower left-hand corner of the Learning Style Graph, you probably prefer Mode 3 learning. You hunger for an opportunity to try out what you're studying. You get involved with new knowledge by testing it out. You investigate how ideas and techniques work, and you put into practice what you learn. You thrive when you have well-defined tasks, guided practice, and frequent feedback.

Mode 4 blends doing and feeling. If most of your learning style profile is in the upper left-hand corner of the Learning Style Graph, you probably prefer Mode 4 learning. You get excited about going beyond classroom assignments. You like to take what you have practiced and find other uses for it. You seek ways to apply this newly gained skill or information at your workplace or in your personal relationships.

It might be easier for you to remember the modes if you summarize each one as a single question:

- Mode 1 means asking, *Why* learn this?
- Mode 2 means asking, *What* is this about?
- Mode 3 means asking, *How* does this work?
- Mode 4 means asking, *What if* I tried this in a different setting?

Combinations. Some learning style profiles combine all four modes. The profile to the left reflects a learner who is focused primarily on gathering information—*lots* of information! People with this profile tend to ask for additional facts from an instructor, or they want to know where they can go to discover more about a subject.

The profile to the left applies to learners who focus more on understanding what they learn and less on gathering lots of information. People with this profile prefer smaller chunks of data with plenty of time to process it. Long lectures can be difficult for these learners.

The profile to the left indicates a learner whose preferences are fairly well balanced. People with this profile can be highly adaptable and tend to excel no matter what the instructor does in the classroom. ■

Remove this sheet before completing the Learning Style Graph.

This page is inserted to ensure that the other writing you do in this book does not show through on page LSI–7.

Remove this sheet before completing the Learning Style Graph.

This page is inserted to ensure that the other writing you do in this book does not show through on page LSI–7.

Developing all four modes of learning

Each mode of learning represents a unique blend of feeling, watching, thinking, and doing. No matter which of these you've tended to prefer, you can develop the ability to use all four modes:

- **To develop Mode 1,** ask questions that help you understand *why* it is important for you to learn about a specific topic. You might also want to form a study group.
- **To develop Mode 2,** ask questions that help you understand *what* the main points and key facts are. Also, learn a new subject in stages. For example, divide a large reading assignment into sections and then read each section carefully before moving on to the next one.
- **To develop Mode 3,** ask questions about *how* a theory relates to daily life. Also allow time to practice what you learn. You can do experiments, conduct interviews, create presentations, find a relevant work or internship experience, or even write a song that summarizes key concepts. Learn through hands-on practice.
- **To develop Mode 4,** ask *what-if* questions about ways to use what you have just learned in several different situations. Also,

seek opportunities to demonstrate your understanding. You could coach a classmate about what you have learned, present findings from your research, explain how your project works, or perform your song.

Developing all four modes offers many potential benefits. For example, you can excel in many types of courses and find more opportunities to learn outside the classroom. You can expand your options for declaring a major and choosing a career. You can also work more effectively with people who learn differently from you.

In addition, you'll be able to learn from instructors no matter how they teach. Let go of statements such as "My teachers don't get me" and "The instructor doesn't teach to my learning style." Replace those excuses with attitudes such as "I am responsible for what I learn" and "I will master this subject by using several modes of learning."

The graph on this page is here for you to turn in to your instructor if required to do so.

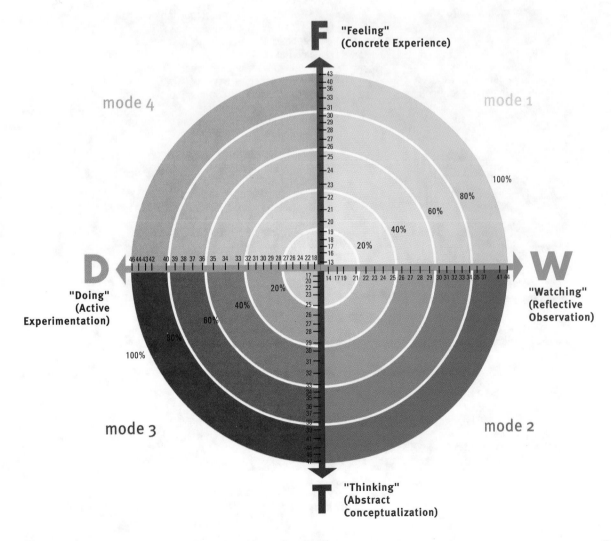

Balancing your preferences

The chart below identifies some of the natural talents people have, as well as challenges for people who have a strong preference for any one mode of learning. For example, if most of your "kite" is in Mode 2 of the Learning Style Graph, then look at the lower right-hand corner of the following chart to see whether it gives an accurate description of you.

After reviewing the description of your preferred learning mode, read all of the sections that start with the words "People with other preferred modes." These sections explain what actions you can take to become a more balanced learner.

Feeling

Doing ← → **Watching**

mode 4

Strengths:
- Getting things done
- Leadership
- Risk taking

Too much of this mode can lead to:
- Trivial improvements
- Meaningless activity

Too little of this mode can lead to:
- Work not completed on time
- Impractical plans
- Lack of motivation to achieve goals

People with other preferred modes can develop Mode 4 by:
- Making a commitment to objectives
- Seeking new opportunities
- Influencing and leading others
- Being personally involved
- Dealing with people

mode 1

Strengths:
- Imaginative ability
- Understanding people
- Recognizing problems
- Brainstorming

Too much of this mode can lead to:
- Feeling paralyzed by alternatives
- Inability to make decisions

Too little of this mode can lead to:
- Lack of ideas
- Not recognizing problems and opportunities

People with other preferred modes can develop Mode 1 by:
- Being aware of other people's feelings
- Being sensitive to values
- Listening with an open mind
- Gathering information
- Imagining the implications of ambiguous situations

mode 3

Strengths:
- Problem solving
- Decision making
- Deductive reasoning
- Defining problems

Too much of this mode can lead to:
- Solving the wrong problem
- Hasty decision making

Too little of this mode can lead to:
- Lack of focus
- Reluctance to consider alternatives
- Scattered thoughts

People with other preferred modes can develop Mode 3 by:
- Creating new ways of thinking and doing
- Experimenting with fresh ideas
- Choosing the best solution
- Setting goals
- Making decisions

mode 2

Strengths:
- Planning
- Creating models
- Defining problems
- Developing theories

Too much of this mode can lead to:
- Vague ideals ("castles in the air")
- Lack of practical application

Too little of this mode can lead to:
- Inability to learn from mistakes
- No sound basis for work
- No systematic approach

People with other preferred modes can develop Mode 2 by:
- Organizing information
- Building conceptual models
- Testing theories and ideas
- Designing experiments
- Analyzing quantitative data

Thinking

Using your
LEARNING STYLE PROFILE
to succeed

USE THE MODES WHILE CHOOSING COURSES

Remember your learning style profile when you're thinking about which classes to take and how to study for each class. Look for a fit between your preferred mode of learning and your course work.

If you prefer Mode 1, for example, then look for courses that sound interesting and seem worthwhile to you. If you prefer Mode 2, then consider classes that center on lectures, reading, and discussion. If you prefer Mode 3, then choose courses that include demonstrations, lab sessions, role-playing, and other ways to take action. And if you enjoy Mode 4, then look for courses that could apply to many situations in your life—at work, at home, and in your relationships.

You won't always be able to match your courses to your learning styles. View those situations as opportunities to practice becoming a flexible learner. By developing your skills in all four modes, you can excel in many types of courses.

USE THE MODES TO EXPLORE YOUR MAJOR

If you enjoy learning in Mode 1, you probably value creativity and human relationships. When choosing a major, consider the arts, English, psychology, or political science.

If Mode 2 is your preference, then you enjoy gathering information and building theories. A major related to math or science might be ideal for you.

If Mode 3 is your favorite, then you like to diagnose problems, arrive at solutions, and use technology. A major related to health care, engineering, or economics could be a logical choice for you.

And if your preference is Mode 4, you probably enjoy taking the initiative, implementing decisions, teaching, managing projects, and moving quickly from planning into action. Consider a major in business or education.

As you prepare to declare a major, remain flexible. Use your knowledge of learning styles to open up possibilities rather than dictate your choices. Also remember that regardless of your preferred mode, you can excel at any job or major; this may just mean developing new skills in other modes.

USE THE MODES OF LEARNING TO EXPLORE YOUR CAREER

Knowing about learning styles becomes especially useful when planning your career.

People who excel at Mode 1 are often skilled at tuning in to the feelings of clients and coworkers. These people can listen with an open mind, tolerate confusion, be sensitive to people's feelings, open up to problems that are difficult to define, and brainstorm a variety of solutions. If you like Mode 1, you may be drawn to a career in counseling, social services, the ministry, or another field that centers on human relationships. You might also enjoy a career in the performing arts.

People who prefer Mode 2 like to do research and work with ideas. They are skilled at gathering data, interpreting information, and summarizing—arriving at the big picture. They may excel at careers that center on science, math, technical communications, or planning. Mode 2 learners may also work as college teachers, lawyers, technical writers, or journalists.

People who like Mode 3 are drawn to solving problems, making decisions, and checking on progress toward goals. Careers in medicine, engineering, information technology, or another applied science are often ideal for them.

People who enjoy Mode 4 like to influence and lead others. These people are often described as "doers" and "risk takers." They like to take action and complete projects. Mode 4 learners often excel at managing, negotiating, selling, training, and teaching. They might also work in a leadership role for a nonprofit organization or government agency.

Keep in mind that there is no strict match between certain learning styles and certain careers. Learning is essential to success in all careers. Also, any career can attract people with a variety of learning styles. For instance, the health care field is large enough to include people who prefer Mode 3 and become family physicians—*and* people who prefer Mode 2 and become medical researchers.

ACCEPT CHANGE—AND OCCASIONAL DISCOMFORT

Seek out chances to develop new modes of learning. As you do, remember that discomfort is a natural part of the learning process. Allow yourself to notice any struggle with a task or lack of interest in completing it. Remember that such feelings are temporary and that you are balancing your learning preferences. By choosing to move through discomfort, you consciously expand your ability to learn in new ways. ■

You're One Click Away ...
from more ideas for using your learning style profile to succeed.

CHAPTER 1

SKILLS *Snapshot*

The Discovery Wheel in the Introduction to this book includes a section labeled Learning Styles. For the next 10 to 15 minutes, go beyond your initial responses to that exercise. Take a snapshot of your skills as they exist today, after reading and doing this chapter.

Begin by reflecting on some recent experiences. Then take another step toward mastery by choosing to follow up on your reflections with a specific action.

DISCOVERY

My score on the Learning Styles section of the Discovery Wheel was . . .

Three things I do well as a student are . . .

Three ways that I'd like to improve as a student are . . .

If asked to describe my learning style in one sentence, I would say that I am . . .

INTENTION

To expand my learning style, I would like to experiment with new strategies for learning, including . . .

Of the strategies I just listed, the one that I intend to focus on in the near future is . . .

ACTION

To use the strategy I just described, the most important thing I can do next is to . . .

At the end of this course, I would like my Learning Styles score on the Discovery Wheel to be . . .

Taking Charge of Your Time & Money

Use this **Master Student Map** to ask yourself

WHY THIS CHAPTER MATTERS . . .

- A lack of planning and problems with money can quickly undermine your success in school.

WHAT IS INCLUDED . . .

HOW YOU CAN USE THIS CHAPTER . . .

- Discover the details about how I currently manage time and money.
- Set goals, including financial goals, that make a difference in the quality of my life.
- Know exactly what to do today, this week, and this month to achieve my goals.
- Eliminate procrastination.

WHAT IF . . .

- I could meet my goals with time and money to spare?

JOURNAL ENTRY 5

Discover what you want from this chapter

The most important goal for me to accomplish this school year is . . .

A's in all classes

Right now my biggest challenge in managing money is . . .

Tracking my spendings

Ideas from this chapter that I want to use include . . .

© Ruslan Ivantsov/Shutterstock.com

21

POWER process

Be here now

Being right here, right now is such a simple idea. It seems obvious. Where else can you be but where you are? When else can you be there but when you are there?

The answer is that you can be somewhere else at any time—in your head. It's common for our thoughts to distract us from where we've chosen to be. When we let this happen, we lose the benefits of focusing our attention on what's important to us in the present moment.

To "be here now" means to do what you're doing when you're doing it. It means to be where you are when you're there. Students consistently report that focusing attention on the here and now is one of the most powerful tools in this book.

We all have a voice in our head that hardly ever shuts up. If you don't believe it, conduct this experiment: Close your eyes for 10 seconds, and pay attention to what is going on in your head. Please do this right now.

Notice something? Perhaps a voice in your head was saying, "Forget it. I'm in a hurry." Another might have said, "I wonder when 10 seconds is up?" Another could have been saying, "What little voice? I don't hear any little voice."

That's the voice.

This voice can take you anywhere at any time—especially when you are studying. When the voice takes you away, you might appear to be studying, but your brain is somewhere else.

All of us have experienced this voice, as well as the absence of it. When our inner voices are silent, time no longer seems to exist. We forget worries, aches, pains, reasons, excuses, and justifications. We fully experience the here and now. Life is magic.

Do not expect to be rid of the voice entirely. That is neither possible nor desirable. Inner voices serve a purpose. They enable us to analyze, predict, classify, and understand events out there in the "real" world. The trick is to consciously choose when to be with your inner voice and when to let it go.

Instead of trying to force a stray thought out of your head, simply notice it. Accept it. Tell yourself, "There's that thought again." Then gently return your attention to the task at hand. That thought, or another, will come back. Your mind will drift. Simply notice again where your thoughts take you, and gently bring yourself back to the here and now.

Also remember that planning supports this Power Process. Goals are tools that we create to guide our action in the present. Time management techniques—calendars, lists, and all the rest—have only one purpose. They reveal what's most important for you to focus on right *now*.

The idea behind this Power Process is simple. When you listen to a lecture, listen to a lecture. When you read this book, read this book. And when you choose to daydream, daydream. Do what you're doing when you're doing it. Be where you are when you're there.

Be here now . . . and now . . . and now.

You're One Click Away...
from accessing Power Process Media online and finding out more about how to "be here now."

You've got the time—
and the money

The words *time management* may call forth images of restriction and control. You might visualize a prune-faced Scrooge hunched over your shoulder, stopwatch in hand, telling you what to do every minute. Bad news.

Good news: You *do* have enough time for the things you want to accomplish in life. All it takes is thinking through the possibilities and making conscious choices.

Time is an equal opportunity resource. All of us, regardless of gender, race, creed, or national origin, have exactly the same number of hours in a week. No matter how famous we are, no matter how rich or poor, we all get 168 hours to spend each week—no more, no less.

Time is also an unusual commodity. It cannot be saved. You can't stockpile time like wood for the stove or food for the winter. It can't be seen, heard, touched, tasted, or smelled. You can't sense time directly. Even scientists and philosophers find it hard to describe. Because time is so elusive, it is easy to ignore. That doesn't bother time at all. Time is perfectly content to remain hidden until you are nearly out of it. And when you are out of it, you are out of it.

Time is a nonrenewable resource. If you're out of wood, you can chop some more. If you're out of money, you can earn a little extra. If you're out of love, there is still hope. If you're out of

> Time is an equal opportunity resource. All of us, regardless of gender, race, creed, or national origin, have exactly the same number of hours in a week. No matter how famous we are, no matter how rich or poor, we all get 168 hours to spend each week—no more, no less.

health, it can often be restored. But when you're out of time, that's it. When this minute is gone, it's gone.

Sometimes it seems that your friends control your time; your boss controls your time; your teachers or your parents or your kids or somebody else controls your time. Maybe that is not true, though.

Approach time as if you were in control. When you say you don't have enough time, you might really be saying that you are not spending the time you *do* have in the way that you want. This chapter is about ways to solve that problem.

The same idea applies to money. When you say you don't have enough money, the real issue might be that you are not spending the money you *do* have in ways that align with your values.

Most money problems result from spending more than is available. It's that simple, even though we often do everything we can to make the problem much more complicated. The solution also is simple: Don't spend more than you have. If you are spending more than you have, then increase your income, decrease your spending, or do both.

The point is that you are in control of what you earn and spend. This idea has never won a Nobel Prize in Economics, but you won't go broke applying it.

Everything written about time and money management can be reduced to three main ideas:

1. **Know exactly *what* you want.** State your wants as clear, specific goals. And put them in writing. When our lives lack this quality, we spend most of our time responding to interruptions, last-minute projects, and emergencies. Life feels like a scramble to just survive. We're so busy achieving someone else's goals that we forget about getting what *we* want.

2. **Know *how* to get what you want.** Take action to meet your goals, including financial goals. Determine what you'll do *today* to get what you want in the future. Put those actions in writing as well.

3. **Take action to *get* what you want.** When schedules get tight, we often drop important activities such as exercising and fixing nutritious meals. We postpone them for that elusive day when we'll finally "have the time" or "have the money."

Don't wait for that time to come. *Make* the time to get the results in life that you desire. Use the suggestions and exercises in this chapter to empower yourself.

The most useful strategies for managing time and money are not new. These strategies are all based on the cycle of discovery, intention, and action that you're already practicing in this book. Throw in the ability to add and subtract, and you have everything you need to manage your time and your money. Spend these valuable resources in ways that align with your values. ■

Give your goals some teeth

Many of us have notions about what we want out of life. They are warm, fuzzy ideals such as "I want to be a good person," "I want to be financially secure," or "I want to be happy." Left in such vague terms, however, these notions will seldom lead to any results.

Another option is to translate your ideals into goals. Find out what a goal looks like. Listen to what it sounds like. Pick it up and feel it. Make your goal as real as the teeth on a chain saw.

The key is to state your goals as specific outcomes. Think in detail about how things will be different once your goals are attained. List the changes in what you'll see, feel, touch, hear, do, or have. Whenever possible, state this outcome as a result that you can measure.

Perhaps one of your desires is to get a good education and graduate on time. Translate that into: "Graduate with a B.S. degree in engineering, with honors, by 2014."

Suppose that you want to improve your health. You might translate that into "lose 10 pounds over the next 10 months."

Likewise, a desire to improve your personal finances could translate into "pay off my car loan in 24 months" or "reduce my monthly expenses by 10 percent."

Next, use a process of brainstorming and evaluation to break down each goal into short-term actions. When you analyze a goal down to this level, you're well on the way to meeting it.

You're about to experience the process of setting a goal for yourself. Gather a pen, extra paper, and a watch with a second hand. To get the most benefit, follow the stated time limits. The entire exercise takes about 30 minutes.

Discovery Statement

For 10 minutes write down everything that you want in your life. Write as fast as you can and write whatever comes into your head. Leave no thought out. Don't worry about accuracy. The objective of a brainstorm is to generate as many ideas as possible. Begin your list in the space below and continue on additional paper as needed. Simply brainstorm as many answers as possible to the following sentence:

I discovered that I want . . .

_____

_____

_____

_____

_____

_____

_____

_____

_____

_____

_____

_____

_____

_____

_____

_____

_____

_____

_____

_____

_____

_____

_____

_____

_____

_____

_____

Intention Statement

After you have finished brainstorming, spend the next five minutes looking over your list. Analyze what you wrote. Read the list out loud. If something is missing, add it.

Then look for *one* thing on the list that's important to you right now, even if it's something that might take many years and many steps to achieve. State this as a goal—a specific outcome or result to achieve by a certain date.

Write your goal in the following space.

I intend to . . .

_____

_____

_____

_____

_____

_____

_____

_____

_____

_____

_____

_____

_____

_____

_____

_____

_____

_____

_____

_____

_____

_____

_____

_____

_____

_____

_____

_____

Action Statement

Now spend 10 minutes writing a list of specific actions that you will take to produce the outcome or result you listed above. Be specific. The idea is to list actions that you can include on a daily to-do list or write down on a calendar. For example, a goal to graduate by a certain date could call for actions such as "call the financial aid office to ask about student loans" or "ask my academic advisor about course requirements for my major."

In your list, include actions that you will take only once as well as habits—things that you will do on a regular basis. For example, a goal to graduate with honors can include a habit such as, "I will study two hours for every hour I'm in class."

Create your list of actions in the space below and use separate paper as needed.

For five minutes, review your brainstormed list of actions. Are they specific? Can you see yourself actually *doing* each of them? If anything on your list is vague or fuzzy, go back and revise it.

Congratulations! Take one more minute to savor the feeling that comes with getting clarity about your deepest values and heartfelt desires. You can take the process you just used and apply it to getting *anything* you want in life. The essential steps are the same in each case: State your desire as a specific outcome. Then translate the goal into a list of concrete actions.

You're One Click Away . . .
from an online goal-setting exercise.

_____

_____

Seven ways to take back *your time*

The truth about time management is that it doesn't exist. Think about it: Time cannot be managed. Every human being gets exactly the same allotment of hours: 24 per day, 168 per week.

However, we can manage our *behavior* so that we become more productive during the fixed number of hours that we all have.

You might know people who seem efficient and yet relaxed. These people do not have more time than you do. They simply manage their behavior in productive ways.

Experiment with the following behaviors. Each of them is a strategy for using the time of your life in the way that you choose. Select one strategy to apply right away. When it becomes a habit, come back to this article and choose another one. Repeat this process as often as you like, and reap the rewards.

1. DO IT NOW

Postponing decisions and procrastinating are major sources of stress. An alternative is to handle the task or decision immediately. Answer that e-mail now. Make that phone call as soon as it occurs to you.

Also use waiting time. Five minutes waiting for a subway, 20 minutes waiting for the dentist, 10 minutes between classes—all that time adds up fast. Have short study tasks ready to do during these periods. For example, you can carry 3 × 5 cards with facts, formulas, or definitions and pull them out anywhere.

2. DELEGATE

Asking for help can free up extra hours you need for studying. Instead of doing all the housework or cooking yourself, assign some of the tasks to family members or roommates. Instead of driving across town to deliver a package, hire a delivery service to do it.

It's neither practical nor ethical to delegate certain study tasks, such as writing term papers or completing reading assignments. However, you can still draw on the ideas of other people in completing such tasks. For instance, form a writing group to edit and critique papers, brainstorm topics or titles, and develop lists of sources.

3. SAY NO

Suppose that someone asks you to volunteer for a project and you realize immediately that you don't want to do it. Save time by graciously telling the truth up front. Saying "I'll think about it and get back to you" just postpones the conversation until later, when it will take more time.

Saying no graciously and up front can be a huge timesaver. Many people think that it is rude to refuse a request. But saying no can be done effectively and courteously. When you tell people that you're saying no to a new commitment because you are busy educating yourself, most of them will understand.

Saying no includes logging off e-mail and instant messaging when appropriate. The Internet is the ultimate interrupter. In today's world, responses to e-mails or instant messages are expected almost immediately. To avoid distraction set an "away" alert for instant messages and set specific times during the day to check your e-mail.

Also experiment with doing less. Planning is as much about dropping worthless activities as about adding new ones. See whether you can reduce or eliminate activities that contribute little to your values or goals.

4. USE A CALENDAR

Use a calendar to remind yourself about commitments that will take place on a certain date or at a certain time—classes, meetings, appointments, and the like. You can also schedule due dates for assignments, reviewing sessions for tests, and any other events you want to remember.

Many students use a paper-based calendar that they can carry along with their textbooks and class notes. Other people favor online calendars such as those offered by Google and Yahoo! Experiment with both and see what works best for you.

When using any kind of calendar, schedule fixed blocks of time first. Start with class time and work time, for instance. These time periods are usually determined in advance. Other activities are scheduled around them.

As an alternative to entering class times in your calendar each week, you can simply print out your class schedule and consult it as needed. As a general guideline, schedule about two hours of study time each week for every hour that you spend in class.

Tasks often expand to fill the time we allot for them, so use your calendar to set clear starting and stopping times. Plan a certain amount of time for that reading assignment, set a timer, and stick to it. Feeling rushed or sacrificing quality is not the aim here. The point is to push yourself a little and discover what your time requirements really are.

Avoid scheduling marathon study sessions, however. When possible, study in shorter sessions. Three 3-hour sessions are usually far more productive than one 9-hour session.

Recognize that unexpected things will happen, and leave some holes in your schedule. Build in blocks of unplanned time, and mark these in your calendar as "flex time" or "open time."

5. WRITE REMINDERS

Almost every book about personal productivity mentions a to-do list. This is a list of specific actions—phone calls to make, errands to run, assignments to complete. Also include actions that are directly related to your goals. (See "Journal Entry 6: Give your goals some teeth" on page 24.)

Save your to-do list for actions that do *not* have to be completed on a certain date or at a certain time. Complete your to-do items at times between the scheduled events in your day. Delete items on your list when you complete them, and add new items as you think of them.

You can record your to-do items on sheets of paper. Another option is to put each to-do item on its own 3 × 5 card. This allows for easy sorting into categories. Also, you'll never have to recopy your to-do list. Whenever you complete a to-do item, simply throw away or recycle the card.

Computers offer similar flexibility. Just open up a file and key in all your to-do items. In a single window on your screen, you'll be able to see at least a dozen to-do items at a glance. As with 3 × 5 cards, you can delete and rearrange to your heart's content.

6. DISCOVER YOUR PERSONAL RHYTHMS

Many people learn best during daylight hours. If this is true for you, then schedule study time for your most difficult subjects when the sun is up.

When you're in a time crunch, get up a little early or stay up late. If the time crunch is chronic, experiment with getting up 15 minutes earlier or going to bed 15 minutes later each day on a more permanent basis. Over the course of one year, either choice will yield 91 extra hours of waking activity.

7. GO FOR THE LONG TERM

Experiment with longer-term planning. Thinking beyond today and the current week can help you see how your daily activities relate to longer-range goals. On your calendar, include *any* key dates for the upcoming quarter, semester, or year. These dates can relate to any area of life—academic, career, or family events. Here are some examples:

- Test dates
- Lab sessions
- Due dates for assignments
- Days when classes will be canceled
- Interim due dates, such as when you plan to complete the first draft of a term paper
- Birthdays, anniversaries, and other special occasions
- Medical and dental checkups
- Application due dates for internships
- Concerts and plays
- Due dates for major bills—insurance, taxes, car registration, credit card and installment loan payments, medical expenses, interest charges, and charitable contributions
- Trips, vacations, and holidays ◼

You're One Click Away . . .
from additional ways to become more productive.

Forget about **time management—** *just get things done*

David Allen, author of *Getting Things Done: The Art of Stress-Free Productivity,* says that a lack of time is not the real issue for the people he coaches. Instead, the problem is having only a vague idea of our desired outcomes and the specific actions needed to produce them. Allen offers the following suggestions.

1. Collect. To begin, make a note about every unfinished project, incomplete task, misplaced object—or anything else that's nagging you. List each of these items on a separate 3 × 5 card or piece of paper and dump it into an in-basket.

2. Process. Pick up each note in your in-basket, one at a time, and ask, "Do I truly want or need to do something about this?" If the answer is no, then trash the item. If the answer is yes, then choose immediately how to respond: Do it now, write a reminder to do it later, or file the item away for future reference. The goal is to *empty* your in-basket at least once each week.

3. Organize. Now group your reminders into appropriate categories. Allen recommends using a calendar for scheduled events, a list of current projects, and a list of next actions to take on each project.

4. Review. Every week, collect any new projects or tasks that are on your mind. Also update your calendar and lists. Ask yourself, "What are all my current projects? And what is the *very next physical action* (such as a phone call or errand) that I can take to move each project forward?"

5. Do. Every day, review your calendar and lists. Based on this information and on your intuition, make moment-to-moment choices about how to spend your time.

David Allen, *Getting Things Done: The Art of Stress-Free Productivity* (New York: Penguin, 2001).

2

JOURNAL ENTRY 7

Discover where your time goes

Do you ever hear yourself saying, "Where did my morning go?" Many people have little idea where their time really goes. But with some heightened awareness and minimal record keeping, you can discover exactly how you spend your time. With this knowledge you can diagnose productivity problems with pinpoint accuracy. You can delete the time-killers and the life-drainers—activities that consume hours yet deliver the least in results or satisfaction. This frees up more time for the activities that you truly value.

If you think you already have a good idea of how you spend time, then predict how many hours you devote each week to sleeping, studying, working, attending classes, and socializing. Use this exercise to monitor your time for one week. Then notice how accurate your predictions were. You'll quickly see the value of collecting accurate data about the way you use time.

Following is a series of steps for monitoring your use of time. To get the most benefit from this exercise, proceed like a scientist. Adopt the hypothesis that you can manage your time in more optimal ways. Then see whether you can confirm or refute that hypothesis by collecting precise data in the laboratory—the laboratory in this case being your life.

1. Choose a specific period to monitor

To get the most benefit from monitoring your time, do it for at least one day. You can extend this practice over several days, a week, or even a month. Monitoring your time over greater intervals can reveal broader patterns in your behavior. You'll get more insight into the way that you spend your most precious resource—you.

2. Plan how to record your data

The key to this exercise is to record the times that you start and stop each activity over a period of 24 hours: sleeping, eating, studying, travelling to and from class, working, watching television, listening to music, sitting in lectures, taking care of the kids, running errands. To promote accuracy and accumulate useful data, track your activity in 30-minute intervals. Tracking 15-minute intervals can be even more useful.

You can record this data in any way that works. Consider these options:

- **Carry a 3 × 5 card** with you each day for recording your activities. Every time that you start a new activity, describe it in a word or two and write down the time you started.

- **Use a daily calendar** that includes slots for scheduling appointments at each hour of the day. Instead of scheduling events ahead of time, simply note how you actually spend each hour.

- **Use time-tracking software.** For the latest products, key the words *time tracking* into a search engine.

- **Create your own system for time monitoring.** For example, before you go to bed, review your day and write down your activities along with starting and stopping times. (See the illustration on this page.)

Sample Time Monitor		
Activity	Start	Stop
Sleep	11:00 pm	6:00 am
Jog/Stretch	6:00 am	7:00 am
Shower/Dress	7:00 am	7:30 am
Breakfast	7:30 am	8:00 am
Travel to Campus	8:30 am	9:00 am
History	9:00 am	10:20 am
Check Email	10:30 am	11:00 am
English Lit	11:00 am	12:00 pm
Lunch/Review for Psych test	12:00 pm	1:00 pm
Work-Study Job	1:00 pm	4:00 pm
Run Errands	4:00 pm	5:00 pm
Travel Home	5:00 pm	5:30 pm
Watch TV/Relax	5:30 pm	6:30 pm
Dinner/Socialize	6:30 pm	8:00 pm
Read Chapter 4/English	8:00 pm	9:00 pm
Make Flashcards for Psych test	9:00 pm	10:00 pm
Review notes from today's History/English Lectures	10:00 pm	11:00 pm

Note: Keep this exercise in perspective. No one says that you have to keep track of the rest of your life in 15-minute intervals. Eventually you can monitor selected activities in your life and keep track of them only for as long as you choose.

3. Record your data

Now put your plan into action. For a minimum of one day, collect data about how much time you spend on each activity.

4. List how much time you spent on each activity

At the end of the day or week, add up the total hours you devoted to each activity. Examples might include eight hours for sleeping, two hours for watching a movie, three hours of class, and six hours for studying. Make sure the grand total of all activities is 24 hours per day or 168 hours per week.

5. Group your activities into major categories

After you've monitored your time for at least one week, group your activities together into broader categories. Examples are *sleep, class, study,* and *meals.* Another category, *grooming,* might include showering, putting on makeup, brushing your teeth, and getting dressed. *Travel* can include walking, driving, taking the bus, and riding your bike. Other categories might be *exercise, entertainment, work, television, domestic,* and *children.* Use categories that make sense for you.

6. Summarize your data

Use the blank two-column chart on this page to summarize the results of the previous steps. Include each category of activity and the number of hours for each category. First, look at the sample chart. Then, using the blank chart provided, fill in your own information.

Categories of Activity	Hours Spent on Each Activity
Class	
Study/Reading for Classes	
Meals (including cooking)	
Free Time	
Exercise	
Clean Apartment	
Laundry	
Call Family	
Work	
Personal Maintenance	
Sleep	
Total	

Categories of Activity	Hours Spent on Each Activity
	Total_____

Also consider using a pie chart to represent your categories of activity. This can be useful for two reasons. First, a circle is a fixed shape, reinforcing the idea that you have only a fixed amount of time to work with: 24 hours a day, 168 hours per week. Second, seeing your life represented on a pie chart tempts you to adjust the sizes of the slices—each slice being a category of activity. You make this adjustment by consciously choosing to devote more or less time to each category. Look at the sample chart below and then fill in your own pie chart using the information from your chart.

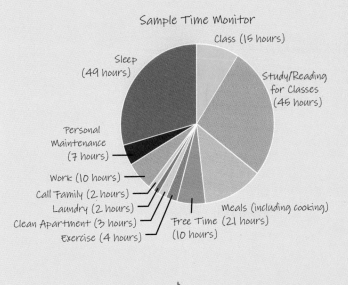

Sample Time Monitor

Class (15 hours)
Study/Reading for Classes (45 hours)
Meals (including cooking) (21 hours)
Free Time (10 hours)
Exercise (4 hours)
Clean Apartment (3 hours)
Laundry (2 hours)
Call Family (2 hours)
Work (10 hours)
Personal Maintenance (7 hours)
Sleep (49 hours)

7. Reflect on your time monitor

Complete the following sentences.

After monitoring my time, I discovered that . . .

I play too many video games

I was surprised that I spent so much time on . . .

Video games

I was surprised that I spent so little time on . . .

Going outside / doing real world activities

I intend to spend more time on . . .

exercising / things away from the computer screen.

I intend to spend less time on . . .

Video games

You're One Click Away . . .
from an online version of this exercise.

Procrastination unplugged

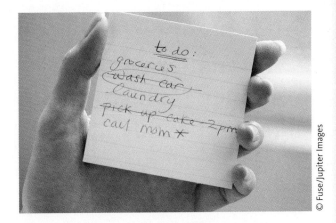

© Fuse/Jupiter Images

The terms *self-discipline, willpower,* and *motivation* are often used to describe something missing in ourselves. Time after time, we invoke these words to explain another person's success—or our own shortcomings: "If I were more motivated, I'd get more involved in school." "Of course she got an A. She has self-discipline." "If I had more willpower, I'd lose weight."

It seems that certain people are born with lots of motivation, whereas others miss out on it.

An alternative way of thinking is to stop assuming that motivation is mysterious, determined at birth, or hard to come by. In fact, perhaps the whole concept of motivation is just a myth. Maybe what we call motivation is something that you already possess—the ability to do a task even when you don't feel like it.

We don't need the concept of motivation to change our behavior. Rather, immediate action can flow from genuine commitment. With that idea in mind, test the following suggestions.

CHECK FOR ATTITUDES THAT PROMOTE PROCRASTINATION

Certain attitudes fuel procrastination and keep you from experiencing the rewards in life that you deserve. In their book *Procrastination: Why You Do It and What to Do About It*, psychologists Jane Burka and Lenora Yuen list these examples:

> I must be perfect.
> Everything I do should go easily and without effort.
> It's safer to do nothing than to take a risk and fail.
> If it's not done right, it's not worth doing at all.
> If I do well this time, I must always do well.
> If I succeed, someone will get hurt.[1]

If you find such beliefs running through your mind, write them down. Getting a belief out of your head and on to paper can rob that belief of its power. Also write a more effective belief that you want to

10 things you can do in 10 minutes (or less)

- Preview a textbook chapter.
- Write a Discovery or an Intention Statement.
- Reread an article in this book.
- Do an exercise (or part of an exercise) in this book.
- Create your weekly budget.
- Take a brisk walk or climb several flights of stairs for exercise.
- Do a spiritual practice, such as meditation or prayer.
- Write and use an affirmation.
- Write a goal or action plan. Review your calendar or to-do list. (Refer to "Journal Entry 6: Give your goals some teeth.")
- Nothing. Just chill. Stare out the window. Breathe deeply and notice how good it feels.

adopt. For example: "Even if I don't complete this task perfectly, it's good enough for now, and I can still learn from my mistakes."

ACCEPT YOUR FEELINGS OF RESISTANCE—THEN TAKE ACTION

If you wait to exercise until you feel energetic, you might wait for months. Instead, get moving now and watch your feelings change. After five minutes of brisk walking, you might be in the mood for a 20-minute run. Don't wait to feel "motivated" before you take action. Instead, apply the principle that action *creates* motivation.

This principle can be applied to any task you've been putting off. You can move into action no matter how you feel about a task. Simply notice your feelings of resistance, accept them, and then do one small task related to your goal. Then do one more task, and another. Keep at it, one task at a time, and watch procrastination disappear. ■

You're One Click Away . . .
from more ways to prevent procrastination.

Put an end
to money worries

"I can't afford it" is a common reason that students give for dropping out of school. Actually, "I don't know how to pay for it" or "I don't think it's worth it" are probably more accurate ways to state the problem.

No matter what the money problem, the solution usually includes two actions. First discover the facts about how much money you have and how much money you spend. Second, commit to live within your means—that is, spend no more than you have.

DISCOVER THE FACTS

Money likes to escape when no one is looking. And usually no one *is* looking. That's why the simple act of noticing the details about money can be so useful—even if this is the only idea from this chapter that you ever apply.

To discover the facts, record all the money you receive and spend over the course of each month. This sounds like a big task. But if you use a simple system, you can turn it into a habit.

One option is to carry 3×5 cards. Every time you receive money, write the date, the source of income, and the amount on a card. Be sure to use a separate card for each amount. Do the same for money that you spend. On separate cards, list the date, the amount you spent, and what you paid for.

At the end of the month, sort your cards into income and expense categories and then total the amounts for each category. There's a payoff for this action. When you know how much money you really earn, you'll know how much you really have to spend. And if you know what your biggest expenses are, you'll know where to start cutting back if you overspend.

Of course, 3×5 cards are just one option. You can also use a computer, apps for your smartphone, and online banking services. Or carefully file all your receipts and paycheck stubs, and use them to tally up your monthly income and expenses.

Whatever tools you choose, start using them today.

LIVE WITHIN YOUR MEANS

There are three broad strategies for living within your means: increase your income, decrease your expenses, or do both.

Increase income. If you work while you're in school, you'll gain experience, establish references, and expand your contacts for getting a new job or making a career change. Also, regular income in any amount can make a difference in your monthly cash flow.

To find a job while you're in school, talk to someone in the financial aid office who helps students find work. This person can also discuss ways to pay for your education. If you're working full-time while going to school, then use the suggestions in this

> No matter what the money problem, the solution usually includes two actions: discover the facts and live within your means.

chapter for managing your time. They will help you balance the demands of the classroom and the workplace.

Once you graduate and land a job in your chosen field, continue your education. Gain additional skills and certifications that lead to higher earnings.

Also excel as an employee. Be as productive as possible. Look for ways to boost sales, increase quality, or accomplish tasks in less time. These achievements can help you earn a raise. And a positive work experience can pay off for years by leading to recommendations and contacts for a new job.

Decrease expenses. When you look for places to cut expenses, start with the items that cost the most. Consider housing, for example. Sometimes a place a little farther from campus, or a smaller house or apartment, will be much less expensive. You can also keep your housing costs down by finding a roommate.

Another high-ticket item is a car. You might find that it makes more sense to use public transportation or car pool.

Also cook for yourself. This single suggestion could save many a sinking budget.

These are only a few suggestions. You can create many more strategies. The bottom line is this: Before you spend money on anything, ask whether you could get the same benefit from another source for free or for a lower cost. ■

You're One Click Away . . .
from finding more strategies for financial freedom

Use credit
with care

A good credit rating will serve you for a lifetime. With this asset, you'll be able to borrow money any time you need it. A poor credit rating, however, can keep you from getting a car or a house in the future. You might also have to pay higher insurance rates, and you could even be turned down for a job.

To take charge of your credit, borrow money only when truly necessary. If you do borrow, then make all of your payments, and make them on time. This is especially important for managing credit cards and student loans.

USE CREDIT CARDS WITH CAUTION

Pay off the balance each month. An unpaid credit card balance is a sure sign that you are spending more money than you have. To avoid this outcome, keep track of how much you spend with credit cards each month. Set a goal to pay off the entire card balance each month, on time, and avoid finance or late charges.

Scrutinize credit card offers. Finding a card with a lower interest rate can make a dramatic difference. However, look carefully at credit card offers. Low rates might be temporary. After a few months, they could double or even triple. Also look for annual fees, late fees, and other charges buried in the fine print.

Avoid cash advances. Due to their high interest rates and fees, credit cards are not a great source of spare cash. Even when you get cash advances on these cards from an ATM, it's still borrowed money. As an alternative, get a debit card tied to a checking account. Use that card when you need cash on the go.

Check statements against your records. File your credit card receipts each month. When you get the bill for each card, check it against your receipts for accuracy. Mistakes in billing are rare, but they can happen. In addition, checking your statement reveals the interest rate and fees that are being applied to your account.

Use just one credit card. To simplify your financial life and take charge of your credit, consider using only one card. Choose one with no annual fee and the lowest interest rate. Consider the bottom line, and be selective. If you do have more than one credit card, pay off the one with the highest interest rate first. Then consider cancelling that card.

MANAGE STUDENT LOANS

Choose schools with costs in mind. If you decide to transfer to another school, you can save thousands of dollars the moment you sign your application for admission. In addition to choosing schools on the basis of reputation, consider how much they cost and the financial aid packages that they offer.

Avoid debt when possible. The surest way to manage debt is to avoid it altogether. If you do take out loans, borrow only the amount that you cannot get from other sources—scholarships, grants, employment, gifts from relatives, and personal savings. Predict what your income will be when the first loan payments are due, and whether you'll make enough money to manage continuing payments.

Also set a target date for graduation, and stick to it. The fewer years you go to school, the lower your debt.

Shop carefully for loans. Go the financial aid office and ask whether you can get a Stafford loan. These are fixed-rate, low-interest loans from the federal government. For more information on the loans that are available to you, visit www.studentaid.ed.gov.

If your parents are helping to pay for your education, they can apply for a PLUS loan. There is no income limit, and parents can borrow up to the total cost of their children's education.

If at all possible, avoid loans from privately owned companies. These companies often charge higher interest rates and impose terms that are less favorable to students.

While you're shopping around, ask about options for repaying your loans. Lenders might allow you to extend the payments over a longer period or adjust the amount of your monthly payment based on your income.

You're One Click Away . . .
from finding more strategies online for credit mastery.

YOUR TIME, YOUR MONEY, and your values

Want a clue to your values? Look at the way you manage time and money. The amount you spend on fast food shows how much you value convenience. The amount you spend on clothes shows how much you value appearance. And the amount of time you spend in class shows how much you value education.

You might not think about values when you pull out a credit card or make a choice about how to spend a Saturday night. Even so, your values are at work.

TWO ELEMENTS OF VALUES

Think of any value as having two aspects. One is invisible—a belief about what matters most in life. You can define this belief by naming something you want and asking, "*Why* do I want that?" Keep asking until you reach a point where the question no longer makes sense. At that point, you'll bump into one of your values.

Suppose that you want to start dating. Why do you want that? Perhaps you want to find someone who will really listen to you and also share his deepest feelings. Why do you want *that*? Perhaps because you want to love and be loved. If someone asks why you want *that*, you might say, "I want that because . . . well, I just want it." At that point, the *why?* question no longer applies. To you, love is an end in itself. You desire love simply for its own sake. Love is one of your values.

The second aspect of any value is a behavior. If you value love, you will take action to meet new people. You'll take the time to develop close friendships. You'll look for a spouse or life partner. You'll build a long-term relationship that is based, in part, on a shared vision of ways to spend and earn money. These behaviors are visible signs that you value love.

THE POWER OF ALIGNMENT

We experience peace of mind when our behaviors align with our values. However, this is not always the case. If you ever suspect that there's a conflict between your values and your behavior, then look at your calendar, to-do list, or money life for clues.

For example, someone says that he values health. After monitoring his expenses, he discovers that he spent $200 last month on fast food. Also, he spent about 1 hour total during that month on exercising at the gym. He's discovered a clear source of conflict. He can resolve that conflict by redefining his values or changing his behavior.

Money management and time management gives us plenty of opportunities for critical thinking. For example, think about the wisdom of choosing to spend money on the latest video game or digital gadget rather than a textbook or other resource needed for your education. Games and gadgets can deliver many hours of entertainment before they break down. Compare that to the value of doing well in a course, graduating with better grades, and acquiring skills that increase your earning power for the rest of your career.

Sometimes we live values that are not our own. Values creep into our lives due to peer pressure or advertising. Movies, TV, and magazines pump us full of images about the value of owning more *stuff*—bigger houses, bigger cars, better clothes. All that stuff costs a lot of money, and it takes a lot of time to maintain. The process of acquiring it can drive us into debt—and into jobs that pay well but take over our time and deny our values. When this happens, we miss the power of aligning behaviors and values.

ASK THIS QUESTION

One way to align your behaviors with your beliefs is to ask one question whenever you spend time or money: *Is this activity or this expense consistent with my values?* Over time, this question can lead to daily changes in your behavior that make a big difference in your peace of mind.

The power of this strategy is magnified when you track the details of your activities, income, and expenses. This allows you to make choices about time and money with your eyes open. It's all about living on purpose and behaving with integrity. With the facts at hand, you can manage money and time in ways that demonstrate your values. ■

Free fun

Sometimes it seems that the only way to spend time having fun is to spend money. Not true. Search out free entertainment on campus and in your community. Beyond this, your imagination is the only limit. Some suggestions are listed below. If you think they're silly or boring, create better ideas of your own.

Browse a bookstore. Volunteer at a child care center. Draw. Exercise. Find other people who share your hobby, and start a club. Give a massage. Do yoga with a friend. Play Frisbee golf. Make dinner for your date. Picnic in the park. Take a long walk. Ride your bike. Listen to music that you already own but haven't heard for a while. Take a candlelight bath. Play board games. Have an egg toss. Test-drive new cars. Donate blood. Make yourself breakfast in bed.

You're One Click Away . . .
frome finding more options online for free fun.

2

✔ CRITICAL THINKING EXERCISE 2

Reflect on your spending

Review the article "Put an end to money worries" on page 32. Then use the suggestions in that article to actually keep track of your income and expenses for one month.

If doing this for an entire month seems like too much work, then commit to keeping these records for just one week or even a few days. As you gain experience with monitoring the details of your money life, you can gradually extend the period to one month.

Next, reflect on what you're learning. To start creating a new future with money, complete the following statements.

After monitoring my income and expenses, I was surprised to discover that . . .

When it comes to money, I am skilled at . . .

Saving money and buying only what I need.

When it comes to money, I am *not* so skilled at . . .

Tracking my finances to know exactly how much/where I spend

I could increase my income by . . .

* *more hours at work*
* *Second Job*
* *Spend less on vices*

I could spend less money on . . .

Cigs, Alcohol, Video Games

The most powerful step I can take right now to take charge of my money is . . .

Keep track of my earning/spending

Finally, take a moment to congratulate yourself for completing this exercise. No matter how the numbers add up, you are learning to take conscious control of your money. Repeat this exercise every month. It will keep you on a steady path to financial freedom.

2 SKILLS Snapshot

Take a snapshot of your current skills at working with time and money. Also think about the next step you'll take to develop more mastery in these areas of your life.

DISCOVERY

My score on the Time and Money section of the Discovery Wheel on page 9 was . . .

I would describe my ability to set and achieve goals as . . .

My strategies for overcoming procrastination currently include . . .

Right now my main sources of income are . . .

My three biggest expenses each month are . . .

INTENTION

I plan to graduate by (month and year) . . .

I plan to pay for my education next year by . . .

When it comes to mastering time and money, the most important goal for me to achieve this year is . . .

ACTION

To achieve the goal I just described, the next action I will take is . . .

At the end of this course, I would like my Time and Money score on the Discovery Wheel to be . . .

Achieving Your Purpose for Reading

Use this **Master Student Map** to ask yourself

WHY THIS CHAPTER MATTERS . . .

- Higher education requires extensive reading of complex material.

WHAT IS INCLUDED. . .

HOW YOU CAN USE THIS CHAPTER . . .

- Experiment with a three-phase strategy for reading more effectively.
- Comprehend difficult texts with more ease.
- Keep up with my online reading.

WHAT IF . . .

- I could finish my reading with time to spare and easily recall the key points?

JOURNAL ENTRY 8

Discover what you want from this chapter

Recall a time when you encountered problems with reading, such as finding words you didn't understand or pausing to reread paragraphs more than once. In the space below, describe what happened.

I discovered that I . . .

_____

_____

_____

_____

Now list at least three specific reading skills that you intend to gain from this chapter.

I intend to . . .

_____

_____

_____

_____

© Ruslan Ivantsov/Shutterstock.com

POWER process

Notice your pictures and let them go

One of the brain's primary jobs is to manufacture images. We use mental pictures to make predictions about the world, and we base much of our behavior on those predictions.

Pictures can sometimes get in our way. Take the student who plans to attend a school he hasn't visited. He chose this school for its strong curriculum and good academic standing, but his brain didn't stop there. In his mind, the campus has historic buildings with ivy-covered walls and tree-lined avenues. The professors, he imagines, will be as articulate as Barack Obama and as entertaining as Conan O'Brien. The cafeteria will be a cozy nook serving everything from delicate quiche to strong coffee. He will gather there with fellow students for hours of stimulating, intellectual conversation. The library will have every book, while the computer lab will boast the newest technology.

The school turns out to be four gray buildings downtown, next to the bus station. The first class he attends is taught by an overweight, balding professor wearing a purple and orange bird-of-paradise tie. The cafeteria is a nondescript hall with machine-dispensed food, and the student's apartment is barely large enough to accommodate his roommate's tuba. This hypothetical student gets depressed. He begins to think about dropping out of school.

The problem with pictures is that they can prevent us from seeing what is really there. That is what happened to the student in this story. His pictures prevented him from noticing that his school is in the heart of a culturally vital city—close to theaters, museums, government offices, clubs, and all kinds of stores. The professor with the weird tie is not only an expert in his field but also a superior teacher. The school cafeteria is skimpy because it can't compete with the variety of inexpensive restaurants in the area.

Our pictures often lead to our being angry or disappointed. We set up expectations of events before they occur. Sometimes we don't even realize that we have these expectations. The next time you discover you are angry, disappointed, or frustrated, look to see which of your pictures aren't being fulfilled.

When you notice that pictures are getting in your way, in the gentlest manner possible let your pictures go. Let them drift away like wisps of smoke picked up by a gentle wind.

This Power Process can be a lifesaver when it comes to reading. Some students enter higher education with pictures about all the reading they'll be required to do before they graduate. They see themselves feeling bored, confused, and worried about keeping up with assignments. If you have such pictures, be willing to let them go. This chapter can help you recreate your whole experience of reading, which is crucial to your success.

Sometimes when we let go of old pictures, it's helpful to replace them with new, positive pictures. These new images can help you take a fresh perspective. Your new pictures might not feel as comfortable and genuine as your old ones. That's okay. Give it time. It's your head, and you're ultimately in charge of the pictures that live there.

You're One Click Away . . .
from accessing Power Process Media online and finding out more about how to "notice your pictures and let them go."

Muscle READING

Picture yourself sitting at a desk, a book in your hands. Your eyes are open, and it looks as if you're reading. Suddenly your head jerks up. You blink. You realize your eyes have been scanning the page for 10 minutes, and you can't remember a single thing you have read.

Or picture this: You've had a hard day. You were up at 6 A.M. to get the kids ready for school. A coworker called in sick, and you missed your lunch trying to do his job as well as your own. You picked up the kids, then had to shop for dinner. Dinner was late, of course, and the kids were grumpy.

Finally, you get to your books at 8 P.M. You begin a reading assignment on something called "the equity method of accounting for common stock investments." "I am preparing for the future," you tell yourself, as you plod through two paragraphs and begin the third.

Suddenly, everything in the room looks different. Your head is resting on your elbow, which is resting on the equity method of accounting. The clock reads 11:00 P.M. Say good-bye to 3 hours. Sometimes the only difference between a sleeping pill and a textbook is that the textbook doesn't have a warning on the label about operating heavy machinery.

You can use a system called Muscle Reading to avoid mental minivacations and reduce the number of unscheduled naps during study time—even after a hard day. Muscle Reading is a way to decrease difficulty and struggle by increasing energy and skill.

Muscle Reading is a three-phase technique. Each phase includes specific strategies.

PHASE ONE:
Before you read
Step 1: **Preview**
Step 2: **Outline**
Step 3: **Question**

PHASE TWO:
While you read
Step 4: **Focus**
Step 5: **Flag Answers**

PHASE THREE:
After you read
Step 6: **Recite**
Step 7: **Review**
Step 8: **Review again**

To remember the Muscle Reading strategies, memorize three short sentences:

P_{ry} O_{ut} Questions.

Focus and Flag Answers.

Recite, Review, and Review again.

These three sentences correspond to the three phases of the Muscle Reading technique. Each sentence is an acrostic. The first letter of each word stands for one of the steps listed above.

Take a moment to invent images for each of those sentences.

For *Phase 1*, visualize or feel yourself prying out questions from a text. These questions are ones you want answered based on a brief survey of the assignment. Make a mental picture of yourself scanning the material, spotting a question, and reaching into the text to pry it out. Hear yourself saying, "I've got it. Here's my question."

Then for *Phase 2*, focus on finding answers to your questions. Feel free to underline, highlight, or mark up your text in other ways. Flag the most important points with double stars, double arrows, or double underlines. Make them so obvious that they lift up from the page.

Finally, you enter *Phase 3*. Hear your voice reciting what you have learned. Listen to yourself making a speech or singing a song about the material as you review it.

To jog your memory, write the first letters of the Muscle Reading acrostic in a margin or at the top of your notes. Then check off the steps you intend to follow. Or write the Muscle Reading steps on 3 × 5 cards and then use them for bookmarks.

This is not to say that Muscle Reading will make your education a breeze. Muscle Reading might even look like more work at first. Muscle Reading might take a little time to learn. At first, you might feel it's slowing you down. That's natural when you're gaining a new skill. Mastery comes with time and practice.

Effective textbook reading is an active, energy-consuming, sit-on-the-edge-of-your-seat business. That's why this strategy is called Muscle Reading. ■

3

PHASE 1 Before you read

STEP 1 PREVIEW

Before you start reading, preview the entire assignment. You don't have to memorize what you preview to get value from this step. Previewing sets the stage for incoming information by warming up a space in your mental storage area.

If you are starting a new book, look over the table of contents and flip through the text page by page. If you're going to read one chapter, flip through the pages of that chapter. Even if your assignment is merely a few pages in a book, you can benefit from a brief preview of the table of contents.

Read all chapter headings and subheadings. Like the headlines in a newspaper, these are usually printed in large, bold type. Often headings are brief summaries in themselves.

Keep an eye out for summary statements. If the assignment is long or complex, read the summary first. Many textbooks have summaries in the introduction or at the end of each chapter.

When previewing, seek out familiar concepts, facts, or ideas. These items can help increase comprehension by linking new information to previously learned material. Take a few moments to reflect on what you already know about the subject—even if you think you know nothing. This technique prepares your brain to accept new information.

Look for ideas that spark your imagination or curiosity. Inspect drawings, diagrams, charts, tables, graphs, and photographs.

Imagine what kinds of questions will show up on a test. Previewing helps to clarify your purpose for reading. Ask yourself what you will do with this material and how it can relate to your long-term goals. Will you be reading just to get the main points? Key supporting details? Additional details? All of the above? Your answers will guide what you do with each step that follows.

Keep your preview short. If the entire reading assignment will take less than an hour, your preview might take 5 minutes. Previewing is also a way to get yourself started when an assignment looks too big to handle. It is an easy way to step into the material.

STEP 2 OUTLINE

With complex material, take time to understand the structure of what you are about to read. Outlining actively organizes your thoughts about the assignment and can help make complex information easier to understand.

If your textbook provides chapter outlines, spend some time studying them. When an outline is not provided, sketch a brief one in the margin of your book or at the beginning of your notes on a separate sheet of paper. Later, as you read and take notes, you can add to your outline.

Headings in the text can serve as major and minor entries in your outline. For example, the heading for this article is "Phase 1: Before you read," and the subheadings list the three steps in this phase. When you outline, feel free to rewrite headings so that they are more meaningful to you.

The amount of time you spend on this outlining step will vary. For some assignments, a 10-second mental outline is all you might need. For other assignments (fiction and poetry, for example), you can skip this step altogether.

STEP 3 QUESTION

Before you begin a careful reading, determine what you want from the assignment. Then write down a list of questions, including any questions that resulted from your preview of the materials.

Another useful technique is to turn chapter headings and subheadings into questions. For example, if a heading is "Transference and Suggestion," you can ask yourself, "What are *transference* and *suggestion?* How does *transference* relate to *suggestion?*" Make up a quiz as if you were teaching this subject to your classmates.

If there are no headings, look for key sentences and turn them into questions. These sentences usually show up at the beginnings or ends of paragraphs and sections.

Have fun with this technique. Make the questions playful or creative. You don't need to answer every question that you ask. The purpose of making up questions is to get your brain involved in the assignment. Take your unanswered questions to class, where they can be springboards for class discussion.

Demand your money's worth from your textbook. If you do not understand a concept, write specific questions about it. The more detailed your questions, the more powerful this technique becomes.

• •

Have fun with this technique. Make the questions playful or creative. You don't need to answer every question that you ask. The purpose of making up questions is to get your brain involved in the assignment. Take your unanswered questions to class, where they can be springboards for class discussion.

• •

 **You're One Click Away . . .**
from finding examples of Phase 1 strategies online.

PHASE 2 While you read

STEP 4 FOCUS

You have previewed the reading assignment, organized it in your mind or on paper, and formulated questions. Now you are ready to begin reading.

It's easy to fool yourself about reading. Just having an open book in your hand and moving your eyes across a page doesn't mean that you are reading effectively. Reading takes mental focus.

As you read, be conscious of where you are and what you are doing. Use the "Power Process: Be here now." When you notice your attention wandering, gently bring it back to the present moment. There are many ways to do this.

To begin, get in a position to stay focused. If you observe chief executive officers, you'll find that some of them wear out the front of their chair first. They're literally on the edge of their seat. Approach your reading assignment in the same way. Sit up. Keep your spine straight. Avoid reading in bed, except for fun.

Avoid marathon reading sessions. Schedule breaks and set a reasonable goal for the entire session. Then reward-

FIVE SMART WAYS
to highlight a text

Step 5 in Muscle Reading mentions a powerful tool: highlighting. It also presents a danger—the ever-present temptation to highlight too much text. Excessive highlighting leads to wasted time during reviews. Get the most out of all that money you pay for books and the time you spend reading. Highlight in an efficient way that leaves texts readable for years to come and provides you with an easy reviewing method.

Read carefully first. Read an entire chapter or section at least once before you begin highlighting. Don't be in a hurry to mark up your book. Get to know the text first. Make two or three passes through difficult sections before you highlight.

Make choices up front about what to highlight. Perhaps you can accomplish your purposes by highlighting only certain chapters or sections of a text. When you highlight, remember to look for passages that directly answer the questions you posed during Step 3 of Muscle Reading. Within these passages, highlight individual words, phrases, or sentences rather than whole paragraphs. The important thing is to choose an overall strategy before you put highlighter to paper.

Recite first. You might want to apply Step 6 of Muscle Reading before you highlight. Talking about what you read—to yourself or with other people—can help you grasp the essence of a text. Recite first; then go back and highlight. You'll probably highlight more selectively.

Underline, then highlight. Underline key passages lightly in pencil. Then close your text and come back to it later. Assess your underlining. Perhaps you can highlight less than you underlined and still capture the key points.

Use highlighting to monitor your comprehension. Critical thinking plays a role in underlining and highlighting. When highlighting, you're making moment by-moment decisions about what you want to remember from a text. You're also making inferences about what material might be included on a test. Take your critical thinking a step further by using highlighting to check your comprehension. Stop reading periodically and look back over the sentences you've highlighted. See whether you are making accurate distinctions between main points and supporting material. Highlighting too much—more than 10 percent of the text—can be a sign that you're not making this distinction and that you don't fully understand what you're reading.

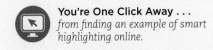
You're One Click Away . . .
from finding an example of smart highlighting online.

> It's easy to fool yourself about reading. Just having an open book in your hand and moving your eyes across a page doesn't mean that you are reading effectively. Reading takes mental focus.

yourself with an enjoyable activity for 10 or 15 minutes every hour or two.

For difficult reading, set more limited goals. Read for a half hour and then take a break. Most students find that shorter periods of reading distributed throughout the day and week can be more effective than long sessions.

Visualize the material. Form mental pictures of the concepts as they are presented. If you read that a voucher system can help control cash disbursements, picture a voucher handing out dollar bills. Using visual imagery in this way can help deepen your understanding of the text while allowing information to be transferred into your long-term memory.

Read material out loud, especially if it is complicated. Some of us remember better and understand more quickly when we hear an idea.

Get a "feel" for the subject. For example, let's say you are reading about a microorganism—a paramecium—in your biology text. Imagine what it would feel like to run your finger around the long, cigar-shaped body of the organism. Imagine feeling the large fold of its gullet on one side and the tickle of the hairy little cilia as they wiggle in your hand.

In addition, predict how the author will answer your key questions. Then read to find out if your predictions were accurate.

STEP 5 FLAG ANSWERS

As you read, seek out the answers to your questions. You are a detective, watching for every clue. When you do find an answer, flag it so that it stands out on the page.

Deface your books. Have fun. Flag answers by highlighting, underlining, writing comments, filling in your outline, or marking up pages in any other way that helps you. Indulge yourself as you never could with your grade school books.

Marking up your books offers other benefits. When you read with a highlighter, pen, or pencil in your hand, you involve your kinesthetic senses of touch and motion. Being physical with your books can help build strong neural pathways in your memory.

You can mark up a text in many ways. For example:

- Place an asterisk (*) or an exclamation point (!) in the margin next to an especially important sentence or term.
- Circle key terms and words to look up later in a dictionary.
- Write short definitions of key terms in the margin.
- Write a Q in the margin to highlight possible test questions, passages you don't understand, and questions to ask in class.
- Write personal comments in the margin—points of agreement or disagreement with the author.
- Write mini-indexes in the margin—that is, the numbers of other pages in the book where the same topic is discussed.
- Write summaries in your own words.
- Rewrite chapter titles, headings, and subheadings so that they're more meaningful to you.
- Draw diagrams, pictures, tables, or maps that translate text into visual terms.
- Number each step in a list or series of related points.
- In the margins, write notes about the relationships between elements in your reading. For instance, note connections between an idea and examples of that idea.
- If you infer an answer to a question or come up with another idea of your own, write that down as well.

Avoid marking up a text too soon. Wait until you complete a chapter or section to make sure you know the key points. Then mark up the text. Sometimes, flagging answers after you read each paragraph works best.

Also remember that the purpose of making marks in a text is to call out important concepts or information that you will review later. Flagging key information can save lots of time when you are studying for tests. With this in mind, highlight or underline sparingly—usually less than 10 percent of the text. If you mark up too much on a page, you defeat the purpose: to flag the most important material for review.

Finally, jot down new questions, and note when you don't find the answers you are looking for. Ask these questions in class, or see your instructor personally. Demand that your textbooks give you what you want—answers. ■

You're One Click Away . . .
from finding examples of Phase 2 strategies online.

PHASE 3 After you read

STEP 6 RECITE

Talk to yourself about what you've read. Or talk to someone else. When you finish a reading assignment, make a speech about it. When you recite, you practice an important aspect of metacognition—synthesis, or combining individual ideas and facts into a meaningful whole.

One way to get yourself to recite is to look at each underlined point. Note what you marked; then put the book down and start talking out loud. Explain as much as you can about that particular point.

To make this technique more effective, do it in front of a mirror. It might seem silly, but the benefits can be enormous. Reap them at exam time.

A related technique is to stop reading periodically and write a short, free-form summary of what you just read. In one study, this informal "retrieval practice" helped students recall information better than other study techniques.[1]

Classmates are even better than mirrors. Form a group and practice teaching one another what you have read. One of the best ways to learn anything is to teach it to someone else.

In addition, talk about your reading whenever you can. Tell friends and family members what you're learning from your textbooks.

Talking about your reading reinforces a valuable skill—the ability to summarize. To practice this skill, pick one chapter (or one section of one chapter) from any of your textbooks. State the main topic covered in this chapter. Then state the main points that the author makes about this topic.

For example, the main topic up to this point in this chapter is Muscle Reading. The main point about this topic is that Muscle Reading includes three phases—steps to take before you read, while you read, and after you read. For a more detailed summary, you could name each of the steps.

Note: This topic-point method does not work so well when you want to summarize short stories, novels, plays, and other works of fiction. Instead, focus on action. In most stories, the main character confronts a major problem and takes a series of actions to solve it. Describe that problem and talk about the character's key actions—the turning points in the story.

STEP 7 REVIEW

Plan to do your first complete review within 24 hours of reading the material. Sound the trumpets! This point is critical: A review within 24 hours moves information from your short-term memory to your long-term memory.

Review within 1 day. If you read it on Wednesday, review it on Thursday. During this review, look over your notes and clear up anything you don't understand. Recite some of the main points again.

This review can be short. You might spend as little as 15 minutes reviewing a difficult 2-hour reading assignment. Investing that time now can save you hours later when studying for exams.

Muscle Reading— a leaner approach

Keep in mind that Muscle Reading is an overall approach, not a rigid, step-by-step procedure. Here's a shorter variation that students have found helpful. Practice it with any chapter in this book:

- **Preview and question.** Flip through the pages, looking at anything that catches your eye—headings, subheadings, illustrations, photographs. Turn the title of each article into a question. For example, "How Muscle Reading works" can become "How does Muscle Reading work?" List your questions on a separate sheet of paper, or write each question on a 3 × 5 card.

- **Read to answer your questions.** Read each article. Then go back over the text and underline or highlight answers to the appropriate questions on your list.

- **Recite and review.** When you're done with the chapter, close the book. Recite by reading each question—and answering it—out loud. Review the chapter by looking up the answers to your questions. (It's easy—they're already highlighted.) Review again by quizzing yourself one more time with your list of questions.

STEP 8 REVIEW AGAIN

The final step in Muscle Reading is the weekly or monthly review. This step can be very short—perhaps only 4 or 5 minutes per assignment. Simply go over your notes. Read the highlighted parts of your text. Recite one or two of the more complicated points.

The purpose of these reviews is to keep the neural pathways to the information open and to make them more distinct. That way, the information can be easier to recall. You can accomplish these short reviews anytime, anywhere, if you are prepared.

Conduct a 5-minute review while you are waiting for a bus, for your socks to dry, or for the water to boil. Three-by-five cards are a handy review tool. Write ideas, formulas, concepts, and facts on cards, and carry them with you. These short review periods can be effortless and fun.

Sometimes longer review periods are appropriate. For example, if you found an assignment difficult, consider rereading it. Start over, as if you had never seen the material before. Sometimes a second reading will provide you with surprising insights.

Decades ago, psychologists identified the primacy-recency effect, which suggests that we most easily remember the first and last items in any presentation.[2] Previewing and reviewing your reading can put this theory to work for you. ■

You're One Click Away . . .
from finding examples of Phase 3 strategies online.

JOURNAL ENTRY 9   *Discovery/Intention Statement*

Experimenting with Muscle Reading

After reading the steps included in Muscle Reading, reflect on your reading skills. Are you a more effective reader than you thought you were? Less effective? Record your observations below.

I discovered that I . . .

_____

_____

_____

_____

_____

_____

_____

_____

_____

_____

_____

_____

_____

_____

Many students find that they only do the "read" step with their textbooks. You've just read about the advantages of eight additional steps you should perform. Depending on the text, reading assignment, your available time, and your commitment level to the material, you may discover through practice which additional steps work best for you. Right now, make a commitment to yourself to experiment with all or several of the additional Muscle Reading steps by completing the following Intention Statement.

I intend to use the following Muscle Reading steps for the next 2 weeks in my _____ class:

❑ Preview

❑ Outline

❑ Question

❑ Focus

❑ Flag answers

❑ Recite

❑ Review

❑ Review again

Ways to **overcome** *confusion*

Sometimes ordinary reading methods are not enough. It's easy to get bogged down in a murky reading assignment. The solution starts with a First Step: When you are confused, tell the truth about it.

Successful readers monitor their understanding of reading material. They do not see confusion as a mistake or a personal shortcoming. Instead, they take it as a cue to change reading strategies and process ideas at a deeper level.

Read it again. Somehow, students get the idea that reading means opening a book and dutifully slogging through the text—line by line, page by page. They move in a straight line from the first word until the last. Actually, this method can be an ineffective way to read much of the published material you'll encounter in college.

Feel free to shake up your routine. Make several passes through tough reading material. During a preview, for example, just scan the text to look for key words and highlighted material. Next, skim the entire chapter or article again, spending a little more time and taking in more than you did during your preview. Finally, read in more depth, proceeding word by word through some or all of the text. Difficult material—such as the technical writing in science texts—is often easier the second time around. Isolate difficult passages and read them again, slowly.

This suggestion comes with one caution. If you find yourself doing a lot of rereading, then consider a change in reading strategies. For example, you might benefit from reciting after each paragraph or section rather than after each chapter.

Look for essential words. If you are stuck on a paragraph, mentally cross out all of the adjectives and adverbs. Then read the sentences without them. Find the important words—usually verbs and nouns.

Hold a mini-review. Pause briefly to summarize—either verbally or in writing—what you've read so far. Stop at the end of a paragraph and recite, in your own words, what you have just read. Jot down some notes, or create a short outline or summary.

Read it out loud. Make noise. Read a passage out loud several times, each time using a different inflection and emphasizing a different part of the sentence. Be creative. Imagine that you are the author talking.

Talk to someone who can help. Admit when you are stuck. Then bring questions about reading assignments to classmates and members of your study group. Also, make an appointment with your instructor. Most teachers welcome the opportunity to work individually with students. Be specific about your confusion. Point out the paragraph that you found toughest to understand.

Stand up. Changing positions periodically can combat fatigue. Experiment with standing as you read, especially if you get stuck on a tough passage and decide to read it out loud.

Skip around. Jump to the next section or to the end of a tough article or chapter. You might have lost the big picture. Simply seeing the next step, the next main point, or a summary might be all you need to put the details in context. Retrace the steps in a chain of ideas, and look for examples. Absorb facts and ideas in whatever order works for you—which may be different than the author's presentation.

Find a tutor. Many schools provide free tutoring services. If your school does not, other students who have completed the course can assist you.

Use another text. Find a similar text in the library. Sometimes a concept is easier to understand if it is expressed another way. Children's books—especially children's encyclopedias—can provide useful overviews of baffling subjects.

Note where you get stuck. When you feel stuck, stop reading for a moment and diagnose what's happening. At these stop points, mark your place in the margin of the page with an "S" for *Stuck*. A pattern to your marks over several pages might indicate a question you want to answer before going further.

Construct a word stack. Sometimes the source of confusion is an unfamiliar word. When you come across one, write it down on a 3×5 card. Below the word, copy the sentence in which it was used, along with the page number. You can look up each word immediately, or you can accumulate a stack of these cards and look up the words later. Write the definition of each word on the back of the 3×5 card, adding. Add the diacritics—marks that tell you how to pronounce the word.

Divide unfamiliar words into parts. Another strategy for expanding your vocabulary is to divide an unfamiliar word into syllables and look for familiar parts. This strategy works well if you make it a point to learn common prefixes (beginning syllables) and suffixes (ending syllables). For example, the suffix *-tude* usually refers to a condition or state of being. Knowing this makes it easier to conclude that *habitude* refers to a repeated way of doing something. Likewise, *similitude* means being similar or having a quality of resemblance.

Infer the meaning of words from their context. You can often deduce the meaning of an unfamiliar word simply by paying attention to its context—the surrounding words, phrases, sentences, paragraphs, or images. Later, you can confirm your deduction by consulting a dictionary.

Practice looking for context clues such as these:

- *Definitions.* A key word might be defined right in the text. Look for phrases such as *defined as* or *in other words.*

- *Examples.* Authors often provide examples to clarify a word meaning. If the word is not explicitly defined, then study the examples. They're often preceded by the phrases *for example, for instance,* or *such as.*

- *Lists.* When a word is listed in a series, pay attention to the other items in the series. They might define the unfamiliar word through association.

- *Comparisons.* You might find a new word surrounded by synonyms—words with a similar meaning. Look for synonyms after words such as *like* and *as.*

- *Contrasts.* A writer might juxtapose a word with its antonym. Look for phrases such as *on the contrary* and *on the other hand.*

Stop reading. When none of the above suggestions work, do not despair. Admit your confusion and then take a break. Catch a movie, go for a walk, study another subject, or sleep on it. The concepts you've already absorbed might come together at a subconscious level as you move on to other activities. Allow some time for that process. When you return to the reading material, see it with fresh eyes. ■

You're One Click Away . . .
from more strategies for overcoming confusion.

Five ways to read with children underfoot

It is possible to have both effective study time and quality time with your children. The following suggestions come mostly from students who are also parents. The specific strategies you use will depend on your schedule and the ages of your children.

Find a regular playmate for your child.
Some children can pair off with close friends and safely retreat to their rooms for hours of private play. You can check on them occasionally and still get lots of reading done.

Create a special space for your child.
Set aside one room or area of your home as a play space. Childproof this space. The goal is to create a place where children can roam freely and play with minimal supervision. Consider allowing your child in this area *only* when you study. Your homework time then becomes your child's reward. If you're cramped for space, just set aside some special toys for your child to play with during your study time.

Use television responsibly.
Whenever possible, select educational programs that keep your child's mind active and engaged. Also see whether your child can use headphones while watching television. That way, the house stays quiet while you study.

Schedule time to be with your children when you've finished studying.
Let your children in on the plan: "I'll be done reading at seven-thirty. That gives us a whole hour to play before you go to bed."

Ask other adults for help.
Getting help can be as simple as asking your spouse, partner, neighbor, or fellow student to take care of the children while you study. Offer to trade child care with a neighbor: You will take his kids and yours for 2 hours on Thursday night if he'll take them for 2 hours on Saturday morning.

Find community activities and services.
Ask whether your school provides a child care service. In some cases, these services are available to students at a reduced cost.

Getting THE MOST from ONLINE READING

Suppose that you kept track of the number of hours that you spend online each week. The total might surprise you. If you're a student, a large part of that online time is probably devoted to reading. This might include:

- E-mails
- Instant messages
- Web pages
- PDF files
- Web-based discussion groups
- Web-based course materials

You can apply all three phases of Muscle Reading to online reading. However, if you approach online reading only with the strategies you use for printed documents, you might waste time trying to find the information you want. In addition, you could miss out on key points and find it hard to remember what you read. Use the following strategies to prevent those problems and get the most from your time online.

CHOOSE YOUR TOOLS

You interact physically with printed documents by turning pages. You might use a finger or a pencil to mark your place in the text as you read. Also, you might write notes in the margins. When you're online, you interact with documents in different ways—by clicking on links, typing in text boxes, and scrolling up and down or across pages.

In addition, modern Web browsers have tools that can help you with online reading. For instance:

- Tabbed browsing allows you to open up several Web pages at a time and move between them with a single click.
- Full-screen browsing allows you to expand a window so that it fills your entire computer screen.
- Increasing the font size makes it easier to read small type.
- Decreasing font size can help you fit more text and images on a screen, showing you the "big picture" of a Web page.
- Ad blocking and pop-up blocking frees you from distracting advertisements and windows that appear without your permission.

To find these and related features, check the menus in your browser, including the Preferences menu.

KEEP YOUR FOCUS

To get the most from online reading, disable or ignore instant messaging and e-mail notifications. Also tune out social networking Web sites such as Facebook, Google+, and Twitter. (Save them as a reward for completing your online reading.)

Many Web pages are cluttered with images, videos, and animations. These can be fun to consume—and they can distract you from your purpose for reading. To strip away everything but the main text on a Web page, use a tool such as Readability (www .readability.com). You can install Readability as a browser extension or as a bookmarklet that sits in the Bookmarks bar on your browser.

Instapaper (www.instapaper.com/extras) and Readable (readable.tastefulwords.com) also offer bookmarklets for cleaning up Web pages.

If you're using an iPhone or iPad with Safari as your Web browser, look for a Reader button in the toolbar. Click on this button to remove clutter.

Also remove desktop clutter. Most of us find it easier to be productive at work when we clear away clutter and work at a clean desk. To be more productive at online reading, remove clutter from your computer desktop by closing these:

- Applications that you don't need for online reading
- Windows that you're not actively using
- Tabs in your browser for Web pages that you don't need anymore

CHOOSE YOUR PATHWAY

Remember that the information you find on a series of Web pages is not presented in a linear way. To succeed with online reading, actively seek out the content that aligns with your purpose for reading. Look for answers to the questions you listed during the first phase of Muscle Reading.

Scan headings. Headings are words that appear in large type, bold type, or both on a Web page. Sometimes you'll see subheadings as well—words in smaller bold type.

Headings and subheadings describe what you'll find in the text and images that follow. Use them to quickly locate the content you want. You might find a direct answer to one of your questions right in a heading on a Web page.

Think through the link. Skilled readers make many predictions when they're online. The idea is to plan a step or two ahead of where you are in an online document. Predict what kind of material you will find in one—or more—layers behind a link.

Suppose you're scanning Web pages for information about endangered species of animals in your state. You say to yourself, "It would be great if I could find an interactive map." Then you find this link on a Web page: Endangered species by state. "That's what I need," you say to yourself. So you click on the link and wait for the new Web page to load. This is an example of "thinking through the link": You make a prediction as you read and then take a related action.

Some links will lead to dead ends, however—pages that have nothing to do with your predictions. To improve your skills at thinking through links:

- Hit the "Back" button on your browser to return to the previous page and look for other links.
- Go to the home page for the Web site and look for other links that are more relevant to your purpose.
- Look for a search box on the Web page and fill it with key words from the questions you want to answer.

To refine your predictions, also look for common types of links. These are often located at the top or bottom of a Web page. For example:

- *About* links lead you to pages that explain the purpose and general scope of a Web site.
- *Related* links lead to pages with similar content.
- *FAQ* links lead to pages with a list of common questions about a topic and their answers.
- *Help* links lead to pages that help you solve problems with using a Web site.
- *Contact* links lead to pages with an address, phone number, and e-mail address for a Web site's authors.

Skip content freely. Some students feel that it's their obligation to read every word that appears on a Web page. They're afraid of missing something. Let go of that obligation. Feel free to skip Web content that fails to answer your questions. Remember that the author's purpose for writing might be different from your purpose for reading.

Of course, there are times when you'll want to read an entire Web page or Web-based document because it's assigned. In that case, slow down to take your time and dwell on the details.

Ask: Am I getting lost? Suppose you have a book in your hands and want to find a sentence that you read earlier. You can just skim as you flip through the previous pages. When you're online, however, things aren't so simple. In just a few minutes of clicking through links, you might race through dozens of Web pages. Winding your way back through them can be tricky.

To retrace your online reading path:

- Use your browser's Back and Forward buttons.
- Scan the pages listed under your browser's History menu.
- Keep a tab in your browser open to a Web site's home page or site map.
- Use your browser's Find command to search Web pages for a specific word or phrase.

CHOOSE YOUR PACE

Whether you're online or offline, vary your reading speed based on your purpose. Skilled readers are not just fast—they're flexible. They shift to low gear and slow down when text is difficult. They speed up when reviewing easy material. And they race past content that doesn't match their purpose.

Also remember that long sessions at a computer screen can be hard on your eyes. To prevent eyestrain during online reading, slow down your pace even more, take frequent, short breaks to stand up or take a walk. Look away from the screen at something across the room or outside the window. Or simply close your eyes for a few seconds.

BOOKMARK YOUR ONLINE READING

Bookmarks are lists of Web pages you've visited. When you find a page you'll want to check later, bookmark it. Every browser offers a way to store, organize, and search your bookmarks. Just look for the Bookmarks menu in your Web browser.

You can also have fun with social bookmarking Web sites. These let you store, organize, annotate, and search bookmarks that are stored online. In addition, you can share your public bookmarks with other people who visit the site. Some social bookmarking sites are:

- Delicious (delicious.com)
- Diigo (diigo.com)
- Pinboard (pinboard.in)

If you run across articles and blog posts that you want to read later, also consider using an application such as Pocket (getpocket.com). This will create a personal "to read" list that you can synchronize across your computer, tablet, and smartphone. Readability and Instapaper offer similar features.

SUPPLEMENT ONLINE READING WITH PEOPLE CONTACT

One possible disadvantage of going online is isolation, especially when a course is entirely Web-based. Form a study group to discuss your online reading. If you find links to an online discussion group or chat room, then take advantage of those features.

Leaving your Web browser behind to connect with people can take your online reading to a new level. ■

You're One Click Away . . .
from more strategies for online reading.

CRITICAL THINKING EXERCISE 3

"Dear author—I don't necessarily agree"

Two cornerstones of critical thinking are the abilities to test logic and examine evidence. Some strategies for doing both are explained in Chapter 7: "Thinking Clearly & Communicating Your Ideas." You can start testing logic right now by asking the following questions about what you read:

- Does the author define her key terms?

- Do any of the author's main points contradict each other?

- Has the author clearly stated her assumptions (the points that she simply accepts as true without trying to prove them)?

- Is the author's material free of logical fallacies, such as jumping to conclusions or making personal attacks?

Choose a current reading assignment—a nonfiction piece rather than a novel, short story, or poem. Focus on a particular chapter or section of this assignment and test it by asking the above questions. If you answered no to any of the above questions, then explain your reasons for doing so in the space below:

_____

_____

_____

_____

_____

_____

_____

_____

_____

_____

_____

_____

Now review the same chapter or section and examine evidence. In the space below, list the author's main points. Did she present enough facts, examples, or expert testimony to support each one? If you answered no to this question, then explain your reasons for doing so in the space below:

_____

_____

_____

_____

_____

_____

_____

_____

_____

_____

_____

_____

_____

_____

_____

_____

_____

3

 You're One Click Away . . .
from more ways to think critically about your reading.

3 SKILLS Snapshot

After studying this chapter, you might want to make some changes to the way you read. First, take a snapshot of your current reading habits and reflect on the reading skills you've already developed. Complete the following sentences.

DISCOVERY

My score on the Reading section of the Discovery Wheel on page 9 was . . .

If someone asked me how well I keep up with my assigned reading, I would say that . . .

To get the most out of a long reading assignment, I start by . . .

When I take notes on my reading, my usual method is to . . .

When it's important for me to remember what I read, I . . .

When I don't understand something that I've read, I overcome confusion by . . .

INTENTION

I'll know that I've reached a new level of mastery with reading when . . .

Stated as a goal, my intention is to . . .

ACTION

To reach my goal, the most important thing I can do next is to . . .

At the end of this course, I would like my Reading score on the Discovery Wheel to be . . .

Participating in Class & Taking Notes

4

Use this **Master Student Map** to ask yourself

WHY THIS CHAPTER MATTERS . . .

- Note taking helps you understand course content and directly affects how well you do on tests.

WHAT IS INCLUDED . . .

HOW YOU CAN USE THIS CHAPTER . . .

- Experiment with several formats for note taking.
- Take effective notes in special situations.

WHAT IF . . .

- I could take notes that remain informative and useful for weeks, months, or even years to come?

JOURNAL ENTRY 10

Discover what you want from this chapter

Recall a recent incident in which you had difficulty taking notes. Perhaps you were listening to an instructor who spoke quickly, or you got confused and stopped taking notes altogether. Describe your experience here.

I discovered that I . . .

_____

_____

_____

_____

Now, preview this chapter to find at least three strategies that you can use right away to take better notes. List the strategies and the page numbers where you can read more about them

I intend to . . .

_____

_____

_____

_____

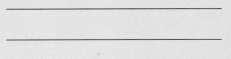

© Ruslan Ivantsov/Shutterstock.com

I create it all

This article describes a powerful tool for times of trouble. In a crisis, "I create it all" can lead the way to solutions. The main point of this Power Process is to treat experiences, events, and circumstances in your life *as if* you created them.

"I create it all" is one of the most unusual and bizarre suggestions in this book. It certainly is not a belief. Use it when it works. Don't when it doesn't.

Keeping that in mind, consider how powerful this Power Process can be. It is really about the difference between two distinct positions in life: being a victim or being responsible.

A victim of circumstances is controlled by outside forces. We've all felt like victims at one time or another. Sometimes we felt helpless.

In contrast, we can take responsibility. Responsibility is "response-ability"—the ability to choose a *response* to any event. You can choose your *response* to any event, even when the event itself is beyond your control.

Many students approach grades from the position of being victims. When the student who sees the world this way gets an "F," she reacts something like this:

"Another 'F'! That teacher couldn't teach her way out of a wet paper bag. She can't teach English for anything. There's no way to take notes in that class. And that textbook—what a bore!"

The problem with this viewpoint is that in looking for excuses, the student is robbing herself of the power to get any grade other than an "F." She's giving all of her power to a bad teacher and a boring textbook.

There is another way, called *taking responsibility*. You can recognize that you choose your grades by choosing your actions. Then you are the source, rather than the result, of the grades you get. The student who got an "F" could react like this:

"Another 'F'! Oh, shoot! Well, hmmm . . . What did I do to create it?"

Now, that's power. By asking, "How did I contribute to this outcome?" you are no longer the victim. This student might continue by saying, "Well, let's see. I didn't review my notes after class. That might have done it." Or "I went out with my friends the night before the test. Well, that probably helped me fulfill some of the requirements for getting an 'F.'"

The point is this: When the "F" is the result of your friends, the book, or the teacher, you probably can't do anything about it. However, if you *chose* the "F," you can choose a different grade next time. You are in charge.

You're One Click Away . . .
from accessing Power Process Media online and finding out more about how to "create it all."

iStockphoto.com/Mark Chen

Note-taking
ESSENTIALS

You enter a lecture hall filled with students. For the next hour, one person standing at the front of the room will do most of the talking. Everyone else is seated and silent, taking notes. The lecturer seems to be doing all the work.

Don't be deceived. Look closely and you'll see students taking notes in a way that radiates energy. They're awake and alert. They're writing—a physical activity that expresses mental engagement. These students listen for levels of information, make choices about what to record, and create effective materials to review later.

One way to understand note taking is to realize that taking notes is just one part of the process. Effective note taking consists of three phases.

First, you carefully set the stage for taking notes. This means showing up for class both physically and mentally. Your job is to observe an event, which can be anything from a lecture to a lab experiment or a slide show of an artist's works.

Second, you record your observations of that event. That is, you "take notes." This means listening for the main points and capturing them in the form of key words and images. Master students like to play with various formats for note taking, often discovering that a change in approach can deepen their understanding of course material.

Finally, you return to your notes at a later time to mine them for added value. You review what you have recorded. You memorize, reflect, and apply what you're learning. In addition, you predict test questions and rehearse possible answers. All this activity lifts ideas off the page and turns them into a working part of your mind.

Each phase of the note-taking process is essential, and each depends on the others. Setting the stage determines the quality of your observations. And the quality of the words and images that you capture determines how much value you can extract from your notes.

While in school, you may spend hundreds of hours taking notes. Experimenting with ways to make those notes more effective is a direct investment in your success. Think of your notes as a textbook that *you* create—one that's more in tune with your learning preferences than any textbook you could buy.

Legible and speedy handwriting, knowledge about outlining, a nifty pen, and a new notebook are all great note-taking devices. Technology—including laptop computers, tablets, and smartphones—takes traditional note taking to a whole new level. You can capture key notes with word-processing, outlining,

> While in school, you may spend hundreds of hours taking notes. Experimenting with ways to make those notes more effective is a direct investment in your success

database, or publishing software—and an ever-expanding catalog of "apps." Your notes can become living documents that you access at any time from a variety of devices. You can search, bookmark, tag, and archive the content of your notes as you would do with other digital files.

And all those tools are worthwhile only if you take notes in a way that helps you *think* about what you're reading and experiencing in class.

This is a well-researched aspect of student success in higher education. Study after study points to the benefits of taking notes. The value is added in two ways. First, you create a set of materials that refreshes your memory and helps you prepare for tests. Second, taking notes prompts you to listen effectively during class. You translate new ideas into your own words and images. You impose a personal and meaningful structure on what you see, read, and hear. You move from passive observer to active participant.[1]

It's not that you take notes so that you can learn from them later. Instead, you learn *while* taking notes.

Use the suggestions in this chapter to complete each phase of note taking more effectively. If you put these ideas into practice, you can turn even the most disorganized chicken scratches into tools for learning. ■

Turn POWERPOINTS into POWERFUL NOTES

PowerPoint presentations are common. They can also be lethal for students who want to master course content or those who simply want to stay awake.

Some students stop taking notes during a PowerPoint presentation. This choice can be hazardous to your academic health for three major reasons:

- *PowerPoint presentations don't include everything.* Instructors and other speakers use PowerPoint to organize their presentations. Topics covered in the slides make up an outline of what your instructor considers important. Slides are created to flag the main points and signal transitions between points. However, speakers usually add examples and explanations that don't appear on the slides. In addition, slides will not include any material from class discussion, including any answers that the instructor gives in response to questions.

- *You stop learning.* Taking notes forces you to capture ideas and information in your own words. Also, the act of writing things down helps you remember the material. If you stop writing and let your attention drift, you can quickly get lost.

- *You end up with major gaps in your notes.* When it's time to review your notes, you'll find that material from PowerPoint presentations is missing. This can be a major pain at exam time.

To create value from PowerPoint presentations, take notes on them. Continue to observe, record, and review. See PowerPoint as a way to *guide* rather than to *replace* your own note taking. Even the slickest, smartest presentation is no substitute for your own thinking.

Experiment with the following suggestions. They include ideas about what to do before, during, and after a PowerPoint presentation.

BEFORE THE PRESENTATION

Sometimes instructors make PowerPoint slides available before a lecture. If you have computer access, download these files. Scan the slides, just as you would preview a reading assignment.

Consider printing out the slides and bringing them along to class. (If you own a copy of PowerPoint, then choose the "handouts" option when printing. This will save paper and ink.) You can take notes directly on the pages that you print out as in the figure below. Be sure to add the slide numbers if they are missing.

If you use a laptop computer for taking notes during class, then you might not want to bother with printing. Just open up the Power-Point file and type your notes in the window that appears at the bottom of each slide. After class, you can print out the slides in note view. This will show the original slides plus any text that you added.

DURING THE PRESENTATION

In many cases, PowerPoint slides are presented visually by the instructor *only during class.* The slides are not provided as handouts, and they are not available online for students to print out.

This makes it even more important to take effective notes in class. Capture the main points and key details as you normally would. Use your preferred note-taking strategies.

Be selective in what you write down. Determine what kind of material is on each slide. Stay alert for new topics, main points, and important details. Taking too many notes makes it hard to keep up with a speaker and separate main points from minor details.

In any case, go *beyond* the slides. Record valuable questions and answers that come up during a discussion, even if they are not a planned part of the presentation.

AFTER THE PRESENTATION

If you printed out slides before class and took notes on those pages, then find a way to integrate them with the rest of your notes. For example, add references in your notebook to specific slides. Or create summary notes that include the major topics and points from readings, class meetings, and PowerPoint presentations.

Printouts of slides can provide review tools. Use them as cues to recite. Cover up your notes so that only the main image or words on each slide are visible. See whether you can remember what else appears on the slide, along with the key points from any notes you added.

Also consider "editing" the presentation. If you have the PowerPoint file on your computer, make another copy of it. Open up this copy, and see whether you can condense the presentation. Cut slides that don't include anything you want to remember. Also rearrange slides so that the order makes more sense to you. Remember that you can open up the original file later if you want to see exactly what your instructor presented. ■

How Muscle Reading Works

▸ Phase 1 – Before You Read
  ▪ Pry Out Questions

▸ Phase 2 – While You Read
  ▪ Focus and Flag Answers

▸ Phase 3 – After You Read
  ▪ Recite, Review, and Review Again

Set the stage for
note taking

The process of note taking begins well before you enter a classroom or crack open a book. Promote your success by "psyching up"—setting the physical and mental stage to receive what your teachers have to offer.

Also remember that your ability to take notes in any course can instantly improve when you truly show up for class. That means taking a seat in the room *and* focusing your attention while you're there. Use the following suggestions to meet both goals.

COMPLETE REQUIRED READING

Instructors usually assume that students complete reading assignments, and they construct their lectures accordingly. The more familiar you are with a subject, the easier it will be to understand in class.

PACK MATERIALS

A good pen does not make you a good observer, but the lack of a pen or a notebook or other note-taking tools can disrupt your concentration. Make sure you have any materials you will need, including a textbook.

ARRIVE EARLY TO PUT YOUR BRAIN IN GEAR

Arriving at class late or with only seconds to spare can add a level of stress that interferes with listening. Avoid that interference by arriving at least 5 minutes before class begins. Use this spare time to review notes from the previous class session.

SIT IN THE FRONT OF THE CLASSROOM

The closer you sit to the front, the fewer the distractions. Also, material on the board is easier to read from up front, and the instructor can see you more easily when you have a question.

TAKE CARE OF HOUSEKEEPING DETAILS

If you're taking notes on paper, then write your name and phone number in each notebook in case you lose it. Class notes become more valuable as a term proceeds. Develop the habit of labeling and dating your notes at the beginning of each class. Number the pages too.

Devote a specific section of your notebook to listing assignments for each course. Keep all details about test dates here also, along with a course syllabus. You're less likely to forget assignments if you compile them in one place where you can review them all at a glance.

Leave blank space. Notes tightly crammed on the page are hard to read and difficult to review. Leave plenty of space on the page.

Later, when you review, you can use the blank space to clarify points, write questions, or add other material.

Use a three-ring binder for paper-based notes. Three-ring binders give you several benefits. First, pages can be removed and spread out when you review. Second, the three-ring-binder format will allow you to insert handouts right into your notes easily. Third, you can insert your own out-of-class notes in the correct order.

Use only one side of a piece of paper. When you use one side of a page, you can review and organize all your notes by spreading them out side by side.

LIMIT DISTRACTIONS

Listening well can be defined as the process of overcoming distraction. In the classroom, you may have to deal with external distractions—noises from the next room, other students' conversations, or a lecturer who speaks softly. Internal distractions can be even more potent—for example, stress, memories about last night's party, or daydreams about what you'll do after class.

When the distraction is external, the solution may be obvious. Move closer to the front of the room, ask the lecturer to speak up, or politely ask classmates to keep quiet. Internal distractions can be trickier. Some solutions follow.

Flood your mind with sensory data. Notice the shape of your pen. Feel the surface of your desk. Bring yourself back to class by paying attention to the temperature or the quality of light in the room.

Notice and release daydreams. If your attention wanders, don't grit your teeth and try to stay focused. Just notice when your attention has wandered and gently bring it back.

Pause for a few seconds and write distracting thoughts down. If you're thinking about the errands you want to run later, list them on a 3×5 card. Once your distractions are out of your mind and safely stored on paper, you can gently return your attention to taking notes.

Let go of judgments about lecture styles. Human beings are judgment machines. We evaluate everything, especially other people. We notice the way someone looks or speaks and we instantly make up a story about her. We do this so quickly that we don't even realize it.

Don't let your attitude about an instructor's lecture style, habits, or appearance get in the way of your education. You can decrease the power of your judgments if you pay attention to them and let them go.

You can even let go of judgments about rambling, unorganized lectures. Take the initiative and organize the material yourself. While taking notes, separate the key points from the examples and supporting evidence. Note the places where you got confused, and make a list of questions to ask.

Participate in class activities. Ask questions. Volunteer for demonstrations. Join in class discussions. Be willing to take a risk or look foolish if that's what it takes for you to learn. Chances are, the question you think is "dumb" is also on the minds of several of your classmates.

Relate the class to your goals. If you have trouble staying awake in a particular class, write at the top of your notes how that class relates to a specific goal. Identify the payoff for reaching that goal.

REMEMBER THAT YOU CAN LISTEN AND DISAGREE

When you hear something you disagree with, notice your disagreement and let it go. If your disagreement is persistent and strong, make note of this and then move on. Internal debate can prevent you from receiving new information. Just absorb it with a mental tag: "I don't agree, and my instructor says ..."

When you review your notes later, think critically about the instructor's ideas. List questions or note your disagreements.

Also, avoid "listening with your answer running." This refers to the habit of forming your response to people's ideas *before* they've finished speaking. Let the speaker have his say, even when you're sure you'll disagree.

GIVE THE SPEAKER FEEDBACK

Speakers thrive on attention. Give lecturers verbal and nonverbal feedback—everything from simple eye contact to insightful comments and questions. Such feedback can raise an instructor's energy level and improve the class.

BRACKET EXTRA MATERIAL

Bracketing refers to separating your own thoughts from the lecturer's as you take notes. This is useful in two circumstances.

First, bracket your own opinions. For the most part, avoid making editorial comments in your lecture notes. The danger is that when you return to your notes, you may mistake your own ideas for those of the speaker. Clearly label your own comments, such as questions to ask later or strong disagreements. Pick a symbol, like brackets, and use consistently.

Second, bracket material that confuses you. Invent your own signal for getting lost during a lecture. For example, write a circled question mark in the margin of the paper. Or simply leave space for the explanation that you will get later. This space will also be a signal that you missed something. Be honest with yourself when you don't understand. ■

You're One Click Away . . .
from more ways to set the stage for note taking.

Cope with fast-talking teachers

Ask the instructor to slow down. This obvious suggestion is easily forgotten. If asking him to slow down doesn't work, ask him to repeat what you missed. Also experiment with the following suggestions.

Take more time to prepare for class.
Familiarity with a subject increases your ability to pick out key points. Before class, take detailed notes on your reading and leave plenty of blank space. Take these notes with you to class and simply add your lecture notes to them.

Be willing to make choices.
Focus your attention on key points. Instead of trying to write everything down, choose what you think is important. Occasionally you will make a wrong choice and neglect an important point. Worse things could happen.

Exchange copies of notes with classmates.
Your fellow students might write down something you missed. At the same time, your notes might help them.

Leave empty spaces in your notes.
Allow plenty of room for filling in information you missed. Use a symbol that signals you've missed something, so you can remember to come back to it.

See the instructor after class.
Take your class notes with you and show the instructor what you missed.

Learn shorthand.
Some note-taking systems, known as shorthand, are specifically designed for getting ideas down fast. Books and courses are available to help you learn these systems.

Ask questions even if you're totally lost.
There may be times when you feel so lost that you can't even formulate a question. That's okay. Just report this fact to the instructor. Or just ask any question. Often this will lead you to the question that you really want to ask.

✔ CRITICAL THINKING EXERCISE 4

Listen for key points

Key points are the major ideas in a lecture—the "bottom-line" or "takeaway" messages. Lecturers usually provide verbal clues that they're coming up to a key point. Listen for phrases such as:

The following three factors . . .
The most important thing is . . .
What I want you to remember is . . .
In conclusion . . .

To illustrate and support key points, speakers offer supporting material in the form of examples, facts, statistics, quotations, anecdotes, and other details.

In short, there are two levels of material in a lecture: (1) key points and (2) details that support the key points. Your ability to examine evidence depends on making this distinction.

You can make this distinction in your notes with simple visual cues. For example:

- Highlight key points. As you take notes, graphically emphasize the key points. Underline them, write them in uppercase letters, write them in a different color of ink, or go over them with a highlighter. In your notes, record only the most vivid or important details used to support each key point.

- Use numbered lists to record a sequence of key points. When you want to indicate a series of events or steps that take place in time, number each one in chronological order.

- Format your notes in two columns. In the left-hand column, list the key points. On the right, include the most important details that relate to each point.

To experiment with these suggestions right away, complete the following steps to evaluate your note taking:

1. Select a page or two of class notes that you've taken recently.

2. Circle, underline, or highlight the key points.

3. If you were not able to distinguish the key points from supporting material in your notes, then do some revision. Recopy your notes using the two-column format described above. Show your revised notes to a classmate or to your instructor and ask for feedback.

Finally, reflect on this exercise. Complete the following sentences.

In reviewing my notes, I discovered that . . .

_____

_____

_____

_____

_____

To take more effective notes in the future, I intend to . . .

_____

_____

_____

_____

_____

_____

_____

_____

_____

_____

 You're One Click Away . . .
from more ways to capture key points and supporting details.

CAPTURE *key words*

When it comes to notes, more is not necessarily better. Your job is not to write down all of a lecturer's words or even most of them. Taking effective notes calls for split-second decisions about which words are essential to record and which are less important.

An easy way to sort the less important from the essential is to take notes using key words. Key words or phrases contain the essence of communication. They include technical terms, names, numbers, equations, and words of degree: *most, least, faster,* and the like.

Key words are laden with associations. They evoke images and associations with other words and ideas. One key word can initiate the recall of a whole cluster of ideas. A few key words can form a chain: From those words, you can reconstruct an entire lecture.

FOCUS ON NOUNS AND VERBS

In many languages, there are two types of words that carry the essential meaning of most sentences—nouns and verbs. For example, the previous sentence could be reduced to: *nouns + verbs carry meaning. Carry* is a verb; most of the remaining words are nouns.

There are additional ways to subtract words from your notes and still retain the lecturer's meaning:

Eliminate adverbs and adjectives. The words *extremely interesting* can become *interesting* in your notes—or simply an exclamation mark (!)

Note the topic followed by a colon and key point. For instance, *There are seven key principles that can help you take effective notes* becomes *Effective notes: 7 principles.*

Use lists. There are two basic types. A numbered list expresses steps that need to be completed in a certain order. A simple bulleted list includes ideas that are related but do not have to follow a sequential order.

Look for models. To find more examples of key words, study newspaper headlines. Good headlines include a verb and only enough nouns to communicate the essence of an event or idea.
Example: Reducing speech to key words

To see how key words can be used in note taking, take yourself to an imaginary classroom. You are enrolled in a course on world religion, and today's lecture is an introduction to Buddhism. The instructor begins with these words:

Okay, today we're going to talk about three core precepts of Buddhism. I know that this is a religion that may not be familiar to many of you, and I ask that you keep an open mind as I proceed. Now, with that caveat out of the way, let's move ahead.

First, let's look at the term anicca. *By the way, this word is spelled a-n-i-c-c-a. Everybody got that? Great. All right, well, this is a word in an ancient language called Pali, which was widely spoken in India during the Buddha's time—about 600 years before the birth of Jesus. Anicca is a word layered with many meanings and is almost impossible to translate into English. If you read books about Buddhism, you may see it rendered as impermanence, and this is a passable translation.*

Impermanence is something that you can observe directly in your everyday experience. Look at any object in your external environment and you'll find that it's constantly changing. Even the most solid and stable things—like a mountain, for example—are dynamic. You could use time-lapse photography to record images of a mountain every day for 10 years, and if you did, you'd see incredible change—rocks shifting, mudslides, new vegetation, and the like.

Following is one way to reduce this section of the lecture to key words:

Buddhism: 3 concepts
#1 = anicca *= impermanence.*
Anicca = Pali = ancient Indian language (600 yrs b4 Jesus).
Example of anicca: time-lapse photos @ changes in mountain.

In this case the original 209 words of the lecture have been reduced to 28. However, this example might be a little sparse for your tastes. Remember that it shows only one possible option for abbreviating your notes. Don't take it as a model to imitate strictly.

A CAVEAT: USE COMPLETE SENTENCES AT CRUCIAL POINTS

Sometimes key words aren't enough. When an instructor repeats a sentence slowly and emphasizes each word, she's sending you a signal. Also, technical definitions are often worded precisely because even a slightly different wording renders the definitions useless or incorrect. Write down key sentences word for word.

ADDITIONAL SUGGESTIONS FOR CAPTURING THE ESSENTIAL INFORMATION

Write notes in paragraphs with complete sentences. When it is difficult to follow the organization of a lecture or to put information into outline form, create a series of informal paragraphs. Use complete sentences for precise definitions, direct quotations, and important points that the instructor emphasizes by repetition or other signals—such as the phrase "This is an important point." For other material, focus on capturing key words.

Listen for introductory, concluding, and transition words and phrases. Examples are "the following three factors," "in conclusion," "the most important consideration," "in addition to," and "on the other hand." These phrases and similar ones signal relationships, definitions, new subjects, conclusions, cause and effect relationships, and examples. They reveal the structure of the lecture. You can use these phrases to organize your notes.

Take notes in different colors. You can use colors as highly visible organizers. For example, you can signal important points with red. Or use one color for notes about the text and another color for lecture notes. Besides, notes that are visually pleasing can be easier to review.

Copy material from the board and a PowerPoint presentation. Record all formulas, diagrams, and problems that the teacher presents on the board or in a PowerPoint presentation. Copy dates, numbers, names, places, and other facts. If it's presented visually in class, put it in your notes. You can even use your own signal or code to flag that material.

Plan to get notes for classes you miss. For most courses, you'll benefit by attending every class session. If you miss a class, catch up as quickly as possible. Early in each term, connect with other students who are willing to share notes. Also contact your instructor. Perhaps there is another section of the same course that you can attend so you won't miss the lecture information. If there is a Web site for your class, check it for assignments and the availability of handouts you missed. ■

You're One Click Away . . .
from more strategies for reducing ideas to their essence.

Short and sweet—Remember to abrevi8

Abbreviations can be useful in note taking as well as texting—if you use them consistently. Some abbreviations are standard. If you make up your own abbreviations, write a key explaining them in your notes.

Avoid vague abbreviations. When you use an abbreviation like *comm.* for *committee,* you run the risk of not being able to remember whether you meant *committee, commission, common, commit, community, communicate, or communist.*

The following seven principles explain how to use abbreviations in your notes:

Principle: Leave out articles.

Examples: Omit a, an, the.

Principle: Leave out vowels.

Examples: Talk becomes tlk, said becomes sd, American becomes Amrcn.

Principle: Use mathematical symbols.

Examples: Plus becomes +, minus becomes −, is more than becomes >, is less than becomes <, equals or is becomes =.

Principle: Use arrows to indicate causation and changes in quantity.

Examples: Increase becomes; decrease becomes; causes, leads to, or shows that becomes.->

Principle: Use standard abbreviations and omit the periods.

Examples: Pound becomes lb, Avenue becomes ave.

Principle: Create words from numbers and letters that you can sound out and combine.

Examples: Before becomes b4, too becomes 2.

Principle: Use a comma in place of and.

Example: Freud and Jung were major figures in twentieth-century psychology becomes 20th century psych: Freud, Jung = major figures.

Note: If you key your notes into computer files, you can often use a "find and replace" command to replace abbreviations with full words.

Play with NOTE-TAKING *formats*

. . . .

There are several formats in which to take notes. Experiment with as many as possible to find the one that works best for you.

. . . .

THE CORNELL FORMAT

One option for note taking that has worked for students around the world is the Cornell format. Originally described by Walter Pauk, this approach is now taught across the United States and in other countries as well.[2]

The cornerstone of this system is simple: a wide margin on the left-hand side of the page. Pauk calls this the *cue column,* and using it is the key to the Cornell format's many benefits. To get started with this approach to note taking, take the following steps.

Format your paper. On each page of your notes, draw a vertical line, top to bottom, about two inches from the left edge of the paper. This line creates the cue column—the space to the left of the line. You will use this space later to condense and review your notes.

Pauk also suggests that you leave a 2-inch space at the bottom of the page. He calls this the summary area. This space is also designed to be used at a later stage, as you review your notes.

Take notes, leaving the cue column and summary area blank. As you read or listen to a lecture, take notes on the right-hand side of the page. *Do not write in the cue column or summary area.* You'll use these spaces later.

Fill in the cue column. You can reduce your notes to several kinds of entries in the cue column:

- *Key questions.* Think of the notes you took on the right-hand side of the page as a set of answers. In the cue column, write the corresponding questions. Write one question for each major term or point in your notes.

- *Key words.* Writing key words will speed the review process later. Also, reading your notes and focusing on extracting key words will further reinforce your understanding of the lecture or reading assignment.

- *Headings.* Pretend that you are a copy editor at a newspaper, and that the notes you took are a series of articles about different topics. In the cue column, write a headline for each "article." Use actual newspaper headlines—and headings in your textbooks—as models.

Fill in the summary area. See whether you can reduce all the notes on the page to a sentence or two. Add cross-references to topics elsewhere in your notes that are closely related. Explain briefly why the notes on this page matter; if you think the material is likely to appear on a test, note that fact here. Also use the summary area to list any questions that you want to ask in class.

EXAMPLE: NOTES IN CORNELL FORMAT

CUE COLUMN	NOTES
	INTRO TO PHILOSOPHY 1/10/09
What is the origin of the word Philosophy?	Philosophy—from the Greek philosophia— "lover of wisdom"
What do philosophers do?	Philosophers have different views of their main task:
	--reflect on the nature of ultimate reality
	--create a framework to unite all fields of knowledge
	--critically evaluate all claims to knowledge
	Traditional topics in philosophy = 5 areas:
What are 5 traditional topics in philosophy?	1. Determine when a series of assertions is coherent and consistent (logic)
	2. Determine what is ultimately real (ontology)
	3. Determine what constitutes real knowledge (epistemology)
	4. Determine is what is truly valuable (axiology and aesthetics)
	5. Determine what forms of behavior best sustain human society (ethics and politics)
SUMMARY	
Even though philosophers have differing views of their task, there are 5 traditional topics in philosophy.	

OUTLINES

In addition to the Cornell format, another option for note taking is outlining. The traditional Roman numeral style represents just one option for outlining. By playing with other options, you can discover the power of outlining. Use this tool to reveal relationships between ideas and to categorize large bodies of information.

Outlines consist of *headings*—words, phrases, or sentences arranged in a hierarchy from general to specific:

- In the first or top level of an outline, record the major topics or points that are presented in a lecture or reading assignment.
- In the second level, record the key topics or points that are used to support and explain the first-level headings.
- In the third level, record facts, examples, and other details that relate to each of your second-level headings.

EXAMPLE: NOTES IN OUTLINE FORMAT

Following is an outline of part of this article, based on the above suggestions:

CORNELL FORMAT

Format paper in two vertical columns and summary area at bottom.

Take notes; leave cue column and summary area blank.

Fill in cue column with key questions, key words, or headings.

Fill in summary area.

Notice that the first-level heading in this outline is printed in all uppercase (capital) letters. Second-level headings appear in both uppercase and lowercase letters. You could add a third level of headings to this outline by listing the topic sentences for each paragraph in the article. These third-level headings could be indented and listed underneath the second-level headings.

CONCEPT MAPS

Concept mapping—explained by Joseph Novak and D. Bob Gowin in their book *Learning How to Learn*—is a way to express ideas in a visual form.[3] Here are the key elements:

- A main concept written at the top of a page
- Related concepts arranged in a hierarchy, with more general concepts toward the top of a page and more specific concepts toward the bottom
- Links—lines with words that briefly explain the relationship between concepts.

When you combine concepts with their linking words, you'll often get complete sentences (or sets of coherent phrases). One benefit of concept maps is that they quickly, vividly, and accurately show the relationships between ideas.

EXAMPLE: NOTES IN CONCEPT MAP FORMAT

This is an excerpt from notes on a reading assignment about nutrition.

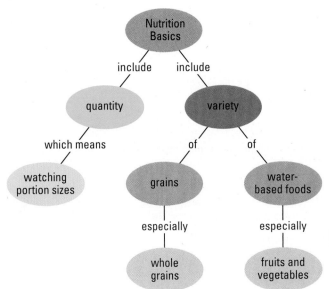

COMBINE FORMATS

Feel free to use different note-taking systems for different subjects and to combine formats. Do what works for you.

For example, combine concept maps along with the Cornell method. You can modify the Cornell format by dividing your notepaper in half. Reserve one-half for concept maps and the other for linear information such as lists, graphs, and outlines, as well as equations, long explanations, and word-for-word definitions.

You can also incorporate a concept map into your paragraph-style notes whenever you feel one is appropriate. In addition, concept maps are useful for summarizing notes taken in the Cornell format. ■

You're One Click Away . . .
from more formats for note taking.

Mine Your Notes
for *added value*

The purpose of taking notes is to consult them later. To some students, that means scanning them once or twice before a test. By that time, however, the notes might raise more questions than they answer. As an alternative, add value to your notes by revising them and predicting test questions.

REVISE YOUR NOTES

Take your first pass through your notes as soon after each class as possible. Use this time to accomplish the following:

- Fix passages that are illegible.
- Check to see that your notes are labeled with the date and the name of the class.
- Make sure that the pages are numbered.
- Expand on passages that are hard to understand.
- Write out abbreviated words or phrases that might be unclear to you later.
- List questions that you need answered in order to make sense of your notes.

PREDICT TEST QUESTIONS

Predicting test questions can do more than help you get better grades. It can also keep you focused on the purpose of the course and help you design your learning strategies. Following are legal and constructive ways to outsmart your teacher and reduce surprises at test time.

Create a signal to flag possible test items in your notes. Use asterisks (**), exclamation marks (!!), or a *T!* in a circle. Place these signals in the margin next to ideas that seem like possible test items.

Look for verbal cues from your teacher. Few teachers will try to disguise the main content of their courses. In fact, most offer repeated clues about what they want you to remember. Many of those clues are verbal:

- *Repetition.* Your teachers may state important points several times or return to those points in subsequent classes. They may also read certain passages word for word from their notes or from a book. Be sure to record all these points fully in your notes.
- *Common terms.* Also note your teachers' "pet phrases"— repeated terms that relate directly to course content. You could

benefit from using these terms in essay exams—along with explanations in your own words to show that you truly understand the concepts.

- *Questions.* Pay attention to questions that the instructor poses to the class. These are potential test questions. Write them down, along with some answers.
- *Emphasis on certain types of content.* Some teachers emphasize details—facts, names, dates, technical terms, and the like. Other teachers focus on broad themes and major events. Be alert to such differences. They are clues to the kind of tests you'll have.
- *Placement of content.* Listen closely to material presented at the beginning and end of a lecture. Skilled speakers will often preview or review their key content at these points.
- *Comments on assigned readings.* When material from reading assignments is also covered extensively in class, it is likely to be on the test. The opposite can also be true: When your teacher emphasizes material that does *not* appear in any assigned reading, that material is likely to be important.

Look for nonverbal cues from your teacher. Sometimes a lecturer's body language will give potent clues to key content. He might use certain gestures when making critical points—pausing, looking down at notes, staring at the ceiling, or searching for words. If the lecturer has to think hard about how to make a point, that's probably an important point. Also note the following.

- *Watch the board or screen.* If an instructor takes time to write something down and display it to the whole class, consider this to be another signal that the material is important. In short: If it's on the board, on a screen, or in a handout, put it in your notes. Use your own signal or code to flag this material.
- *Watch the instructor's eyes.* If an instructor glances at his notes and then makes a point, it is probably a signal that the information is especially important. Anything he reads from his notes is a potential test question.
- *Remember the obvious.* Listen for these words: "This material will be on the test." ◼

You're One Click Away . . .
from more ways to mine value from your notes.

Taking notes
while *reading*

Taking notes while reading requires the same skills that apply to taking class notes: observing, recording, and reviewing. Use these skills to take notes for review and for research.

REVIEW NOTES

Review notes will look like the notes you take in class. Take review notes when you want more detailed notes than writing in the margin of your text allows. You might want to single out a particularly difficult section of a text and make separate notes. Or make summaries of overlapping lecture and text material. Because you can't underline or make notes in library books, these sources will require separate notes, too. To take more effective review notes, use the following suggestions.

Set priorities. Single out a particularly difficult section of a text and make separate notes. Or make summaries of overlapping lecture and text material.

Use a variety of formats. Translate text into Cornell notes, concept maps, or outlines. Translate diagrams, charts, and other visual elements into words. Then reverse the process by translating straight text into visual elements. Combine these formats to create your own.

However, don't let the creation of new formats get in your way. Even a simple list of key points and examples can become a powerful review tool.

Another option is to close your book and just start writing. Write quickly about what you intend to remember from the text, and don't worry about following any format.

Condense a passage to key quotes. Authors embed their essential ideas in key sentences. As you read, continually ask yourself, "What's the point?" Then see whether you can point to a specific sentence on the page to answer your question. Look especially at headings, subheadings, and topic sentences of paragraphs. Write these key sentences word for word in your notes, and put them within quotation marks. Copy as few sentences as you can and still retain the core meaning of the passage.

Condense by paraphrasing. Pretend that you have to summarize a chapter, article, or book on a postcard. Limit yourself to a single paragraph—or a single sentence—and use your own words. This is a great way to test your understanding of the material.

Take a cue from the table of contents. Look at the table of contents in your book. Write each major heading on a piece of paper, or key those headings into a file on your computer. Include page numbers. Next, see whether you can improve on the table of contents. Substitute your own headings for those that appear in the book. Turn single words or phrases into complete sentences, and use words that are meaningful to you.

Adapt to special cases. The style of your notes can vary according to the nature of the reading material. If you are assigned a short story or poem, for example, then read the entire work once without taking any notes. On your first reading, simply enjoy the piece. When you finish, write down your immediate impressions. Then go over the piece again. Make brief notes on characters, images, symbols, settings, plot, point of view, or other aspects of the work.

Note key concepts in math and science. When you read mathematical, scientific, or other technical materials, copy important formulas or equations. Recreate important diagrams, and draw your own visual representations of concepts. Also write down data that might appear on an exam.

RESEARCH NOTES

Take research notes when preparing to write a paper or deliver a speech. One traditional method of research is to take notes on index cards. You write one idea, fact, or quotation per card, along with a note about the source (where you found it). The advantage of limiting each card to one item is that you can easily arrange cards according to the sequence of ideas in your outline. If you change your outline, no problem. Just resort your cards.

Taking notes on a computer or other digital device offers the same flexibility as index cards. Just include one idea, fact, or quotation per paragraph along with the source. Think of each paragraph as a separate "card." When you're ready to create the first draft of your paper or presentation, just move paragraphs around so that they fit your outline.

Take care with your sources. No matter whether you use cards or a computer, be sure to *include a source for each note that you take.*

Say, for example, that you find a useful quotation from a book. You want to include that quotation in your paper. Copy the quotation word for word onto a card, or key the quotation into a computer file. Along with the quotation, note the book's author, title, date and place of publication, and publisher. You'll need such information later when you create a formal list of your sources—a bibliography, or a list of endnotes or footnotes.

For guidelines on what information to record about each type of source, check with your instructor. Different instructors might have different preferences, so be sure to ask.

Avoid plagiarism. When people take material from a source and fail to acknowledge that source, they are committing plagiarism. Even when plagiarism is accidental, the consequences can be harsh.

Many cases of plagiarism occur during the process of taking research notes. To prevent this problem, remember that a major goal of taking research notes is to *clearly separate your own words and images from words and images created by someone else*. To meet this goal, develop the following habits:

- If you take a direct quote from one of your sources, then enclose those words in quotation marks and note information about that source.

- If you take an image (photo, illustration, chart, or diagram) from one of your sources, then note information about that source.

- If you summarize or paraphrase *a specific passage* from one of your sources, then use your own words and note information about that source.

- If your notes include any idea that is closely identified with a particular person, then note information about the source.

- When you include one of your own ideas in your notes, then simply note the source as "me."

If you're taking notes on a computer and using Internet sources, be especially careful to avoid plagiarism. When you copy text or images from a Web site, separate those notes from your own ideas. Use a different font for copied material, or enclose it in quotation marks.

You do not need to note a source for these:

- Facts that are considered common knowledge ("The history of the twentieth century includes two world wars").

- Facts that can be easily verified ("The United States Constitution includes a group of amendments known as the Bill of Rights").

- Your own opinion ("Hip-hop artists are the most important poets of our age").

The bottom line: Always present your own work—not materials that have been created or revised by someone else. If you're ever in doubt about what to do, then take the safest course: Cite a source. Give credit where credit is due.

In addition, ask your instructors for their guidelines on avoiding plagiarism. Your school might even have a specific policy on this issue. Search for it in the course catalog or Web site. Then follow it to the letter.

Reflect on your notes Schedule time to review all the information and ideas that your research has produced. By allowing time for rereading and reflecting on all the notes you've taken, you create the conditions for genuine understanding.

Start by summarizing major points of view on your topic. Note points of agreement and disagreement among your sources.

Also see whether you can find direct answers to the questions that you had when you started researching. These answers could become headings in your paper.

Look for connections in your material, including ideas, facts, and examples that occur in several sources. Also look for connections between your research and your life—ideas that you can verify based on personal experience.

The result of all this reflection can be an "aha!" moment that fuels a powerful paper or presentation. Enjoy. ■

> Many cases of plagiarism occur during the process of taking research notes. To prevent this problem, remember that a major goal of taking research notes is to clearly separate your own words and images from words and images created by someone else.

 You're One Click Away . . .
from finding examples of effective research and review notes online.

Transform your note taking

Think back on the last few lectures you have attended. How would you rate your note-taking skills? As you complete this exercise, think of areas that need improvement.

Discovery Statement

First, recall a recent incident in which you had difficulty taking notes. Perhaps you were listening to an instructor who talked fast. Maybe you got confused and stopped taking notes altogether. Or perhaps you went to review your notes after class, only to find that they made no sense at all.

Describe this incident in more detail, noting how it was challenging for you. I discovered that . . .

_____

_____

_____

_____

_____

_____

Intention Statement

Now review this chapter to find at least five strategies that you can use right away to help you take better notes. Sum up each of those strategies in a few words and note the page numbers where these strategies are explained.

Strategy	Page number

Action Statement

Now gear up for action. Describe a specific situation in which you will apply at least one of the strategies you listed previously. If possible, choose a situation that will occur within the next 24 hours.

_____

_____

_____

_____

_____

_____

_____

_____

_____

After experimenting with these strategies, evaluate how well they worked for you. If you thought of a way to modify any of the strategies so that they can work more effectively, describe those modifications here:

_____

_____

_____

_____

_____

_____

_____

_____

_____

_____

_____

_____

_____

4

4 SKILLS Snapshot

Take a snapshot of your note-taking skills as they exist today, after reading and doing this chapter. Begin by reflecting on some of your recent experiences with note taking. Then take the next step toward mastery by committing to a specific action in the near future.

DISCOVERY

My score on the section of the Discovery Wheel on page 9 was . . .

If my attention wanders while taking notes, I refocus by . . .

When I strongly disagree with the opinion of a speaker or author, I respond by . . .

If asked to rate the overall quality of the notes that I've taken in the last week, I would say that . . .

In general, I find my notes to be most useful when they . . .

INTENTION

I'll know that I've reached a new level of mastery with note taking when . . .

My main goal for note-taking is . . .

ACTION

The most important thing I can do next to meet my goal is . . .

By the time I finish this course, I would like my Notes score on the Discovery Wheel to be . . .

Maximizing Your Memory & Mastering Tests

Use this **Master Student Map** to ask yourself

WHY THIS CHAPTER MATTERS . . .

- Adopting a few simple techniques can make a major difference in how well you prepare for tests—and how you perform on them.

WHAT IS INCLUDED. . .

HOW YOU CAN USE THIS CHAPTER . . .

- Enhance my memory and use study time more effectively.
- Gain strategies for raising my scores on tests.
- Separate my self-image from my test scores.

WHAT IF . . .

- I could let go of fear about tests—or anything else?

© Ruslan Ivantsov/Shutterstock.com

JOURNAL ENTRY 12

Discover what you want from this chapter

Think about an upcoming test; it can be one in any of your courses. Describe this test and how you feel about taking it.

I discovered that I . . .

_____

_____

_____

_____

_____

Next, preview this chapter to find at least three strategies that you can use during the next week to prepare for the test you just described. List those strategies below, and note the page numbers where you can find out more about each one.

I intend to . . .

_____

_____

_____

_____

_____

DETACH

This Power Process helps you release the powerful, natural student within you. It is especially useful whenever negative emotions are getting in your way.

Attachments are addictions. When we are attached to something, we think we cannot live without it, just as a drug addict feels he cannot live without drugs. We believe our well-being depends on maintaining our attachments.

We can be attached to just about anything: beliefs, emotions, people, roles, objects. The list is endless.

One person, for example, might be so attached to his car that he takes an accident as a personal attack. Pity the poor unfortunate who backs into this person's car. He might as well have backed into the owner himself.

Another person might be attached to her job. Her identity and sense of well-being depend on it. She could become depressed if she got fired.

When we are attached and things don't go our way, we can feel angry, sad, afraid, or confused.

Suppose you are attached to getting an "A" on your physics test. You feel as though your success in life depends on getting that "A." As the clock ticks away, you work harder on the test, getting more stuck. That voice in your head gets louder: "I must get an 'A.' I MUST get an 'A.' I MUST GET AN 'A!'"

Now is a time to detach. See whether you can just *observe* what's going on, letting go of all your judgments. When you just observe, you reach a quiet state above and beyond your usual thoughts. This is a place where you can be aware of being aware. It's a tranquil spot, apart from your emotions. From here, you can see yourself objectively, as if you were watching someone else.

That place of detachment might sound far away and hard to reach. You can get there in three ways.

First, pay attention to your thoughts and physical sensations. If you are confused and feeling stuck, tell yourself, "Here I am, confused and stuck." If your palms are sweaty and your stomach is one big knot, admit it.

Second, practice relaxation. Start by simply noticing your breathing. Then breathe more slowly and more deeply. See whether you can breathe the relaxing feeling into your whole body.

Third, practice seeing current events from a broader perspective. In your mind, zoom out to a bigger picture. Ask yourself how much today's test score will matter to you in one week, one month, one year, or one decade from today. You can apply this technique to any challenge in life.

Caution: Giving up an *attachment* to being an "A" student does not mean giving up *being* an "A" student. Giving up an attachment to a job doesn't mean giving up the job. When you detach, you get to keep your values and goals. However, you know that you will be okay even if you fail to achieve a goal.

Remember that you are more than your goals. You are more than your thoughts and feelings. These things come and go. Meanwhile, the part of you that can *just observe* is always there and always safe, no matter what happens.

Behind your attachments is a master student. Release that mastery. Detach.

You're One Click Away. . .
from accessing Power Process Media online and finding out more about how to "detach."

iStockphoto.com/iSci

Grades: The truth

> Grades are *not* a measure of your intelligence or creativity, an indication of your ability to contribute to society, nor a measure of your skills or your worth as a human being.

On the surface, tests don't look dangerous. Yet sometimes we treat them as if they are land mines.

Suppose a stranger walks up to you on the street and says, "Amiri Baraka first published under another name. What was it?"* Would you tense up or break out in a cold sweat? Would your breathing become shallow?

Probably not, even if you've never heard of Amiri Baraka. But if you find this question on a test and you don't know the answer, your hands might get clammy. That's because there are lots of misconceptions about grades.

Grades are *not* a measure of your intelligence or creativity.

Grades are *not* an indication of your ability to contribute to society.

Grades are *not* a measure of your skills or your worth as a human being.

Some people think that a test score measures what a student has accomplished in a course. This is also false.

The truth is that is that a test score is simply a measure of what you scored on a test. If you are anxious about a test and blank out, the grade cannot measure what you've learned. The reverse is also true: If you are good at taking tests and you are a lucky guesser, the score won't be an accurate reflection of what you know.

Yet we tend to give test scores the power to determine how we feel about ourselves. Common thoughts include "If I fail a test, I am a failure" or "If I do badly on a test, I am a bad person."

If you do badly on a test, you are a person who did badly on a test. That's all. Even if you score low on an important test—such as an entrance test for college or medical school, bar exams, or CPA exams—this usually means only a delay.

If you experience test anxiety, then you might find this whole line of reasoning hard to swallow. Test anxiety is a common problem among students. It can surface in many ways, masquerading as a variety of emotions:

- *Anger:* "The teacher never wanted me to pass this stupid course anyway."
- *Blame:* "If only the class were not so boring."
- *Fear:* "I'll never have enough time to study."

Believing in any of these statements leaves us powerless. We become victims of things that we don't control—the teacher, the textbook, or the wording of the test questions.

Another option is to ask: "What can I do to experience my next test differently? How can I prepare more effectively? How can I manage stress before, during, and after the test?" When you answer such questions, you take back your power.

The key is to approach each test as a performance. From this point of view, preparing for a test means *rehearsing*. Study in the way that an actor prepares for a play—by simulating the conditions you'll encounter in the exam room. Do the kinds of tasks that you'll actually perform during a test: answering questions, solving problems, composing essays, and the like.

Carrying around misconceptions about tests and grades can put undue pressure on your performance. It's like balancing on a railroad track. Many people can walk along the rail and stay balanced for long periods. Yet the task seems entirely different if the rail is placed between two buildings, 52 stories up.

It is easier to do well on exams if you don't put too much pressure on yourself. Don't give the test some magical power over your own worth as a human being.

The way to deal with tests is to practice for them and keep your perspective. Keep the railroad track on the ground. ■

You're One Click Away...
from more information about integrity in test taking.

Be ready for your *next test*

When getting ready for tests, remember a key word—*review*. First create effective materials for review. Then use them often.

Write review checklists. To begin your test preparation, make a list of what to review in each subject. Include items such as these:

- Reading assignments by chapters or page numbers
- Dates of lectures and major topics covered in each lecture
- Skills to master
- Key course content—definitions, theories, formulas, sample problems, and laboratory findings

A review checklist is not a review sheet; it is a to-do list. These checklists contain the briefest possible description of each type of material that you intend to review. When you conduct your final review sessions, cross items off each checklist as you study them.

AMERICAN HISTORY TEST
Date: 11/1
Materials:
☐ Lecture notes: 9/14–10/29
☐ Textbook, pages 190–323
☐ The Federalist, chapters 1, 2, 4, 6
Topics:
☐ Hamilton and bank policies
☐ Frontier crisis
☐ Jay's treaty and foreign policy

Create summary notes. Summary notes are materials that you create specifically to review for tests. They are separate from notes that you take throughout the term on lectures and readings. Summary notes tie together content from all sources—readings, lectures, handouts, lab sessions, and any other course elements.

You can create summary notes with a computer. Key in all your handwritten notes and edit them into outline form. Or simply create an annotated table of contents for your handwritten notes. Note the date of each lecture, major topics, and main points. Even if you study largely from summary notes, keep the rest of your notes on file. They'll come in handy as backup sources of information.

Create flash cards. Flash cards are like portable test questions. Write them on 3×5 cards. On one side of the cards, write key terms or questions. On the other side, write definitions or answers. Buy an inexpensive card file and arrange your flash cards by subject. Carry a pack of flash cards with you whenever you think you might

have spare time to review. Also keep a few blank cards with you to make flash cards as you recall new information.

Create a mock test. Make some predictions about what will be on the exam. Write your own exam questions and take this "test" several times before the actual test. Design your mock test to look like the real thing. If possible, write out your answers in the room where the test will actually take place.

Do daily reviews. Daily reviews include the short pre- and post-class reviews of reading and lecture notes. This is a powerful tool for moving ideas from short-term to long-term memory.

Do weekly reviews. Review each subject at least once a week. Revisit assigned readings and lecture notes. Do something that forces you to rehearse the material. For example, look over any course summaries you've created and see whether you can re-create them from memory.

Do major reviews. Major reviews are usually conducted during the week before finals or other major exams. *To uncover gaps in knowledge, start major reviews at least three days before the test.*

Major reviews take several hours at a stretch. During long sessions, study the most difficult subjects at the beginning, when you are most alert. When you find it difficult to focus your attention, quit for the day and come back to it tomorrow. ∎

You're One Click Away...
from more strategies for test preparation.

Five things to do in a study group

Compare notes. Make sure you all heard the same thing in class and that you all recorded the important information.

Take a mock test and share results. Ask each group member to bring four or five sample test questions to a meeting. Create a mock test from these questions, take the test under timed conditions, and share answers.

Practice teaching each other. Teaching is a great way to learn something. Turn the material you're studying into a list of topics. Then assign specific topics for each person to teach the group.

Create wall-sized concept maps to summarize a textbook or series of lectures. Work on large sheets of butcher paper, or tape together pieces of construction paper.

Pair off to do "book reports." One person can summarize an assigned reading. The other person can act like an interviewer on a talk show, posing questions and asking for further clarification.

Memory superchargers—
the "six Rs"

To the conscious mind, a memory appears as a discrete mental event—an image, a series of words, the record of a sensation. On a biological level, each of those events involves millions of nerve cells firing chemical messages to each other. Memory is the *probability* that those nerve cells will fire together again in the future. The whole art of improving memory is increasing that probability.

Following are six strategies you can use for this purpose. They all begin with the letter *R*—a convenient hook for your memory.

RELAX

Stress in all its forms—including fear and anxiety—interferes with memory. Remember that you can reduce tension at any time simply by noticing your breathing. This will make it deeper and more regular. For a deeper relaxation, deliberately slow down your breathing. Take in more air with each inhalation and release more air with each exhalation.

Observe the peaks and valleys in your energy flow during the day, and adjust study times accordingly. Perhaps you experience surges in memory power during the later afternoon evening. You might find that you naturally feel more relaxed and alert during certain hours during the day. Study your most difficult subjects at these times, when your energy peaks.

REDUCE

Start by reducing distraction. The simple act of focusing your attention at key moments can do wonders for your memory. Test this idea for yourself: The next time you're introduced to someone, direct 100 percent of your attention to hearing that person's name. Do this consistently and see what happens to your ability to remember names.

Study in a quiet place that is free from distraction. If there's a party at your house, go to the library. If you have a strong attraction to food, don't torture yourself by studying next to your refrigerator. Also remember that 2 hours of studying in front of the television might equal only 10 minutes of studying where it is quiet.

Next, reduce the amount of material to master. During your stay in higher education, you will be exposed to thousands of facts and ideas. No one expects you to memorize all of them. To a large degree, the art of memory is the art of selecting what to remember in the first place. Choose what's essential to remember from reading assignments and lectures. Extract core concepts and key examples. Ask yourself what you'll be tested on, as well as what you want to remember.

RELATE

The data already in your memory are arranged according to a scheme that makes sense to you. When you introduce new data, relate them to similar data:

Create visual associations. Invent a mental picture of the information you want to remember. You can remember how a personal computer stores files by visualizing the hard disk as a huge filing cabinet. This cabinet is divided into folders that contain documents.

Associate course material with something you want. If you're bogged down in quadratic equations, stand back for a minute. Think about how that math course relates to your goal of becoming an electrical engineer, or to gaining skills that open up new career options for you.

Use mnemonics. These are verbal associations that can increase your ability to recall everything from grocery lists to speeches. There are several varieties, such as these:

- *Acrostics:* For instance, the first letters of the words in the sentence **E**very **g**ood **b**oy **d**oes **f**ine (E, G, B, D, and F) are the music notes of the lines of the treble-clef staff.

- *Acronyms:* You can make up your own acronyms to recall a series of facts. A common mnemonic acronym is Roy G. Biv, which has helped thousands of students remember the colors of the visible spectrum (**r**ed, **o**range, **y**ellow, **g**reen, **b**lue, **i**ndigo, and **v**iolet). IMPAT helps biology students remember the stages of cell division (**i**nterphase, **p**rophase, **m**etaphase, **a**naphase, and **t**elophase).

- *"Catchy" lists:* Theodore Cheney, author of *Getting the Words Right*, suggests that you remember the "three Rs" when editing a paper: *Reduce* the paper to eliminate extraneous paragraphs, *rearrange* the paragraphs that remain into a logical order, and *reword* individual sentences so that they include specific nouns and active verbs.[1]

- *Rhymes:* This simple technique is widely applied. Advertisers often use jingles—songs with rhyming lyrics—to promote products. You can invent original rhymes to burn course material into your long-term memory. Rhymes have been used for centuries to teach basic facts. "I before e, except after c" has helped many a student on spelling tests.

- *Mnemonics:* Although mnemonics can be useful, they do have two potential drawbacks. First, they rely on rote memorization rather than understanding the material at a deeper level or

5

thinking critically about it. Second, the mnemonic device itself is sometimes complicated to learn and time-consuming to develop. To get the most from mnemonic devices, keep them simple.

RESTRUCTURE

Structure refers to the way that things are organized. When you're faced with a long list of items to remember, look for ways to organize them. Group them into larger categories or arrange them in chronological order.

You can apply this suggestion to long to-do lists. Write each item on a separate 3×5 card. Then create a pile of cards for calls to make, errands to run, and household chores. Within each of these categories, you can also arrange the cards in the order you intend to do them.

The same concept applies to the content of your courses. When reading a novel, for example, organize ideas and facts in categories such as plot, characters, and setting:

To remember the plot, create a timeline. List key events on 3×5 cards and arrange the cards to parallel the order of events in the book.

Group the people in the story into major and minor characters. Again, use 3×5 cards to list each character's name along with an identifying feature.

If geographical setting is important, create a map of the major locations described in the story.

You can also play with different ways to restructure material by using *graphic organizers*. These are preformatted charts that prompt you to visualize relationships among facts and ideas.

One example is a *topic-point-details* chart. At the top of this chart, write the main topic of a lecture or reading assignment. In the left column, list the main points you want to remember. And in the right column, list key details related to each point. Following is the beginning of a chart based on this article:

20 MEMORY TECHNIQUES	
Point	Details
1. Be selective	Choose what not to remember. Look for clues to important material.
2. Make it meaningful	Organize by time, location, category, continuum, oralphabet.
3. Create associations	Link new facts with facts you already know.
4. Learn actively	Sit straight. Stand while studying. Recite while walking.
5. Relax	Release tension. Remain alert.

You could use a similar chart to prompt critical thinking about an issue. Express that issue as a question, and write it at the top. In the left column, note the opinion about the issue. In the right column, list notable facts, expert opinions, reasons, and examples that support each opinion. The example below is about tax cuts as a strategy for stimulating the economy:

STIMULATE THE ECONOMY WITH TAX CUTS?	
Opinion	Support
Yes	Savings from tax cuts allow businesses to invest money in new equipment. Tax cuts encourage businesses to expand and hire new employees.
No	Years of tax cuts under the Bush administration failed to prevent the mortgage credit crisis. Tax cuts create budget deficits.
Maybe	Tax cuts might work in some economic conditions. Budget deficits might be only temporary.

Sometimes you'll want to remember the main actions in a story or historical event. Create a time line by drawing a straight line.

3/19/03 U.S. invades Iraq	3/30/03 Rumsfeld announces location of WMD	4/9/03 Soldiers topple statue of Saddam	5/1/03 Bush declares mission accomplished	5/29/03 Bush: We found WMD

Place points in order on that line to represent key events. Place earlier events toward the left end of the line and later events toward the right. Following is the start of a time line of events relating the U.S. war with Iraq:

When you want to compare or contrast two things, play with a Venn diagram. Represent each thing as a circle. Draw the circles so that they overlap. In the overlapping area, list characteristics that the two things share. In the outer parts of each circle, list the unique characteristics of each thing. The following diagram compares the two types of journal entries included in this book—Discovery Statements and Intention Statements:

The graphic organizers described here are just a few of the many kinds available. To find more examples, do an Internet search using the key words *graphic organizer*. Have fun, and invent graphic organizers of your own.

RECITE

Recitation is simply speaking about ideas and facts that you want to remember. Some points to remember about recitation include the following.

Discovery Statements
- Describe specific thoughts
- Describe specific feelings
- Describe current and past behaviors

(overlap)
- Are a type of journal entry
- Are based on telling the truth
- Can be written at any time on any topic
- Can lead to action

Intention Statements
- Describe future behaviors
- Can include timelines
- Can include rewards

second nature. Learn the material so well that you could talk about it in your sleep.

This technique—overlearning the material—is especially effective for problem solving in math and science courses. Do the assigned problems, then do more problems. Find another text and work similar problems. Make up your own problems and work those. When you pretest yourself in this way, the potential rewards are speed, accuracy, and greater confidence at exam time. ∎

You're One Click Away. . .
from more memory strategies.

The "out loud" part is important. Reciting silently, in your head, may be useful—in the library, for example—but it can be less effective than making noise. Your mind can trick itself into thinking it knows something when it doesn't. Your ears are harder to fool.

When you repeat something out loud, you also anchor the concept in two different senses. First, you get the physical sensation in your throat, tongue, and lips when voicing the concept. Second, you hear it. In terms of memory, the combined result is synergistic.

Use your own words. Say that you want to remember that the "acceleration of a falling body due to gravity at sea level equals 32 feet per second per second." You might say, "Gravity makes an object accelerate 32 feet per second faster for each second that it's in the air at sea level." Putting an idea in your own words forces you to think about it.

Recite in writing. Like speaking, the act of writing is multisensory, combining sight and touch. The mere act of writing down a series of terms and their definitions can help you remember the terms—even if you lose the written list. In addition, writing down what you know quickly reveals gaps in your learning, which you can then go back and fill in. When you're done writing summaries of books or lectures, read what you've written out loud—two forms of recitation.

Recite with visuals. Create diagrams, charts, maps, timelines, bulleted lists, numbered lists, and other visuals. Even the traditional outline is a visual device that separates major and minor points.

REPEAT

Repetition is a popular memory device because it works. Repetition blazes a trail through the pathways of your brain, making the information easier to recall. Repeat a concept out loud until you know it. Then say it five more times.

Students often stop studying when they think they know material just well enough to pass a test. Another option is to pick a subject apart, examine it, add to it, and go over it until it becomes

Keep your brain fit for life

Consider these research-based suggestions from the Alzheimer's Association:[2]

Stay mentally active. Take a hiking class or start a garden. Start reading maps of new locations and plan a cross-country trip. Play challenging games and do crossword puzzles. Go to museums, theaters, concerts, and other cultural events.

Stay socially active. Having a network of supportive friends can reduce stress levels. In turn, stress management helps to maintain connections between brain cells. Stay socially active by working, volunteering, and joining clubs.

Stay physically active. Physical activity promotes blood flow to the brain and reduces the risk of diseases that impair brain function. Exercise that includes mental activity—such as planning a jogging route and watching for traffic signals—offers added benefits.

Adopt a brain-healthy diet. A diet rich in dark-skinned fruits and vegetables boosts your supply of antioxidants—natural chemicals that nourish your brain. These foods include: raisins, berries, kale, spinach, brussels and alfalfa sprouts, and broccoli. Avoid foods high in saturated fat and cholesterol, which may increase the risk of Alzheimer's disease.

Protect your heart. In general, what's good for your heart is good for your brain. Protect both organs by eating well, exercising regularly, managing your weight, staying tobacco-free, and getting plenty of sleep. These habits reduce your risk of heart attack, stroke, and other cardiovascular conditions that interfere with blood flow to the brain.

TEST-TAKING ERRORS—
and ways to avoid them

If you think of a test as a sprint, remember that there are at least three ways that you can trip: study errors, errors due to carelessness, and errors that result from getting stuck on a question.

STUDY ERRORS

This kind of error is due to studying material that was not included on the test—or spending too little time on material that *did* appear on the test. Some solutions:

- Ask your teacher about specific topics that will be included on a test.
- Practice predicting test questions.
- Form a study group with class members to create mock tests.

ERRORS DUE TO CARELESSNESS

You can avoid many common test-taking errors simply with the power of awareness. Learn about these errors up front and then look out for them. You can also catch these errors immediately after your test has been returned to you.

Here are some examples:

- Mistakes due to skipping or misreading test directions
- Missing several questions in a certain section of the test—a sign that you misunderstood the directions or neglected to study certain topics
- Failing to finish problems that you knew how to answer—such as skipping the second part of a two-part question
- Consistently changing answers that were correct to answers that were incorrect
- Spending so much time on certain questions that you failed to answer others
- Making mistakes when you copy an answer from scratch paper to your answer sheet
- Turning in your test and leaving early rather than taking the extra time to proofread your answers

To avoid these types of errors, read and follow directions more carefully. Also, set aside time to proofread your answers.

ERRORS DUE TO GETTING STUCK

You might encounter a question and discover that you don't how to answer it. If this occurs, accept your feelings of discomfort. Take a deep breath. Then use any of the following suggestions.

Read it again, Sam. Eliminate the simplest sources of confusion, such as misreading the question.

Skip the question for now. Simple, but it works. Let your subconscious mind work on the answer while you respond to other questions.

Look for answers in other test questions. A term, name, date, or other fact that escapes you might appear in another question on the test itself. Use other questions to stimulate your memory.

Treat intuitions with care. In quick-answer questions (multiple choice, true/false), go with your first instinct on which answer is correct. If you think your first answer is wrong because you misread the question, do change your answer.

Visualize the answer's "location." Think of the answer to any test question as being recorded someplace in your notes or assigned reading. Close your eyes, take a deep breath, and see whether you can visualize that place—its location in the materials you studied for the test.

Rewrite the question. See whether you can put the question that confuses you into your own words.

Just start writing anything at all. On scratch paper, record any response to the question, noting whatever pops into your head. Instead of just sitting there, stumped, you're doing something—a fact that can reduce anxiety. You may also trigger a mental association that answers the test question.

Write a close answer. If you simply cannot think of an accurate answer to the question, then give it a shot anyway. Answer as best you can, even if you don't think your answer is fully correct. You may get partial credit on some tests.

Eliminate incorrect answers. Cross off the answers that are clearly not correct. The answer you cannot eliminate is probably the best choice.

Before you write, make a quick outline. An outline can help speed up the writing of your detailed essay answer. You're less likely to leave out important facts. And if you don't have time to finish your answer, your outline could win you some points. To use test time efficiently, keep your outline brief. Focus on key words to use in your answer. ■

You're One Click Away...
from more ways to avoid test-taking errors.

CRITICAL THINKING EXERCISE 5

Turn "F" into feedback

When some students get an F as a grade, they interpret that letter as a message: "You are a failure." That interpretation is not accurate. Getting an F means only that you failed a test or an assignment—not that you failed your life.

From now on, experiment with a new way of thinking. Imagine that the letter F when used as a grade represents the word *feedback*. An F is an indication that you didn't understand the material well enough. It's an invitation to do something differently before you get your next grade.

The next time that a graded test is returned to you (no matter what the grade), spend at least five minutes reviewing it. Then write your answers to the following questions in the space provided. Use separate paper as needed.

On what material did the teacher base test questions—readings, lectures, discussions, or other class activities?

_____

_____

_____

_____

_____

_____

What types of questions appeared in the test—objective (such as matching items, true/false questions, or multiple choice), short-answer, or essay?

_____

_____

_____

_____

What types of questions did you miss?

_____

_____

_____

_____

_____

_____

Can you learn anything from the instructor's comments that will help you prepare for the next test?

_____

_____

_____

_____

_____

Can you now correctly answer the questions that you missed?

_____

_____

_____

_____

_____

Did you make any of the mistakes mentioned in "Test-taking errors and ways to avoid them" on page 74?

_____

_____

_____

_____

After answering the above questions, write a brief plan for avoiding test-taking errors in the future.

_____

_____

_____

_____

_____

You're One Click Away. . .
from more strategies for turning tests into feedback.

Relax—it's just a test

To perform gracefully under the pressure of exams, put as much effort into mastering your fear of tests as you do into mastering the content of your courses. Think of test-taking skills as the "silent subject" on your schedule, equal in importance to the rest of your courses. If nervousness about tests is a consistent problem for you, that is an ideal point to begin "test taking 101."

OVERPREPARE FOR TESTS

Performing artists know that stage fright can temporarily reduce their level of skill. That's why they often overprepare for a performance. Musicians will rehearse a piece so many times that they can play it without thinking. Actors will go over their parts until they can recite lines in their sleep.

As you prepare for tests, you can apply the same principle. Read, recite, and review the content of each course until you know it cold. Then review again. The idea is to create a margin of mastery that can survive even the most extreme feelings of fear.

This technique—overlearning the material—is especially effective for problem solving in math and science courses. Do the assigned problems, then do more problems. Find another text and work similar problems. Make up your own problems and work those. When you pretest yourself in this way, the potential rewards are speed, accuracy, and greater confidence at exam time.

ACCEPT YOUR FEELINGS

Telling someone who's anxious about a test to "just calm down" is like turning up the heat on a pan that's already boiling over: The "solution" simply worsens the problem. Fear and anxiety tend to increase with resistance. The more you try to suppress them, the more intensity the feelings gain.

Roughly speaking, the problem has two levels. First, there's your fear about the test. Second, there's your worry *about* the fact that you feel fear.

As an alternative, stop resisting your fear. Simply accept your feelings, whatever they are. See fear as a cluster of thoughts and body sensations. Watch the thoughts as they pass through your mind. Observe the sensations as they wash over you. Let them rise, peak, and pass away. No feeling lasts forever. The moment you accept fear, you take the edge off the feeling and pave the way for its release.

EXAGGERATE YOUR FEAR UNTIL IT DISAPPEARS

Imagine the catastrophic problems that might occur if you fail the test. You might say to yourself, "Well, if I fail this test, I might fail the course, lose my financial aid, and get kicked out of school. Then I won't be able to get a job, so the bank would repossess my car, and I'd start drinking. Pretty soon I'd be a bum on Skid Row, and then. . . ."

Keep going until you see the absurdity of your predictions. Then you can backtrack to discover a reasonable level of concern.

> You might be justified in worrying about failing the entire course if you fail a key test. Ask yourself, "Can I live with that?" Unless you are taking a skills test in parachute packing and the final question involves jumping out of a plane, the answer will almost always be yes.

You might be justified in worrying about failing the entire course if you fail a key test. Ask yourself, "Can I live with that?" Unless you are taking a skills test in parachute packing and the final question involves jumping out of a plane, the answer will almost always be yes.

ZOOM OUT

When you're in the middle of a test, zoom out. Think the way film directors do when they dolly a camera out and away from an action scene.

In your mind, imagine that you're floating away. View the situation as a detached outside observer.

From this larger viewpoint, ask yourself whether this situation is worth worrying about. This is not a license to belittle or avoid problems; it is permission to gain some perspective.

Another option is to zoom out in time. Imagine yourself one week, one month, one year, one decade, or one century from today. Assess how much the current situation will matter when that time comes. Then come back to the test with a more detached perspective. ■

You're One Click Away . . .
from more stress-management strategies.

Math ESSENTIALS

Consider a three-part program for math success. Begin with strategies for overcoming math anxiety. Next, boost your study skills. Finally, let your knowledge shine during tests.

OVERCOME MATH ANXIETY

Many schools offer courses in overcoming math anxiety. Ask your advisor about resources on your campus. Also experiment with the following suggestions.

Connect math to life. Think of the benefits of mastering math courses. You'll have more options for choosing a major and a career. Math skills can also put you at ease in everyday situations—calculating the tip for a waiter, balancing your checkbook, working with a spreadsheet on a computer. If you follow baseball statistics, cook, do construction work, or snap pictures with a camera, you'll use math. And speaking the language of math can help you feel at home in a world driven by technology.

Remember that math is cumulative. This means that concepts build upon each other in a certain order. If you struggled with algebra, you may have trouble with trigonometry or calculus. To ensure that you have an adequate base of knowledge, tell the truth about your current level of knowledge and skill.

Before you register for a math course, locate assigned texts for the prerequisite courses. If the material in those books seems new or difficult for you, see the instructor. Ask for suggestions on ways to prepare for the course.

Change your conversation about math. When students fear math, they often say negative things to themselves about their abilities in this subject. Many times this self-talk includes statements such as *I'll never be fast enough at solving math problems* or *I'm good with words, so I can't be good with numbers.*

Get such statements out in the open, and apply some emergency critical thinking. You'll find two self-defeating assumptions lurking there: *Everybody else is better at math and science than I am* and *Since I don't understand a math concept right now, I'll never understand it.* Both of these statements are illogical.

Replace negative beliefs with logical, realistic statements that affirm your ability to succeed in math: *Any confusion I feel now can be resolved. I learn math without comparing myself to others.* And *I ask whatever questions are needed to aid my understanding.*

BOOST STUDY SKILLS FOR MATH

Choose teachers with care. Whenever possible, find a math teacher whose approach to math matches your learning style. Talk with several teachers until you find one you enjoy.

In some cases, only one teacher will be offering the math course you need. The suggestions that follow can be used to learn from a teacher regardless of her teaching style.

Take math courses back to back. Approach math in the same way that you learn a foreign language. If you take a year off in between Spanish I and Spanish II, you won't gain much fluency. To master a language, you take courses back to back. It works the same way with math, which is a language in itself.

Avoid short courses. Courses that you take during summer school or another shortened term are condensed. You might find yourself doing far more reading and homework each week than you do in longer courses. If you enjoy math, the extra intensity can provide a stimulus to learn. If math is not your favorite subject, then give yourself extra time. Enroll in courses spread out over more calendar days.

Form a study group. During the first week of each math course, organize a study group. Ask each member to bring five problems to group meetings, along with solutions. Also exchange contact information so that you can stay in touch via e-mail, phone, and text messaging.

Make your text top priority. Math courses are often text driven. Budget for math textbooks and buy them as early as possible. Class activities closely follow the book. This fact underscores the importance of completing your reading assignments. Master one concept before going on to the next, and stay current with your reading. Be willing to read slowly and reread sections as needed.

Do homework consistently. Students who succeed in math do their homework daily—from beginning to end, and from the easy problems all the way through the hard problems. If you do homework consistently, you're not likely to be surprised on a test.

Take notes that promote success in math. Though math courses are often text driven, you might find that the content and organization of your notes makes a big difference as well. Take notes during every class and organize them by date. Also number the pages of your notes. Create a table of contents or index for them so that you can locate key concepts quickly.

Participate in class. Success in math depends on your active involvement. Attend class regularly. Complete homework assignments *when they're due*—not just before the test. If you're confused, get help right away from an instructor, tutor, or study group. Instructors' office hours, free on-campus tutoring, and classmates are just a few of the resources available to you. Also support class participation with time for homework. Make daily contact with math.

Ask questions fearlessly. It's a cliché, and it's true: In math, there are no dumb questions. Ask whatever questions will aid your understanding. Keep a running list of them, and bring the list to class.

Read actively. To get the most out of your math texts, read with paper and pencil in hand. Work out examples. Copy diagrams, formulas, and equations. Use chapter summaries and introductory outlines to organize your learning. From time to time, stop, close your book, and mentally reconstruct the steps in solving a problem. Before you memorize a formula, understand the basic concepts behind it.

USE TESTS TO SHOW WHAT YOU KNOW

Practice problem solving. To get ready for math tests, work *lots* of problems. Find out whether practice problems or previous tests are on file in the library, in the math department, or with your math teacher.

Isolate the types of problems that you find the most difficult. Practice them more often. Be sure to get help with these kinds of problems *before* exhaustion or frustration sets in.

To prepare for tests, practice working problems fast. Time yourself. This activity is a great one for math study groups.

Practice test taking. In addition to solving problems, create practice tests:

- Print out a set of problems, and set a timer for the same length of time as your testing period.

- Whenever possible, work on these problems in the same room where you will take the actual test.

- Use only the kinds of supporting materials—such as scratch paper or lists of formulas—that will be allowed during the test.

- As you work problems, use deep breathing or another technique to enter a more relaxed state.

To get the most value from practice tests, use them to supplement—not replace—your daily homework.

Ask appropriate questions. If you don't understand a test item, ask for clarification. The worst that can happen is that an instructor or proctor will politely decline to answer your question.

Write legibly. Put yourself in the instructor's place. Imagine the prospect of grading stacks of illegible answer sheets. Make your answers easy to read. If you show your work, underline key sections and circle your answer.

> There are no secrets involved in getting ready for math tests. Master some stress-management techniques, do your homework, get answers to your questions, and work sample problems.

Do your best. There are no secrets involved in getting ready for math tests. Master some stress-management techniques, do your homework, get answers to your questions, and work sample problems. If you've done those things, you're ready for the test and deserve to do well. If you haven't done all those things, just do the best you can.

Remember that your personal best can vary from test to test, and even from day to day. Even if you don't answer all test questions correctly, you can demonstrate what you *do* know right now.

During the test, notice when solutions come easily. Savor the times when you feel relaxed and confident. If you ever feel math anxiety in the future, these are the times to remember.[3] ∎

You're One Click Away . . .
from more strategies for math mastery.

JOURNAL ENTRY 13

Transform your experience of tests

No matter how you've felt about tests in the past, you can wipe your mental slate clean. Use the following suggestions to transform the ways that you experience tests of all types, from the shortest pop quiz to the longest exam.

Discovery Statement

Mentally re-create a time when you had difficulty taking a test. Do anything that helps you reexperience this event. You could draw a picture of yourself in this situation, list some of the questions you had difficulty answering, or tell how you felt after finding out your score on the test. Briefly describe that experience in the space below.

I discovered that I . . .

_____
_____
_____
_____
_____
_____
_____
_____

Intention Statement

Next, describe how you want your experience of test taking to change. For example, you might write: "I intend to walk into every test I take feeling well rested and thoroughly prepared."

I intend to . . .

_____
_____
_____
_____
_____

Review this chapter, looking for five strategies that can help you turn your intention into reality. List those strategies below and note the page numbers where you read about them.

Strategy	Page number
_____	_____
_____	_____
_____	_____
_____	_____
_____	_____

Action Statement

Finally, prepare for a smooth transition from intention to action. Choose *one* strategy from the above list and describe exactly when and where you will use it.

I will . . .

_____
_____
_____
_____
_____
_____
_____
_____
_____
_____
_____
_____
_____
_____
_____
_____
_____
_____

5

CHAPTER 5 SKILLS *Snapshot*

Take a minute to reflect on your responses to the "Memory & Tests" section of the Discovery Wheel on page 9. Then take your discoveries and intentions about tests to the next level by completing the following sentences:

DISCOVERY

My score on the Memory & Tests section of the Discovery Wheel on page 9 was . . .

To study for a test, what I usually do is to . . .

One strategy that really helps me with remembering material for tests is . . .

If I feel stressed about a test, I usually respond by . . .

INTENTION

I'll know that I've reached a new level of mastery with memory and tests when . . .

By the time I finish this course, I would like my Memory & Tests score on the Discovery Wheel to be . . .

For now, my main goal related to memory and test taking is . . .

NEXT ACTION

To reach my goal, the most important thing I can do next is to . . .

Using Technology to Succeed

6

Use this **Master Student Map** to ask yourself

WHY THIS CHAPTER MATTERS . . .

- You'll use technology to access course content and interact with instructors and other students.

WHAT IS INCLUDED . . .

HOW YOU CAN USE THIS CHAPTER . . .

- Stay on top of my online course work.
- Develop new skills with technology.
- Build relationships through social networking and virtual team work.
- Navigate the Internet with ease and think critically about what I find.

WHAT IF . . .

- I could use technology to increase the value I get from my courses and build skills that I can transfer to the workplace?

© Ruslan Ivantsov/Shutterstock.com

JOURNAL ENTRY 14

Discover what you want from this chapter

The purpose of this chapter is to help you assess the impact of technology on your life—and to align your use of technology with your values and goals. Begin by previewing this chapter and completing the following sentences.

The things that I enjoy about using digital technology such as smartphones and computers include . . .

_____

_____

Some things that concern me about my use of technology are . . .

_____

_____

Three suggestions from this chapter that could help me deal with my concerns are . . .

_____

_____

_____

Love your problems
(and experience your barriers)

We all have problems and barriers that block our progress or prevent us from moving into new areas. Often, the way we respond to our problems places limitations on what we can be, do, and have.

Problems often work like barriers. When we bump up against one of our problems, we usually turn away and start walking along a different path. And all of a sudden—bump!—we've struck another barrier. And we turn away again.

As we continue to bump into problems and turn away from them, our lives stay inside the same old boundaries. Inside these boundaries, we are unlikely to have new adventures. We are unlikely to keep learning.

If we respond to problems by loving them instead of resisting them, we can expand the boundaries in which we live our lives.

The word *love* might sound like an overstatement. In this Power Process, the word means to unconditionally accept the fact that your problems exist. The more we deny or resist a problem, the stronger it seems to become. When we accept the fact that we have a problem, we can find effective ways to deal with it.

Suppose one of your barriers is speaking in front of a group. You fear that you'll forget everything you planned to say.

One option for dealing with this barrier is denial. You could get up in front of a group and pretend that you're not afraid. You could tell yourself, "I'm not going to be scared," and then try to keep your knees from knocking.

A more effective approach is to love your fear. Go to the front of the room, look out into the audience, and say to yourself, "I am scared. I notice that my knees are shaking and my mouth feels dry, and I'm having a rush of thoughts about what might happen if I say the wrong thing. Yup, I'm scared, and I'm not going to fight it. I'm going to give this speech anyway."

The beauty of this Power Process is that you continue to take action—giving your speech, for example—no matter what you feel. You walk right up to the barrier and then *through* it. You might even find that if you totally accept and experience a barrier, such as fear, it shrinks or disappears. When you relax, you reclaim your natural abilities. You can recall memories, learn something new, and even laugh a little. Even if this does not happen right away, you can still open up to a new experience.

Loving a problem does not need *liking* it. Instead, loving a problem means admitting the truth about it. This helps us take effective action—which can free us of the problem once and for all.

You're One Click Away . . .
from accessing Power Process Media online and finding out more ways to love your problems.

Succeeding *as an* online learner

If you are taking an online course, or a course that is heavily supported by online materials, then get ready for new challenges. You can use a variety of strategies to succeed.

Do a trial run with technology. Verify your access to course Web sites, including online tutorials, PowerPoint presentations, readings, quizzes, tests, assignments, bulletin boards, and chat rooms. Ask your instructors for Web site addresses, e-mail addresses, and passwords. Work out any bugs when you start the course and well before that first assignment is due.

If you're planning to use a computer lab on campus, find one that meets course requirements. Remember that on-campus computer labs may not allow you to install all the software needed to access Web sites for your courses or textbooks.

Develop a contingency plan. Murphy's Law of Computer Crashes states that technology tends to break down at the moment of greatest inconvenience. You might not believe this piece of folklore, but it's still wise to prepare for it:

- Find a "technology buddy" in each of your classes—someone who can contact the instructor if you lose Internet access or experience other computer problems.
- Every day, make backup copies of files created for your courses.
- Keep extra printer supplies—paper and toner or ink cartridges—on hand at all times. Don't run out of necessary supplies on the day a paper is due.

Get actively involved with the course. Your online course will include a page that lists homework assignments and test dates. That's only the beginning. Look for ways to engage with the material by submitting questions, completing assignments, and interacting with the instructor and other students.

Take notes on course material. You can print out anything that appears on a computer screen. This includes online course materials—articles, books, manuscripts, e-mail messages, chat room sessions, and more.

The potential problem is that you might skip the note-taking process altogether. ("I can just print out everything!") You would then miss the chance to internalize a new idea by restating it in your own words—a principal benefit of note taking. Result: Material passes from computer to printer without ever intersecting with your brain.

To prevent this problem, take notes in Cornell, mind map, concept map, or outline format. Write Discovery and Intention Statements to capture key insights from the materials and next actions to take. Also talk about what you're learning. Recite key points out loud, and discuss what you find online with other students.

© iStockphoto.com/RichVintage

Of course, it's fine to print out online material. If you do, treat your printouts like mini-textbooks. Apply the steps of Muscle Reading as explained in Chapter 3.

Another potential problem with online courses is the physical absence of the teacher. In a classroom, you get lots of visual and verbal clues to what kinds of questions will appear on a test. Those clues are often missing from an online course, which means that they could be missing from your notes. Ask your online instructor about what material she considers to be most important.

Set up folders and files for easy reference. Create a separate folder for each class on your computer's hard drive. Give each folder a meaningful name, such as *biology—spring2009*. Place all files related to a course in the appropriate folder. Doing this can save you from one of the main technology-related time wasters: searching for lost files.

Also name individual files with care. Avoid changing extensions that identify different types of files, such as .ppt for PowerPoint presentations or .pdf for files in the Adobe Reader portable document format. Changing extensions might lead to problems when you're looking for files later or sharing them with other users.

Take responsibility. If you register for an online course with no class meetings, you might miss the motivating presence of an instructor and classmates. Instead, manufacture your own motivation. Be clear about what you'll gain by doing well in the course. Relate course content to your major and career goals. Don't wait to be contacted by your classmates and instructor. Initiate that contact on your own.

6

Ask for help. If you feel confused about anything you're learning online, ask for help right away. This is especially important when you don't see the instructor face-to-face in class. Some students simply drop online courses rather than seek help. E-mail or call the instructor before you make that choice. If the instructor is on campus, you might be able to arrange for a meeting during office hours.

Manage time and tasks carefully. Courses that take place mostly or totally online can become invisible in your weekly academic schedule. This reinforces the temptation to put off dealing with these courses until late in the term.

Avoid this mistake! Consider the real possibility that an online course can take *more* time than a traditional, face-to-face lecture class. Online courses tend to embrace lots of activities—sending and receiving e-mails, joining discussion forums, commenting on blog posts, and more. New content might appear every day. One key to keeping up with the course is frequent contact and careful time management:

- Early in the term, create a detailed schedule for online courses. In your calendar, list a due date for each assignment. Break big assignments into smaller steps, and schedule a due date for each step.

- Schedule times in your calendar to complete online course work. Give these scheduled sessions the same priority as regular classroom meetings. At these times, check for online announcements relating to assignments, tests, and other course events. Check for course-related e-mails daily.

- If the class includes discussion forums, check those daily as well. Look for new posts and add your replies. The point of these tools is to create a lively conversation that starts early and continues throughout the term.

> Consider the real possibility that an online course can take *more* time than a traditional, face-to-face lecture class. Online courses tend to embrace lots of activities—sending and receiving e-mails, joining discussion forums, commenting on blog posts, and more.

- When you receive an online assignment, e-mail any questions immediately. If you want to meet with an instructor in person, request an appointment several days in advance.

- Give online instructors plenty of time to respond. They are not always online. Many online instructors have traditional courses to teach, along with administration and research duties.

- Download or print out online course materials as soon as they're posted on the class Web site. These materials might not be available later in the term.

- If possible, submit online assignments early. Staying ahead of the game will help you avoid an all-nighter at the computer during finals week.

Find tools that help with online courses. BlackBoard and other portals for online courses offer tools to help you access the content. See whether there are any created specifically for your class.

These tools might include "apps"—software programs designed to run on smart phones, iPods, iPads, and similar devices. Most apps have specific, limited features. They're designed to just do one or two things well. Look for apps that allow you to manage to-do lists, maintain a calendar, create flash cards, take notes, make voice recordings, read ebooks, and listen to audio books.

Many apps are free. Others cost just a few dollars or come in trial versions that you can use for free.

Focus your attention. Some students are used to visiting Web sites while watching television, listening to loud music, or using instant messaging software. When applied to online learning, these habits can reduce your learning and endanger your grades. To succeed with technology, turn off the television, quit online chat sessions, and turn down the music. Whenever you go online, stay in charge of your attention.

Ask for feedback. To get the most from online learning, request feedback from your instructor via e-mail. When appropriate, also ask for conferences by phone or in person.

Sharing files offers another source of feedback. For example, Microsoft Word has a Track Changes feature that allows other people to insert comments into your documents and make suggested revisions. These edits are highlighted on the screen. Use such tools to get feedback on your writing from instructors and peers.

Note: Be sure to check with your instructors to see how they want students enrolled in their online courses to address and label their e-mails. Many teachers ask their online students to use a standard format for the subject area so they can quickly recognize e-mails from them.

Contact other students. Make personal contact with at least one other student in each of your classes—especially classes that involve lots of online course work. Create study groups to share notes, quiz each other, critique papers, and do other cooperative learning tasks. This kind of support can help you succeed as an online learner. ■

8 TECHNOLOGY SKILLS
TO DEVELOP NOW

For master students, technology is a tool for developing a life-long pattern of success. That's as true of a pencil as an iPad. If you develop the following skills, you can use technology of any kind to achieve your personal, academic, and career goals

1 SEARCH WITH KEY WORDS

Key words are the terms that you enter into a search box on a Web page. Your choice of key words determines the quality of results that you get from Internet search engines, such as Google (google.com), and from library catalogs. For better search results:

Use specific key words. Entering *firefox* or *safari* will give you more focused results than entering *Web browser.*

Use unique key words. Whenever possible, use proper names. Enter *Beatles* or *Radiohead* rather than *British rock bands.*

Use quotation marks if you're looking for certain words in a certain order. "Audacity of hope" will return a list of pages with that exact phrase.

When you're not sure of a key word, add a wild card character. In most search engines, that character is the asterisk (*). If you're looking for the title of a film directed by Clint Eastwood and just can't remember the name, enter *clint eastwood directed *.*

Look for more search options. Many search engines also offer advanced search features and explain how to use them. Look for the word *advanced, settings,* or *more* on the site's home page, and click on the link.

2 DISCOVER IDEAS

The Internet offers you a platform for lifelong learning that's nourished by people who share your interests. Connect with them:

- Search for Web sites related to your courses, including articles and blogs by your instructors and the authors of your textbooks.

- Choose other topics that interest you and search for related Web sites.

- Use an RSS reader, such as Google Reader or NetNewsWire, to get updated lists of articles on those Web sites.

- Search Twitter, Facebook, Google+, and other social networking sites to follow the people who post to your favorite sites.

- Pay special attention to well-written blogs, and join the discussion by commenting on the postings.

- E-mail bloggers who write posts that you enjoy.

- Create your own blog to document your learning and invite comments on your posts.

- Create online accounts that allow you to reserve and renew materials at your school library and public library.

3 CAPTURE AND PRESENT IDEAS

Imagine how useful it would be to have your course materials and notes available to you anywhere, any time, from any digital device. Today there are tools—many of them free—that make this possible.

Note-taking applications allow you to "clip" content from Web sites, add your own notes, store them online, share them, and synchronize them across all your digital devices. Some of these applications also allow you to add "offline" content, such as digital photos of business cards and receipts. You can then organize and search through all this content by using tags and keywords.

Note-taking applications come in several forms. Many are available on the Web. Others also exist as applications for your computer, smartphone, or tablet. Examples include Evernote (evernote.com) and Springpad (springpad.com).

Another, more "low-tech" option is to create a plain text file for each of your courses and for your personal journal. Then enter your notes in those files. The benefits of plain text are that it consumes relatively little memory, and almost all software can read it. Whenever you want to find a note in one of these files, just search for it with key words.

In addition to using a Web browser, learn to create and edit documents, presentations, and spreadsheets. The Microsoft Office Suite (including Word, PowerPoint, and Excel) is widely used. However, there are alternatives with similar features, and several are free. Among them are Google Docs (docs.google.com) and OpenOffice (openoffice.org). Whatever option you choose, make sure that it is compatible with Microsoft Office.

4 MANAGE EVENTS AND TASKS

There are three main types of applications for managing your time.

The first includes calendars for scheduling appointments and keeping track of due dates. Your computer, smartphone, or tablet might come with a calendar application built in. There are online alternatives such as Google Calendar (google.com/calendar) and 30 Boxes (30boxes.com). Online calendars often allow you to create public calendars and share them with other people.

Second, consider list managers. Use them to keep track of to-do items and other groups of related ideas. Look for applications that

6

allow you to assign due dates for to-do items, check off completed items, add item to your lists via e-mail or text messaging, search with key words, and send reminders to yourself. Examples are Remember the Milk (rememberthemilk.com) and Workflowy (workflowy.com).

The third type of application includes goal-setting tools. Sample features include the ability to list goals, track your progress toward them as part of an online community, send yourself reminders, and choose from a library of action plans for achieving common goals. For instance, check out 43Things (43things.com) and Lifetick (lifetick.com).

5 TAKE PART IN SOCIAL NETWORKS

Social networks create value. Web sites such as Facebook, Twitter, LinkedIn, and Google+ are places to share personal news, photos, videos, and links to Web content. You can also use these sites to form study groups and promote special events. Meetup.com and similar services help people with similar interests to connect online and then meet in person.

To experience the benefits of social networking, begin the process now. This is especially important for career planning. Develop a network of people who can help you meet your career goals—well before you start applying for jobs.

Whenever you participate in a social network, stay in charge of your safety and personal reputation:

- Post only what you want made public and permanent.
- Avoid posting personal information such as your home address, birth date, and work or class schedule.
- Do not post any financial information, such as bank account numbers, credit card numbers, your social security number, or information about an eBay or PayPal account.

In addition, "friend" people with care, remembering that you do not have to follow every person who chooses to follow you. If you schedule a face-to-face meeting with someone you met online, choose a public place and bring along a friend you trust.

6 WRITE E-MAIL THAT GETS RESULTS

People are drowning in e-mail. Send messages only to the people who need them and who know you. In the same spirit, use the "reply all" feature sparingly, and keep attachments to a minimum.

Write an informative subject line. Rather than offering a generic description of your message, include the main point.

Make the body of your message as short as possible. Focus on one idea or question. Put that in the first paragraph, along with any request for follow-up action. For easier reading, keep paragraphs short as well.

Before hitting the *send* button, review what you've written. Proofread for spelling and grammar errors. Every message you send says something about your attention to detail. Keep the tone professional—more formal than the text messages you send to friends.

7 PRACTICE NETIQUETTE

The word *etiquette* refers to common courtesy in interpersonal relationships. *Netiquette* is a similar word that means using

> Turn off your cell phone during class. If you're taking notes on your laptop, then don't surf the Internet, send text messages, or check your e-mail. Those habits reduce the value you get from your courses and waste your tuition money.

computers, cell phones, and other digital devices in a civil and courteous way.

Remember that online messages lack voice inflection and other nonverbal cues that are present in face-to-face communication. Without these cues, words can be easily misinterpreted. Before sending your message, read it carefully. Make sure it's clear, polite, and respectful.

The cornerstone of netiquette is to remember that anyone you interact with online is a human being. Whenever you're at a keyboard and writing a message, ask yourself: "Would I say this to the person's face?"

Also remember the "Power Process: Be here now" when using technology. Turn off your cell phone during class. If you're taking notes on a laptop, then don't surf the Web, send text messages, or check your e-mail. Those habits reduce the value you get from your courses and waste your tuition money.

8 STAY SAFE AND SECURE

Keep your data secure. Get to know someone at your school's computer center who can answer technology questions. Ask this person how to protect your equipment from malware, including computer viruses.

Be sure back up your data to an external hard drive, an online service such as DropBox (dropbox.com), or both. If a technical glitch wipes out everything on your computer's hard drive, you'll have extra copies of your files on hand. ■

You're One Click Away . . .
from more strategies for developing core technology skills.

Discover the impact of technology on your time and attention

In 2008, Nicholas Carr published a widely quoted article: "Is Google Making Us Stupid?"[1] In it, he complained that his Web-surfing habits were chipping away at his ability to concentrate and read for long periods of time. "Once I was a scuba diver in the sea of words," Carr wrote. "Now I zip along the surface like a guy on a Jet Ski."

No single Web site has the power to make us stupid. Yet the habits that we develop while we're online might affect our ability to "be here now." This issue presents a perfect opportunity to apply the cycle of discovery, intention, and action.

Discovery

Begin by keeping track of the time that you spend online. Do this for at least one day—or better yet, a full week.

Use a simple system for gathering data. For instance, keep a 3 × 5 card and pen in your pocket or purse. On this card, write down the times when you start using the Internet and when you stop. Another option is to use a Web-based time tracker such as SlimTimer (slimtimer.com) or Rescuetime (rescuetime.com). Or simply estimate your online time at the end of each day.

If possible, include short descriptions of how you spend your online time. For example: *visit Facebook, check e-mail, read the news, do course work,* or *watch videos.*

After monitoring your online time, complete the following sentences

I discovered that the average number of minutes I spend online during the day is . . .

_____

The most common things that I do online are . . .

_____

_____

_____

I was surprised to discover that . . .

_____

_____

_____

Intention

Next, think about any changes that you want to make in the amount of time you spend online—and the ways you use that time. For example, you could

- Turn off all notifications for e-mail messages, social networking updates, and text messages while you study.
- Close your Web browser for defined periods each day.
- Check your e-mail only at specific times each day.
- Stay offline entirely during certain times of the day, or on certain days of the week.

Think about the strategies you'd like to use. Then choose one of them to use during the upcoming week. Complete the following sentence:

I intend to . . .

_____

_____

_____

Action

After acting on your intention for one week, come back to this Journal Entry. Reflect on the results of your new habit

During the past week of online activity, I spent less time on . . .

_____

_____

I spent more time on . . .

_____

_____

The most important thing I can do right now to take charge of time and attention while online is to . . .

_____

_____

_____

6

JOIN THE (VIRTUAL) TEAM

In the economy of the twenty-first century, many projects will be done by virtual teams. These consist of people who might live in different cities—or even different countries—and use digital technology to collaborate. If you can succeed at virtual teamwork, you'll add a valuable new skill to your résumé. Start with the suggestions that follow.

PLAN YOUR TEAM PROJECT

The skeleton of any team project consists of four main elements—milestones, actions, reference materials, and "someday" items.

Milestones are due dates for major parts of the project. If your team is developing a new software package, for example, project milestones include the dates of the alpha, beta, and final product releases.

Begin planning with your calendar. Enter the start date for the project and the final due date. Then assign a due date for each project milestone. This calls for a balance of creative and critical thinking. Choose dates that keep the work going at a steady pace—and that are realistic for your team to meet. Also build in some extra time for unexpected delays.

Actions are lists of the tasks that team members will complete in order to meet the milestones and final due date. These are items that you enter on a to-do list. If you're the team leader, keep a master action list for the project. Assign items to specific people, and follow up to make sure that all items get done.

Writing action items is an art in itself. On your action list, start each item with an active verb such as *call, e-mail, print,* or *deliver.* Choose a word that points to a visible behavior.

Reference materials include background information that team members might want to review as they complete action items. Examples are product catalogs, notes from meetings, and articles from Web sites, magazines, and newspapers. Whenever possible, collect these materials in digital form so that you can share them and search them with key words.

Someday items are ideas for other projects that you might want to pursue. Save these ideas. They could prove valuable in the future.

CHOOSE YOUR TECHNOLOGY

To manage the four elements described above, look for tools that allow you to create, edit, and share documents, spreadsheets, drawings, and presentations. Ideally, the technology that you choose will also allow team members to accomplish the following:

- Update files in real time.
- Track changes or version history in shared documents.
- Share calendars and project-related action lists.
- Send instant messages.
- Set up video conferences.
- Create video and audio recordings of team meetings.
- Back up data online (in the "cloud").
- Use mobile devices to access project files.

You can find a growing list of applications for team work. Their capabilities and prices vary widely, though several are generous with features and also free. Some current options include Google+ Hangouts, AnyMeeting (anymeeting.com), Skype (skype .com), and Zoho collaboration applications (zoho.com) For more ideas, do an Internet search with the key words *collaborate online.*

BE A VIRTUAL TEAM PLAYER

As a team member, your technical skills can make huge contribution. Equally important are your "people skills." Effective teams consist of people who know how to resolve conflict, build consensus based on creative and critical thinking, and cooperate to reach a common goal. In virtual teams, the lack of in-person contact creates special challenges to doing these things.

You can help by making the team a priority in your life. Schedule regular times each week to work on your project. Volunteer to take notes on team meetings and post them in a shared document or blog. And when you agree to complete assigned actions, keep your word.

Also be available. Tell people about the best times and ways to reach you, and respect the preferences of your team members. Keep a list of everyone's contact information and schedule team meetings at least several days in advance.

Respect diversity as well. Your team members may come from different cultures, so review the suggestions in "Thriving in a diverse world" on page 111.

Finally, function as a professional whenever you're online. Team members might get to know you mainly through e-mails and instant messages. Consider the impression you're making with your online presence. Avoid slang, idioms, sarcastic humor, and other expressions that can create misunderstanding. A small dose of civility can make a large difference in the quality of your virtual team experience. ■

You're One Click Away . . .
from more strategies for succeeding in virtual teams.

Developing information literacy

An important quality of master students is curiosity, and that means asking questions. Answering them means finding information from appropriate sources, evaluating the information, organizing it, and using it to achieve a purpose. The ability to do this in a world where data are literally at our fingertips is called *information literacy*.

DISCOVER YOUR QUESTIONS

Start by discovering your *main question*. This is the thing that sparked your curiosity in the first place. Answering it is your purpose for doing research.

Your main question will raise a number of smaller, related questions. These are *supporting questions*. They also call for answers.

Suppose that your main question is this: "During the mortgage credit crisis of 2007 to 2010, what led banks to lend money to people with poor credit histories?" Your list of supporting questions might include the following:

- What banks were involved in the mortgage credit crisis?
- How do banks discover a person's credit history?
- What are the signs of a poor credit history?

Listing your main and supporting questions can save hours of time. If you ever feel overwhelmed or get sidetracked, pull out your list of questions. When the information you're finding answers one of those questions, then you're on track. If you're wading through material that's not answering your questions, then it's time to find another source of information or revise your questions.

CONSIDER PRIMARY AND SECONDARY SOURCES OF INFORMATION

Consider the variety of information sources that are available to you: billions of Web pages, books, magazines, newspapers, and audio and video recordings. You can reduce this vast range of materials to a few manageable categories. Start with the distinction between primary and secondary sources.

Primary sources. These can lead to information treasures. Primary sources are firsthand materials—personal journals, letters, speeches, government documents, scientific experiments, field observations, interviews with recognized experts, archeological digs, artifacts, and original works of art.

Primary sources can also include scholarly publications such as the *New England Journal of Medicine, Contemporary Literary Criticism*, and similar publications. One clue that you're dealing with primary source is the title. If it includes the word *journal*,

then you're probably reading a primary source. If you pick up a magazine with pages of full-color advertisements and photos of celebrities, you're not reading a scholarly journal.

Although many kinds of publications can be useful, scholarly journals and other primary sources are unmatched in depth and credibility. In addition, journal articles are often *peer reviewed*. This means that other experts in the field read and review the articles to make sure that they are accurate.

Secondary sources. These sources summarize, explain, and comment on primary sources. Examples are listed here:

- Popular magazines such as *Time* and *Newsweek*.
- Magazines—such as the *Atlantic Monthly* and *Scientific American*—with wide circulation and long articles.
- Nationally circulated newspapers, such as the *Washington Post, New York Times,* and *Los Angeles Times*.
- General reference works such as the *Encyclopaedia Britannica* and the *Oxford Companion to English Literature*.

Secondary sources are useful places to start your research. Use them to get an overview of your topic. Depending on the assignment, these may be all you need for informal research.

GET TO KNOW YOUR LIBRARY

Remember that many published materials are available in print as well as online. For a full range of sources, head to your campus library.

Ask a librarian. One reason for a trip to the library is to find a reference librarian. Tell this person about the questions you want to answer, and ask for good sources of information.

Take a tour. Libraries—from the smallest one in your hometown to the Smithsonian in Washington, D.C.—consist of just three basic elements:

- *Catalogs*—online databases that list all of the library's accessible sources.
- *Collections*—materials, such as periodicals (magazines, journals, and newspapers), books, pamphlets, audiovisual materials, and materials available from other libraries via interlibrary loan.
- *Computer resources*—Internet access; connections to campus-wide computer networks; and databases stored on CD-ROMs,

6

CDs, DVDs, or online. Online databases, which allow you to look at full-text articles from magazines, journals, and newspapers, are sometimes available from your personal computer or smartphone, with a password. Many libraries have access to special databases that are not available on the Internet. Also ask about ebooks that can be delivered straight to your computer.

Before you start your next research project, take some time to investigate all three elements of your school's library. When inspecting a library's collections, look for materials such as the following, making sure to ask about both print and online versions

- *Encyclopedias.* Use leading print and online encyclopedias, such as the *Encyclopaedia Britannica*. Specialized encyclopedias can cover many fields and include, for example, the *Encyclopedia of Psychology, Encyclopedia of the Biological Sciences*, and *McGraw-Hill Encyclopedia of Science, and Technology.*

- *Biographies.* Read accounts of people's lives in biographical works such as *Who's Who, Dictionary of American Biography*, and *Biography Index: A Cumulative Index to Biographical Material in Books and Magazines.*

- *Statistics and government documents.* Among the many useful sources are the *Statistical Abstract of the United States, Handbook of Labor Statistics, Occupational Outlook Handbook*, and U.S. Census Bureau publications.

- *Almanacs, atlases, and gazetteers.* For population statistics and boundary changes, see the *World Almanac and Book of Facts, Atlas of Crime*, the *New York Times Almanac*, or the *CIA World Factbook.*

- *Dictionaries.* Consult the *American Heritage Dictionary of the English Language, Oxford English Dictionary*, and specialized dictionaries such as the *Dictionary of the Social Sciences.*

- *Reference works in specific subject areas.* These references cover a vast range of material. Examples include *The Oxford Companion to Art*; the *Encyclopedia of the Biological Sciences, Countries and Their Cultures*; and the *Concise Oxford Companion to Classical Literature.* Ask a librarian for more information.

- *Periodical articles.* Find articles in periodicals (works issued periodically, such as scholarly journals, popular magazines, and newspapers) by using a periodical index. Some indexes, such as Lexis-Nexis Academic Universe, InfoTrac, OCLC FirstSearch, and New York Times Ondisc, provide the full text of articles.[2]

TURN TO PEOPLE AS SOURCES OF INFORMATION

Making direct contact with people can offer a welcome relief from hours of solitary research time and give you valuable hands-on involvement. Your initial research will uncover the names of experts on your chosen topic. Consider doing an interview with one of these people—in person, over the phone, or via e-mail.

THINK CRITICALLY ABOUT WHAT YOU DISCOVER

Not all information is created equal. Just because it's published in print or online doesn't mean it's accurate.

The first step to evaluating any source of information is to make sure that you understand what it says. Use the techniques of Muscle Reading described in Chapter 3 to comprehend the author's message. Remember to start by previewing the printed document or Web site, which includes posing questions about what you want to discover.

During your research, find several points of view on key issues. Look for viewpoints that are clear, logical, balanced, and supported by facts that you can verify. When authors take care to cite *their* sources of information, that's a positive sign.

As you compare the work of several authors, look for the points on which they agree and disagree. Also look for any unanswered questions. These represent opportunities for you to do some original thinking.

You'll find more guidelines for critical thinking in Chapter 7.

USE INFORMATION

As you do research, remember to keep a list of all your sources of information and avoid plagiarism. (See "Taking notes while reading" on page 63.) Also make time to digest all the information you gather. Ask yourself:

- *Do I have answers to my main question?*

- *Do I have answers to my supporting questions?*

- *What are the main ideas from my sources?*

- *Do I have personal experiences that can help me answer these questions?*

- *If a television talk show host asked me these questions, how would I answer?*

- *On what points do my sources agree?*

- *On what points do my sources disagree?*

- *Do I have statistics and other facts that I can use to support my ideas?*

- *What new questions do I have?*

The beauty of these questions is that they help you use information from other people to stimulate *your* thinking. Discover the pleasures of emerging insights and sudden inspiration. You just might get hooked on the adventure of information literacy. ■

 You're One Click Away . . .
from more strategies for developing information literacy.

CRITICAL THINKING EXERCISE 6

Evaluate information on the Internet

Take this opportunity to practice critical thinking about information on the Internet. Review the history in your Web browser for a site that you visited recently in connection with your course work. Then answer the following questions.

What is the address (URL) of the site you chose?

Notice the *currency* of several pages on the site. When were they published? Is their content time-sensitive?

_____

_____

_____

_____

Now think about *credibility*. Look for information about the author(s) of this site, including their educational background and professional experience. (You might need to navigate to the site's home page to find this information.) Can you find this information, and does it lead you to trust the site? Why or why not?

_____

_____

_____

_____

Also look for evidence of *bias*—that is, political affiliations or funding sources that might determine the site's stand on an issue. For instance, you can predict that a Web site supported by the National Rifle Association will publish pages that promote certain points of view on gun control. Do you see any evidence of bias in the site that you selected? Explain your answer.

_____

_____

_____

_____

_____

_____

Some Web sites have a *content review policy* that adds to their credibility. Return to the site's home page. Do you see any reference to an editorial board or list of qualified experts who review the site's content before it's published? If so, does it increase your trust in the site? Why or why not?

_____

_____

_____

_____

_____

_____

Next, look for evidence of *audience engagement*. How can readers connect with this site? Does it include a Contact page with a phone number, e-mail address, or street address for the author or sponsoring organization? And if the site includes a blog, do you see comments from readers?

_____

_____

_____

_____

_____

Finally, review your answers to the above questions. Based on your thinking, would you recommend this site to other people? Give reasons for your answer.

_____

_____

You're One Click Away . . .
from more strategies for thinking critically about information on the Internet.

6 SKILLS *Snapshot*

CHAPTER

After experimenting with some suggestions from this chapter, take a few minutes to reflect on your responses to the Technology section of the Discovery Wheel exercise on page 9. Complete the following sentences:

DISCOVERY

My score on the Technology section of the Discovery Wheel was . . .

The digital devices (such as a computer or cell phone) that I use on a daily basis include . . .

I could make a major and positive difference in my use of technology if I could learn to . . .

INTENTION

In order to take my skill with technology to the next level, my goal is to . . .

ACTION

The most important thing that I can do right now to achieve my goal is . . .

At the end of this course, I would like my Technology score on the Discovery Wheel to be . . .

Thinking Clearly & Communicating Your Ideas

Use this **Master Student Map** to ask yourself

WHY THIS CHAPTER MATTERS . . .

- Your skills in thinking, writing, and speaking have a direct impact on your success in school and at work.

WHAT IS INCLUDED . . .

HOW YOU CAN USE THIS CHAPTER . . .

- Gain strategies for creative and critical thinking.
- Detect common errors in thinking.
- Write and speak with more confidence.

WHAT IF . . .

- I could make effective decisions, solve problems, and consistently persuade people to adopt my ideas?

JOURNAL ENTRY 16

Discover what you want from this chapter

Spend 5 minutes previewing this chapter. Then complete the following sentences.

When I'm assigned to write a paper or make a presentation, I usually feel . . .

_____

_____

_____

Based on my preview of this chapter, I could become a more effective speaker and writer by . . .

_____

_____

_____

I could think more clearly and make better decisions by . . .

_____

_____

_____

© Ruslan Ivantsov/Shutterstock.com

POWER process

Employ your word

When you give your word, you are creating—literally. The person you are is, for the most part, a result of the agreements you make. Others know who you are by your words and your commitments. And you can learn who you are by observing which commitments you choose to keep and which ones you choose to avoid.

Relationships are built on agreements. When we break a promise to be faithful to a spouse, to help a friend move to a new apartment, or to pay a bill on time, relationships are strained.

The words we use to make agreements can be placed into six different levels. We can think of each level as one rung on a ladder—the ladder of powerful speaking. As we move up the ladder, our speaking becomes more effective.

The first and lowest rung on the ladder is *obligation*. Words used at this level include *I should, he ought to, someone had better, they need to, I must,* and *I had to.* Speaking this way implies that something other than ourselves is in control of our lives. When we live at the level of obligation, we speak as if we are victims.

The second rung is *possibility*. At this level, we examine new options. We play with new ideas, possible solutions, and alternative courses of action. As we do, we learn that we can make choices that dramatically affect the quality of our lives. We are not the victims of circumstance. Phrases that signal this level include *I might, I could, I'll consider, I hope to,* and *maybe.*

From possibility, we can move up to the third level—*preference*. Here we begin the process of choice. The words *I prefer* signal that we're moving toward one set of possibilities over another, perhaps setting the stage for eventual action.

Above preference is a fourth rung called *passion*. Again, certain words signal this level: *I want to, I'm really excited to do that,* and *I can't wait.*

Action comes with the fifth rung—*planning*. When people use phrases such as *I intend to, my goal is to, I plan to,* and *I'll try like mad to,* they're at the level of planning. The Intention Statements you write in this book are examples of planning.

The sixth and highest rung on the ladder is *promising*. This is where the power of your word really comes into play. At this level, it's common to use phrases such as these: *I will, I promise to, I am committed,* and *you can count on it.* Promising is where we bridge from possibility and planning to action. Promising brings with it all of the rewards of employing your word.

You're One Click Away . . .
from accessing Power Process Media online and finding out more about how to "employ your word.".

iStockphoto.com/Clayton Hansen

CRITICAL THINKING: A survival skill

Society depends on persuasion. Advertisers want us to spend money on their products. Political candidates want us to "buy" their stands on the issues. Teachers want us to agree that their classes are vital to our success. Parents want us to accept their values. Authors want us to read their books. Broadcasters want us to spend our time in front of the radio or television, consuming their programs and not those of the competition.

A typical American sees thousands of television commercials each year—and TV is just one medium of communication. There are also writers and speakers who enter our lives through radio shows, magazines, books, billboards, brochures, Web sites, and fund-raising appeals. They all have a product, service, cause, or opinion for us to embrace.

This flood of appeals leaves us with hundreds of choices about what to buy, what to do, and who to be. It's easy to lose our heads in the crosscurrent of competing ideas—unless we develop skills in critical thinking.

When we think critically, we make choices with open eyes. We can detect thinking that's inaccurate, sloppy, or misleading. Critical thinking is a path to freedom from half-truths and deception. This is liberating.

Critical thinking is a skill that will never go out of style. Throughout human history, nonsense has often been taken for the truth. For example, people once believed that:

- Illness results from an imbalance in the four vital fluids: blood, phlegm, water, and bile.

- Racial integration of the armed forces would lead to destruction of soldiers' morale.

- Women are incapable of voting intelligently.

- We will never invent anything smaller than a transistor. (That was before the computer chip.)

The critical thinkers of history arose to challenge such ideas. Those courageous men and women were master students. They held their peers to high intellectual standards.

It's been said that human beings are rational creatures. Yet no one is born as a creative or critical thinker. These are learned skills.

This is one reason that you study so many subjects in higher education—math, science, history, psychology, literature, and more. A broad base of courses helps you develop as a thinker. You see how people with different viewpoints arrive at conclusions, make decisions, and solve problems. You get a foundation for dealing with complex challenges in your career, your relationships, and your community.

One of the reasons that thinking is so challenging—and so rewarding—is that we have a remarkable capacity to fool ourselves. Some of our ill-formed thoughts and half-truths have a source that hits a little close to home. That source is ourselves.

When they discover that their thinking is fuzzy, lazy, based on a false assumption, or dishonest, master students are willing to admit the truth. These students value evidence and logic. When a solid fact contradicts a cherished belief, they are willing to change the belief.

Critical and creative thinking is the basis for much of what you do in school—reading, writing, speaking, listening, note taking, test taking, problem solving, and decision making. Master students have strategies for accomplishing all these tasks. For example, they distinguish between opinion and fact. They ask probing questions and make detailed observations. They uncover assumptions and define their terms. They make assertions carefully, basing them on sound logic and solid evidence. Almost everything that we call *knowledge* is a result of these activities. This means that thinking and learning are intimately linked.

Remember that one kind of thinking—planning—has the power to lift the quality of your daily life. When you plan, you are the equal of the greatest sculptor, painter, or playwright. More than creating a work of art, you are designing your life. You get to practice this artistry by choosing your major, planning your career, and setting long-term goals.

You have the right to question everything that you see, hear, and read. You also have the opportunity to *create* ideas that can transform your life and contribute to the lives of others. Acquiring these abilities is a major goal of a college education.

Use the suggestions in this chapter to claim the thinking powers that are your birthright. The effective thinker is one aspect of the master student who lives inside you. ■

7

Becoming a
CRITICAL THINKER

Thinking is a path to intellectual adventure. Although there are dozens of possible approaches to thinking well, the process boils down to *asking and answering questions.*

There is one place where master students shine. They possess the ability to ask questions that lead to deeper learning.

Remember that your mind is an obedient servant. It will deliver answers at the same level as your questions. Becoming a critical thinker means staying flexible and asking a wide range of questions.

GETTING READY FOR CRITICAL THINKING

A psychologist named Benjamin Bloom named six levels of thinking. (He called them *educational objectives*, or goals for learning.)[1] Each level of thinking calls for asking and answering different kinds of questions.

LEVEL 1: Remembering. At this level of thinking, the key question is *Can I recall the key terms, facts, or events?* To prompt level 1 thinking, an instructor might ask you to do the following:

- List the steps of Muscle Reading.
- State the primary features of a concept map.
- Name the author of this textbook.

To study for a test with level 1 questions, you could create flash cards to review ideas from your readings and class notes. You could also read a book with a set of questions in mind and underline the answers to those questions in the text. Or you could memorize a list of definitions so that you can recite them exactly. These are just a few sample strategies.

Although remembering is important, this is a relatively low level of learning. No critical or creative thinking is involved. You simply recognize or recall something that you've observed in the past.

LEVEL 2: Understanding. At this level, the main question is *Can I explain this idea in my own words?* Often this means giving examples of an idea based on your own experience.

Suppose that your instructor asks you to do the following:

- Explain the main point of the "Power Process: I create it all."
- Summarize the steps involved in creating a concept map.
- Compare outlining with the Cornell format for taking notes, stating how they're alike and how they differ.

Other key words in level 2 questions are *discuss, estimate,* and *restate.* All of these are cues to go one step beyond remembering and to show that you truly *comprehend* an idea.

LEVEL 3: Applying. Learning at level 3 means asking: *Can I use this idea to produce a desired result?* That result might include completing a task, meeting a goal, making a decision, or solving a problem.

Some examples of level 3 thinking are listed here:

- Write a to-do list.
- Write an effective goal statement.
- Choose a mnemonic to remember the names of the Great Lakes.

Some key words in level 3 questions include *apply, solve, construct, plan, predict,* and *produce.*

LEVEL 4: Analyzing. Questions at this level boil down to this: *Can I divide this idea into parts or steps?* For example, you could do the following:

- Divide the steps of Muscle Reading into three major phases.
- Take a list of key events in the Vietnam War and arrange them in chronological order.
- The "Power Process: Surrender" makes a distinction between surrendering and giving up. Explain that distinction.

Other key words in level 4 questions are *classify, separate, distinguish,* and *outline.*

LEVEL 5: Evaluating. Learning at level 5 means asking, *Can I rate the truth, usefulness, or quality of this idea—and give reasons for my rating?* This is the level of thinking you would use to do the following:

- Judge the effectiveness of an Intention Statement.

- Recommend a method for taking lecture notes when an instructor talks fast.

- Rank the Power Processes in order of importance to you—from most useful to least useful.

Level 5 involves genuine critical thinking. At this level you agree with idea, disagree with it, or suspend judgment until you get more information. In addition, you give reasons for your opinion and offer supporting evidence.

Some key words in level 5 questions are *critique, defend*, and *comment*.

LEVEL 6: Creating. To think at this level, ask, *Can I invent something new based on this idea?* For instance, you might do the following:

- Invent your own format for taking lecture notes.

- Prepare a list of topics that you would cover if you were teaching a student success course.

- Imagine that you now have enough money to retire and then write goals you would like to accomplish with your extra time.

- Create a presentation based on ideas found in this chapter. Put the material in your own words, and use visuals to enhance your main points.

Creative thinking often involves analyzing an idea into parts and then combining those parts in a new way. Another source of creativity is taking several ideas and finding an unexpected connection among them. In either case, you are thinking at a high level. You are going beyond agreement and disagreement to offer something unique—an original contribution of your own.

Questions for creative thinking often start with words such as *adapt, change, collaborate, compose, construct, create, design*, and *develop*. You might also notice phrases such as *What changes would you make . . . ? How could you improve . . . ? Can you think of another way to . . . ? What would happen if . . . ?*

GAINING SKILL AS A CRITICAL THINKER

All levels of thinking are useful. Notice that the lower levels of thinking (1 to 4) give you fewer options than the highest levels (5 and 6). Lower levels of thinking are sometimes about finding the "right" answer to a question. At levels 5 and 6, you

might discover several valid answers or create several workable solutions.

Also notice that the levels build on each other. Before you agree or disagree with an idea, make sure that you *remember* it accurately and truly *understand* it. Your understanding will go deeper if you can *apply* and *analyze* the idea as well.

Master students stay aware of their current level of thinking. They can also move to other levels with a clear intention. The following strategies can help.

Find various points of view on any issue. Imagine George Bush, Cesar Chavez, and Barack Obama assembled in one room to debate the most desirable way to reshape our government. Picture Madonna, Oprah Winfrey, and Mark Zuckerberg leading a workshop on how to plan your career. When seeking out alternative points of view, let scenes like these unfold in your mind.

Dozens of viewpoints exist on every important issue—reducing crime, ending world hunger, preventing war, educating our children, and countless other concerns. In fact, few problems have any single, permanent solution. Each generation produces its own answers to critical questions, based on current conditions. Our search for answers is a vast conversation that spans centuries. On each question, many voices are waiting to be heard.

You can take advantage of this diversity by seeking out alternative views with an open mind. When talking to another person, be willing to walk away with a new point of view—even if it's the one that you originally brought to the table, supported with new evidence.

Level 6 Creating	Can I invent something new based on this idea?
Level 5 Evaluating	Can I rate the truth, usefulness, or quality of this idea—and give reasons for my rating?
Level 4 Analyzing	Can I divide this idea into parts or steps?
Level 3 Applying	Can I use this idea to produce a desired result?
Level 2 Understanding	Can I explain this idea in my own words?
Level 1 Remembering	Can I recall the key terms, facts, or events?

© Cengage Learning 2013

Define terms. Imagine two people arguing about whether an employer should limit health care benefits to members of a family. To one person, the word *family* means a mother, father, and children. To the other person, the word *family* applies to any individuals who live together in a long-term, supportive relationship. Chances are the debate will go nowhere until these two people realize that they're defining the same word in different ways.

Conflicts of opinion can often be resolved—or at least clarified—when we define our key terms up front. This is especially true with abstract, emotion-laden terms such as *freedom, peace, progress,* or *justice.* Blood has been shed over the meaning of such words. Define terms with care.

Look for at least three viewpoints. When asking questions, let go of the temptation to settle for just a single answer. Once you have come up with an answer, say to yourself, "Now what's another?" Using this approach can sustain honest inquiry, fuel creativity, and lead to conceptual breakthroughs.

Be prepared: The world is complicated, and critical thinking is a complex business. Some of your answers might contradict others. Resist the temptation to have all of your ideas in a neat, orderly bundle.

Practice tolerance. One path to critical thinking is tolerance for a wide range of opinions. Taking a position on important issues is natural. When we stop having an opinion on things, we've probably stopped breathing.

Problems occur when we become so attached to our current viewpoints that we refuse to consider alternatives. Likewise, it can be disastrous when we blindly follow everything any person or group believes without questioning its validity.

Many ideas that are widely accepted in Western cultures—for example, civil liberties for people of color and the right of women to vote—were once considered dangerous. Viewpoints that seem outlandish today might become widely accepted a century, a decade, or even a year from now. Remembering this idea can help us practice tolerance for differing beliefs and, in doing so, make room for new ideas that might alter our lives.

Look for evidence and logic. Uncritical thinkers shield themselves from new information and ideas. As an alternative, you can follow the example of scientists, who constantly search for evidence that contradicts their theories. Remember that evidence comes in several forms, including facts, expert testimony, and examples.

The aim of using logic is to make statements that are clear, consistent, and coherent. As you examine a speaker's or writer's assertions, you might find errors in logic—assertions that contradict each other or assumptions that are unfounded.

Consider the source. Look again at that article on the problems of manufacturing cars powered by natural gas. It might have been written by an executive from an oil company. Check out the expert who disputes the connection between smoking and lung cancer. That "expert" might be the president of a tobacco company. The underlying principle is that people can have a vested interest in holding certain opinions.

Understand before criticizing. Polished debaters are good at summing up their opponents' viewpoints—often better than the people who *hold* those viewpoints. Likewise, critical thinkers take the time to understand a statement of opinion before agreeing or disagreeing with it.

Effective understanding calls for listening without judgment. Make it a habit to enter another person's world by summarizing her viewpoint in your own words. If you're conversing with that person, keep revising your summary until she agrees that you've stated her position accurately. If you're reading an article, write a short summary of it. Then scan the article again, checking to see whether your synopsis is on target.

Watch for hot spots. Many people have mental "hot spots"—topics that provoke strong opinions and emotions. Examples are abortion, homosexuality, gun control, and the death penalty.

To become more skilled at examining various points of view, notice your own particular hot spots. Make a clear intention to accept your thoughts and feelings about these topics. Then continue applying your critical thinking strategies.

Be willing to be uncertain. Some of the most profound thinkers have practiced the art of thinking by using two magic sentences. One is "I don't know." The other is "I'm not sure yet."

Those are statements that many people do not like to hear. Our society rewards quick answers and quotable sound bites. We're under considerable pressure to utter the truth in 10 seconds or less.

In such a society, it is courageous and unusual to take the time to pause, to look, to examine, to be thoughtful, to consider many points of view—and to be unsure. When a society adopts half-truths in a blind rush for certainty, a willingness to embrace uncertainty can move us all forward.

Write about it. Thoughts can move at blinding speed. Writing slows down that process. Gaps in logic that slip by us in thought or speech cam be fully exposed when we commit ideas to paper. Writing down our thoughts allows us to compare, contrast, and combine points of view more clearly. This is an essential tool for becoming a critical thinker. ■

You're One Click Away . . .
from more strategies for critical thinking.

CRITICAL THINKING EXERCISE 7

Discover the joy of bafflement

The poet Wendell Berry wrote about confusion as an opportunity to learn: "When we no longer know what to do, we have come to our real work, and when we no longer know which way to go, we have begun our real journey. The mind that is not baffled is not employed. The impeded stream is the one that sings."[2] We're all going to experience periods of confusion. You can start preparing for them now—and even learn to welcome confusion as a path to thinking.

This three-step exercise is about becoming confused on purpose—and seeing what possibilities open up as a result. In the process you will generate and collect new ideas—one of the core thinking skills.

1. In the space below, write something that you're sure is true about yourself (for instance: "I'm sure that I will never take a philosophy course").

_____

_____

_____

_____

_____

_____

2. Next, take the same statement and put a question mark after it (for example: "I would never take a philosophy course?"). You might need to rephrase the question for grammatical sense.

_____

_____

_____

_____

_____

3. Are you feeling confused? If so, great. Go a little deeper. Brainstorm some questions related to the one you just wrote. ("In what ways would taking a philosophy course serve my success in school?" "Could taking a philosophy course help me with designing software?") Write your questions in the space below.

_____

_____

_____

_____

_____

_____

_____

_____

4. Finally, circle one of the questions you wrote in step 3. For 10 minutes, brainstorm answers to this question. Write down all your ideas. Don't worry about whether they're logical or practical. Just see whether you can get into a zone of pure creative thinking. Start writing in the space below and continue on separate paper.

_____

_____

_____

_____

_____

_____

7

Don't fool yourself:
Common mistakes in logic

© Zoran Vukmanov Simokov/Shutterstock.com

Over the last few thousand years, philosophers have listed some classic land mines in the field of logic. These common mistakes in thinking are called *fallacies*. The study of fallacies could fill a yearlong course. Following are some examples to get you started. Knowing about them can help you avoid getting fooled.

JUMPING TO CONCLUSIONS

Jumping to conclusions is the only exercise that some lazy thinkers get. This fallacy involves drawing conclusions without sufficient evidence.

Consider the bank officer who hears about a student's failing to pay back an education loan. After that, the officer turns down all loan applications from students. This person has formed a rigid opinion on the basis of hearsay. Jumping to conclusions—also called *hasty generalization*—is at work here.

Following are more examples of this fallacy:

- *When I went to Mexico for spring break, I felt sick the whole time. Mexican food makes people sick.*

- *Google's mission is to "organize the world's information." Their employees must be on a real power trip.*

- *During a recession, more people go to the movies. People just want to sit in the dark and forget about their money problems.*

Each item in the above list includes two statements, and the second statement does not necessarily follow from the first. More evidence is needed to make any possible connection.

ATTACKING THE PERSON

This fallacy flourishes at election time. Consider the example of a candidate who claims that her opponent failed to attend church regularly during the campaign. Candidates who indulge in personal attacks about private matters are attempting an intellectual sleight of hand. They want to divert our attention from the truly relevant issues.

APPEALING TO AUTHORITY

A professional athlete endorses a brand of breakfast cereal. A famous musician features a soft drink company's product in a music video. The promotional brochure for an advertising agency lists all of the large companies that have used its services.

In each case, the people involved are trying to win your confidence—and your dollars—by citing authorities. The underlying assumption is usually this: *Famous people and organizations buy our product. Therefore, you should buy it too.* Or: *You should accept this idea merely because someone who's well-known says it's true.*

Appealing to authority is usually a substitute for producing real evidence. It invites sloppy thinking. When our only evidence for a viewpoint is an appeal to authority, it's time to think more thoroughly.

POINTING TO A FALSE CAUSE

The fact that one event follows another does not necessarily mean that the two events have a cause-and-effect relationship. All we can actually say is that the events might be correlated. For example, as children's vocabularies improve, they can get more cavities. This does not mean that cavities are the result of an improved vocabulary. Instead, the increase in cavities is due to other factors, such as physical maturation and changes in diet or personal care.

THINKING IN ALL-OR-NOTHING TERMS

Consider these statements: *Doctors are greedy. You can't trust politicians. Students these days are in school just to get high-paying jobs; they lack idealism. Homeless people don't want to work.*

These opinions imply the word *all*. They gloss over individual differences, claiming that all members of a group are exactly alike. They also ignore key facts—for instance, that some doctors volunteer their time at free medical clinics and that many homeless people are children who are too young to work. All-or-nothing thinking is one of the most common errors in logic.

BEGGING THE QUESTION

Speakers and writers beg the question when their colorful language glosses over an idea that is unclear or unproven. Consider this statement: *Support the American tradition of individual liberty and oppose mandatory seat belt laws!* Anyone who makes such a statement "begs" (fails to answer) a key question: Are laws that require drivers to use seat belts actually a violation of individual liberty? ■

You're One Click Away . . .
from more ways to avoid getting fooled.

Ways to Create *ideas*

Anyone can think creatively. Use the following techniques to generate ideas about anything—from solutions to math problems to plans for remodeling a house.

FOCUS AND LET GO

Focusing and letting go are alternating parts of the same process. First, focus on a problem or question for a short period of time. This uses the resources of your conscious mind. Then take a break and completely let go of finding a solution or answer. This gives your subconscious mind time to work. When you alternate focusing and relaxing, the conscious and subconscious parts of your brain work in harmony.

CULTIVATE CREATIVE SERENDIPITY

The word *serendipity* was coined by the English author Horace Walpole from the title of an ancient Persian fairy tale, "The Three Princes of Serendip." The princes had a knack for making lucky discoveries. Serendipity is that knack, and it involves more than luck. It is the ability to see something valuable that you weren't looking for.

History is full of people who make serendipitous discoveries. Country doctor Edward Jenner noticed "by accident" that milkmaids seldom got smallpox. The result was his discovery that mild cases of cowpox immunized them. Penicillin was also discovered by accident. Scottish scientist Alexander Fleming was growing bacteria in a laboratory petri dish. A spore of *Penicillium notatum*, a kind of mold, blew in the window and landed in the dish, killing the bacteria. Fleming isolated the active ingredient, which saved thousands of lives.

You can train yourself in the art of serendipity. Multiply your contacts with the world. Resolve to meet new people. Join a study or discussion group. Read. Go to plays, concerts, art shows, lectures, and movies. Watch television programs you normally wouldn't watch.

Keep your eyes open. You might find a solution to an accounting problem in a popular film. You might discover a topic for your next paper at the corner convenience store.

KEEP IDEA FILES

We all have ideas. People who treat their ideas with care are often labeled "creative." They are the people who recognize ideas *and* keep track of them.

One way to keep track of ideas is to write them down on 3 × 5 cards. In addition, keep a journal. Record observations about the world around you, conversations with friends, important or offbeat ideas—anything.

To fuel your creativity, read voraciously. Clip articles. Consume books. Then the resulting ideas with your computer, tablet, smartphone, or pen and paper.

PLAY WITH IDEAS

Once you gather ideas, look at them from several angles. Switch your attention from one aspect of an issue to another. Examine each fact you collect, and avoid getting stuck on one particular part of a problem. Turn a problem upside down by picking a solution first and then working backward. Ask other people to look at the data. Solicit opinions.

Also look for the obvious solutions or the self-evident "truths" about the problem—then toss them out. Ask yourself, "Well, I know X is true, but if X were *not* true, what would happen?" Or ask the reverse: "If that *were* true, what would follow next?"

Put unrelated facts next to each other and invent a relationship between them, even if it seems absurd at first. Make imaginary pictures with the data. Condense it. Categorize it. Put it in chronological order. Put it in alphabetical order. Put it in random order. Order it from most to least complex. Reverse all of those orders. Look for opposites.

It has been said that there are no new ideas—only new ways to combine old ideas. Creativity is the ability to discover those combinations.

REFINE IDEAS AND FOLLOW THROUGH

Many of us ignore the part of the creative process that involves refining ideas and following through. How many great money-making schemes have we had that we never pursued? How many good ideas have we had for short stories that we never wrote? How many times have we said to ourselves, "You know, what they ought to do is attach two handles to one of those things, paint it orange, and sell it to police departments. They'd make a fortune." And we never realize that we are "they." Genius resides in the follow-through—the application of perspiration to inspiration. ∎

You're One Click Away . . .
from more strategies for creative thinking.

Strategies
for effective writing

Effective writing is essential to your success. Papers, presentations, essay tests, e-mail, blog posts, social networking sites—and even the occasional text message—call on your ability to communicate ideas with force and clarity. You can do that with the following strategies.

Schedule and list writing tasks. Divide the ultimate goal—such as a finished paper—into smaller steps that you can tackle right away. Estimate how long it will take to complete each step. Start with the date your final product is due and work backward to the present.

Say that the due date is December 1, and you have about 3 months to write the paper. Plan to get a first draft done by October 1 and a second draft done by November 1. That gives you time for big revisions and last-minute corrections.

One general guideline is to allow 50 percent of your project time for planning, researching, and writing the first draft. Then devote the remaining 50 percent to revising.

Choose a topic. The most common pitfall is selecting a vague topic. "Harriet Tubman" is not a useful topic for your American history paper because it's too broad. Writing about her could take hundreds of pages. Instead, consider "Harriet Tubman's activities as a Union spy during the Civil War." This topic statement is more specific. It can also function as a working title for your paper.

Write a thesis statement. Clarify what you want to say by summarizing it in one concise and complete sentence. For example: "Harriet Tubman's activities with the Underground Railroad led to a relationship with the Union army during the Civil War." This sentence, called a *thesis statement*, refines your working title. It also helps in making a preliminary outline.

A thesis statement that's clear and to the point can make your paper easier to write. Remember, you can always rewrite your thesis statement as you learn more about your topic.

Consider your purpose. If you want someone to *think* differently, then make your writing clear and logical. Support your assertions with evidence.

If you want someone to *feel* differently, consider crafting a story. Write about a character your audience can empathize with, and tell how that character resolves a problem that the audience can relate to.

And if your purpose is to move the reader into *action*, explain exactly what steps to take. Also offer solid benefits for doing so

Do initial research. At this stage, the objective of your research is not to uncover specific facts about your topic. That comes later. For now, you want to gain an overview of the subject. Discover the structure of your topic—its major divisions and branches.

Outline. To start an outline, gather a stack of 3 × 5 cards. Brainstorm ideas you want to include in your paper. Write one phrase or sentence per card. Then experiment with the cards. Group them into separate stacks, each stack representing one major category. After that, arrange the stacks in a logical order. Finally, arrange the cards *within* each stack in a logical order. Rearrange them until you discover an organization that you like.

If you write on a computer or tablet, you can do the same thing. Use the outlining feature of your word-processing software.

Do in-depth research. Again, you can use 3 × 5 cards. They work wonders when you conduct research. Just write down one fact, quotation, or idea per card. This makes it easy to organize your ideas.

There are plenty of alternatives to 3 × 5 cards, of course. You can use word processing, outlining, or note-taking applications for your computer, tablet, or smartphone.

For more ideas, see "Taking notes while reading" on page 63.

Rearrange your notes to follow you outline. If you've planned your writing project and completed your research, you've already done much of the hard work. Now you can relax into writing your first draft.

To create your draft, gather your notes and arrange them to follow your outline. Then write about the ideas in your notes. Write in paragraphs, with one idea per paragraph. If you have organized your notes logically, related facts will appear close to one another.

Remember that the first draft is not for keeps. You can worry about quality later, when you revise. Your goal at this point is simply to generate lots of material.

Many writers prefer to get their first draft down quickly. Their advice is just to start writing and keep writing until you've covered the material in your outline. Of course, you can pause occasionally to glance at your notes.

Some people find that it works well to forget the word *writing* at this stage. Instead, they ease into the task with activities that help generate ideas. You can free associate, cluster, meditate, daydream, doodle, draw diagrams, visualize the event you want to describe, or talk into a voice recorder. Do anything that gets your ideas flowing.

The goal is to avoid stopping to edit your work. You can save that for the next step.

This part of the writing takes place outside our conscious awareness. Many people report that ideas come to them while they're doing something totally unrelated to writing. Often this happens after they've been grappling with a question and have reached a point where they feel stuck. It's like the composer who said, "There I was, sitting and eating a sandwich, and all of a sudden this darn tune pops into my head."

You can trust your deep mind. It's writing while you eat, sleep, and brush your teeth.

Plan to revise several times. Once you've finished a first draft, let it sit for at least 24 hours. Then start revising. Make a clean copy of each revision, and let each revised draft sit for at least another 24 hours.

Keep in mind the saying "Write in haste; revise at leisure." When you revise, slow down and take a microscope to your work.

Cut. The first and most important step in revising is to look for excess baggage. Approach your first draft as if it were a chunk of granite from which you will chisel the final product. In the end, much of your first draft will be lying on the floor. What is left will be the clean, clear, polished product.

Sometimes the cuts are painful. Sooner or later, every writer invents a phrase that is truly clever but makes no contribution to the purpose of the paper. Grit your teeth and let it go.

Note: For maximum efficiency, make the larger cuts first—sections, chapters, pages. Then go for the smaller cuts—paragraphs, sentences, phrases, words. Stay within the word limit that your instructor assigns.

Paste. In deleting both larger and smaller passages in your first draft, you've probably removed some of the original transitions and connecting ideas. Your next task is to rearrange what's left of your paper so that it flows logically. Look for consistency within paragraphs and for transitions from paragraph to paragraph and section to section.

If your draft doesn't hang together, reorder the ideas. Imagine yourself with scissors and glue, cutting the paper into scraps—one scrap for each major point or event. Then paste these scraps down in a new, more logical order.

> # Keep in mind the saying "Write in haste; revise at leisure." When you revise, slow down and take a microscope to your work.

Fix. Now it's time to look at individual words and phrases. Define any terms that the reader might not know, putting them in plain English whenever you can.

In general, rely on vivid nouns and active verbs. Using too many adjectives and adverbs weakens your message and adds unnecessary bulk to your writing.

Also scan your paper for any passages that are written in the language of texting or instant messaging. Rewrite those into full sentences.

Proofread. In a sense, any paper is a sales effort. If you hand in a paper that is wearing wrinkled jeans, its hair tangled and unwashed, and its shoes untied, your instructor is less likely to buy it. To avoid this situation, format your paper following accepted standards for margin widths, endnotes, title pages, and other details. Also ask your instructor about when and on how to cite the sources used in writing your paper. Finally, look over your paper with an eye for spelling and grammar errors.

When you're through proofreading, take a minute to savor the result. You've just witnessed something of a miracle—the mind attaining clarity and resolution. That's the *aha!* in writing. ■

You're One Click Away . . .
from finding more paths online to effective writing.

7

Planning *and* delivering
A PRESENTATION

Analyze your audience. Developing a presentation is similar to writing a paper. Begin by choosing your topic, purpose, and thesis statement as described in "Strategies for effective writing" on page 102.

Also remember that audiences generally have one question in mind: *So what?* Or, *Why does this matter to me?* They want to know that your presentation relates to their desires.

To convince people that you have something worthwhile to say, write down the main point of your presentation. See whether you can complete this sentence: *I'm telling you this because. . . .*

Communicate your message in three parts. Presentations are usually organized into three main sections: the introduction, the main body, and the conclusion.

In your introduction, state your main point in a way that gets attention. Then give your audience a hint of what's coming next. For example: "More people have died from hunger in the past 5 years than have been killed in all of the wars, revolutions, and murders in the past 150 years. Yet there is enough food to go around. I'm honored to be here with you today and share a solution to this problem."

In the main body of your presentation, develop your ideas in the same way that you develop a written paper. Cover each point in order. Support each point with facts, quotations, and interesting stories. During this part of your presentation, transitions are especially important. Use meaningful pauses and phrases to let people know where you're at and where you're going: "On the other hand, until the public realizes what is happening to children in these countries. . . ." Or, "The second reason hunger persists is . . ."

For the conclusion, summarize your key points and draw your conclusion in a way that no one will forget. A simple standby is this: "In conclusion, I want you to remember three points. . . ."

Create speaking notes. Some professional speakers recommend writing out your speech in full and then putting key words or main points on a few 3 × 5 cards. Number the cards so that if you drop them, you can quickly put them in order again. As you finish the information on each card, move it to the back of the pile. Write information clearly and in letters large enough to be seen from a distance.

Other speakers prefer to use standard outlined notes instead of cards. Another option is concept mapping. Even an hour-long speech can be mapped on one sheet of paper.

Whatever method you choose, use suggestions from Chapter 5 to remember your main points.

Create supporting visuals. Presentations often include visuals such as flip charts or slides created with presentation software. These materials can reinforce your main points.

Remember that effective visuals complement rather than replace your speaking. If you use too many visuals—or visuals that are too complex—your audience might focus on them and forget about you.

Practice your presentation. The key to successful public speaking is practice. When you practice, do so in a loud voice, which helps your audience to hear you.

Keep practicing. Avoid sounding as if you were reading a script. When you know your material well, you can deliver it in a natural way. Practice your presentation until you could deliver it in your sleep. Then run through it a few more times.

Watch the time. Time yourself as you practice. Aim for a lean presentation—just enough to make your point and avoid making your audience restless. Leave your listeners wanting more. The goal is to be brief and then to be seated.

Overcome fear of public speaking. Michael Motley, a professor at the University of California–Davis, distinguishes between two orientations to speaking. People with a *performance orientation* believe that the speaker must captivate the audience by using formal techniques that differ from normal conversation. In contrast, speakers with a *communication orientation* see public speaking simply as an extension of one-to-one conversation. The goal is not to perform but to communicate your ideas to an audience in the same ways that you would explain them to a friend.[3] In other words, focus on the content of your presentation—not on yourself. ■

You're One Click Away . . .
for more strategies for effective presentations.

Take the next step in finding your speaking voice

What do you want to improve about your presentation skills? Thinking about past speeches you have made can help you with future presentations you make in the classroom and in the workplace. Being honest about your current skills will open you up to new strategies that will help you succeed.

Think beyond this textbook, as well. Look to successful speakers in your community or in the public eye. In light of their strengths, consider the speaking skills that you'd like to gain.

Discovery Statement
Think back to the last time you were called upon to speak before a group. In the space below, write down what you remember about that situation.

For example, describe the physical sensations you experienced before and during your presentation, the overall effectiveness of your presentation, and any feedback you received from the audience.

I discovered that . . .

_____
_____
_____
_____
_____
_____
_____

Intention Statement
Based on what you wrote above, what would you like to do differently the next time you speak? Describe the most important thing that you could do to become a more effective speaker.

I intend to . . .

_____
_____
_____

Action Statement
Now, review this chapter for five suggestions that could help you make your intention a reality. Summarize each suggestion here along with the related page number.

Strategy   **Page number**

_____   _____
_____   _____
_____   _____
_____   _____

Finally, choose *one* strategy from the list that you will definitely use for your next presentation.

I will . . .

_____
_____
_____
_____
_____
_____
_____
_____
_____
_____
_____
_____
_____
_____
_____

7

CHAPTER 7 SKILLS *Snapshot*

Take a minute to reflect on your responses to the *Thinking & Communicating* section of the Discovery Wheel on page 9. Reflect on the progress you've made since you did that exercise, and clarify your intentions to develop further mastery. Complete the following sentences:

DISCOVERY

My self-score on the Thinking & Communicating section of the Discovery Wheel was . . .

When asked to evaluate different opinions on an issue or choose among potential solutions to a problem, the first thing I do is . . .

When I hear an accomplished public speaker, the skill that I would most like to acquire is . . .

The biggest obstacle I face right now in becoming an effective writer is . . .

INTENTION

By the time I finish the course, I visualize giving myself a score of ___ on the Thinking & Communicating section of the Discovery Wheel.

I'll know that I've reached a new level of mastery with my thinking and communication skills when . . .

ACTION

To reach that level of mastery, the most important thing I can do next is to . . .

Creating Positive Relationships

Use this **Master Student Map** to ask yourself

WHY THIS CHAPTER MATTERS . . .

- Your "people skills"—including listening deeply and speaking compassionately—are as important to your success as technical skills.

WHAT IS INCLUDED . . .

HOW YOU CAN USE THIS CHAPTER . . .

- Choose conversations that align with my values.
- Make and keep agreements as a tool for creating my future.
- Prevent and resolve conflict with other people.
- Study and work effectively with people from different cultures.

WHAT IF . . .

- I could consistently create the kind of relationships that I've

© Ruslan Ivantsov/Shutterstock.com

JOURNAL ENTRY 18

Discover what you want from this chapter

Think of a time when you experienced an emotionally charged conflict with another person. What happened? Was the conflict ever resolved? Describe your experience here.

_____

_____

_____

_____

Now scan this chapter for ideas that can help you get your feelings and ideas across more skillfully in similar situations. List at least three ideas below, along with the page numbers where you intend to read more about them.

_____

_____

_____

_____

⏻ POWER process

Choose your conversations and your community

Conversations can exist in many forms. One form involves people talking out loud to each other. At other times, the conversation takes place inside our own heads, and we call it *thinking*. We are even having a conversation when we read a magazine or a book, watch television or a movie, or write a letter or a report. These observations have three implications that wind their way through every aspect of our lives.

One implication is that conversations exercise incredible power over what we think, feel, and do. They shape our attitudes, our decisions, our opinions, our emotions, and our actions. If you want clues as to what a person will be like tomorrow, listen to what she's talking about today.

Second, given that conversations are so powerful, it's amazing that few people act on this fact. Most of us swim in a constant sea of conversations, almost none of which we carefully and thoughtfully choose.

The real power of this process lies in a third discovery: We can choose our conversations. Certain conversations create real value for us. They give us fuel for reaching our goals. Other conversations distract us from what we want. They might even create lasting unhappiness and frustration.

Suppose that you meet with an instructor to ask about some guidelines for writing a term paper. She launches into a tirade about your writing skills and lack of preparation for higher education. This presents you with several options. One possibility is to talk about what a jerk the instructor is and give up on the idea of learning to write well. Another option is to refocus the conversation on what you can do to improve your writing skills, such as working with a writing tutor or taking a basic composition class. These two sets of conversations will have vastly different consequences for your success in school.

Another important fact about conversations is that the people you associate with influence them dramatically. If you want to change your attitudes about anything—prejudice, politics, religion, humor—choose your conversations by choosing your community. Spend time with people who speak about and live consistently with the attitudes you value. Use conversations to change habits. Use conversations to explore new ways of seeing the world and to create new options in your life.

When we choose our conversations, we discover a tool of unsurpassed power. This tool has the capacity to remake our thoughts—and thus our lives. It's as simple as choosing the next article you read or the next topic you discuss with a friend.

Start choosing your conversations today, and watch what happens.

You're One Click Away . . .
from accessing Power Process Media online and finding out more about how to "choose your conversations."

Create relationships with integrity

© iStockphoto.com/stefanovilvan

Relationships are built on integrity. When we break a promise to be faithful to a spouse, help a friend move to a new apartment, or pay a bill on time, relationships are strained. When we keep our word, relationships work.

WAYS TO MAKE AND KEEP AGREEMENTS

Integrity means making agreements that we fully intend to keep. However, the only way to ensure that we keep *all* of our agreements is either to make none—or to play it safe and only make agreements that pose no risk.

Examining our agreements can improve our effectiveness. Perhaps we took on too much—or too little. Perhaps we did not use all the resources that were available to us—or we used too many. Perhaps we did not fully understand what we were promising. When we learn from our mistakes and our successes, we can build more relationships with integrity.

By making ambitious agreements, we can also stretch ourselves to new possibilities. If we stretch too far and end up breaking an agreement, we can quickly admit our mistake, deal with the consequences, and negotiate a new agreement.

MOVE UP THE LADDER OF POWERFUL SPEAKING

The words used to talk about our agreements fall into several different levels. Think of each level as one rung on a ladder—the ladder of powerful speaking. As we move up this ladder, our speaking leads to more effective action.

Obligation. The lowest rung on the ladder is *obligation*. Words used at this level include *I should, he ought to, someone better, they need to, I must,* and *I had to.* Speaking this way implies that we have few choices—that we are not in control of our lives. When we live at the level of obligation, we feel passive and helpless to change anything.

Note: When we move to the next rung, we leave behind obligation and advance to self-responsibility. All of the remaining rungs reinforce this characteristic.

Possibility. The next rung up is *possibility*. At this level, we examine new options. We play with new ideas, potential solutions, and alternate courses of action. As we do, we become aware of choices that can dramatically affect the quality of our lives. We are not the victims of circumstance. Phrases that signal this level include *I might, I could, I'll consider, I hope to,* and *maybe.*

Preference. From possibility we can move up to *preference*. Here we start to actively *make* choices. The words *I prefer* signal that we're moving toward one set of possibilities over another, perhaps setting the stage for eventual action.

Passion. Above preference is a rung called *passion*. Again, certain words signal this level: *I want to, I'm really excited to do that, I can't wait.* Possibility and passion are both exciting places to be. Even at these levels, though, we're still far from action. Many of us want to achieve lots of things and have no specific plan for doing so.

Planning. We move closer to action with the next rung—*planning*. When people use phrases such as *I intend to, my goal is to, I plan to,* and *I'll try like mad to,* they're at the level of planning. The Intention Statements you write in this book are examples of planning.

Promising. The highest rung on the ladder is *promising*. This is where the power of your word really comes into play. At this level, it's common to use phrases such as these: *I will, I promise to, I am committed, you can count on it.* This is where we bridge from possibility and planning to action. Promising brings many rewards, including relationships built with integrity.

8

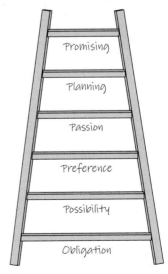

You're One Click Away . . .
from more ways to make and keep powerful agreements.

CLASSROOM CIVILITY—
what's in it for you

This topic might seem like common sense, yet some students forget that simple behaviors create a sense of safety, mutual respect, and community.

Consider an example: A student arrives 15 minutes late to a lecture and lets the door slam behind her. She pulls a fast-food burger out of a crackling paper bag. Then her cell phone rings at full volume—and she answers it. Behaviors like these send a message to everyone in the room: "I'm ignoring you."

Without civility, you lose. Even a small problem with classroom civility can create a barrier for everyone. Learning gets interrupted. Trust breaks down. Your tuition dollars go down the drain. You deserve to enter classrooms that are free of discipline problems and bullies. Many schools have formal policies about classroom civility. Find out what policies apply to you. The consequences for violating them can be serious and may include dismissal or legal action.

With civility, you win. When you treat instructors with respect, you're more likely to be treated that way in return. A respectful relationship with an instructor could turn into a favorable reference letter, a mentorship, a job referral, or a friendship that lasts for years after you graduate. Politeness pays.

Classroom civility does not mean that you have to be passive or insincere. You can present your opinions with passion and even disagree with an instructor in a way that leaves everyone enriched rather than threatened.

Lack of civility boils down to a group of habits. Like any other habits, these can be changed. The following suggestions reflect common sense, and they make an uncommon difference.

Attend classes regularly and on time. If you know that you're going to miss a class or be late, let your instructor know. Take the initiative to ask your instructor or another student about what you missed.

If you arrive late, do not disrupt class. Close the door quietly and take a seat. When you know that you will have to leave class early, tell your instructor before class begins, and sit near an exit. If you leave class to use the restroom or handle an emergency, do so quietly.

During class, participate fully. Take notes and join in discussions. Turn off your cell phone or any other electronic device that you don't need for class. Remember that sleeping, texting, or doing work for another class is a waste of your time and money. Instructors notice distracting activities and take them as a sign of your lack of interest and commitment. So do employers.

Before packing up your notebooks and other materials, wait until class has been dismissed. Instructors often give assignments or make a key point at the end of a class period. Be there when it happens.

Communicate respect. When you speak in class, begin by addressing your instructor as *Ms., Mrs., Mr., Dr., Professor,* or whatever the teacher prefers.

Discussions gain value when everyone gets a chance to speak. Show respect for others by not monopolizing class discussions. Refrain from side conversations and profanity. When presenting viewpoints that conflict with those of classmates or your instructor, combine the passion for your opinion with respect for the opinions of others. Similarly, if you disagree with a class requirement or grade you received, then talk to your instructor about it after class in a respectful way. In a private setting, your ideas will get more attention.

Respect gets communicated in small details. Don't make distracting noises. Cover your mouth if you yawn or cough. Avoid wearing inappropriate clothing. And even if you meet your future spouse in class, refrain from public displays of affection.

Embrace diversity. Master students—and teachers—come in endless variety. They are old and young, male and female. They come from every culture, race, and ethnic group. Part of civility is staying open to the value that other people have to offer.

See civility as a contribution. Every class you enter has the potential to become a community of people who talk openly, listen fully, share laughter, and arrive at life-changing insights. These are master student qualities. Every time you demonstrate them, you make a contribution to your community. ∎

Thriving in a diverse world

Higher education could bring you into the most diverse environment of your life. Your fellow students could come from many different ethnic groups, cultures, and countries. Few institutions in our society can match the level of diversity found in higher education.

To get the most from your education, use this environment to your advantage. Through your encounters with many types of people, you can gain new perspectives and new friends. You can also acquire skills for living in multicultural neighborhoods and working in a global economy.

Cultivate friends from other cultures. Do this through volunteering, serving on committees, or any other activities in which people from other cultures are involved. Through these experiences, your understanding of diversity and "cultural competence" will unfold in a natural, spontaneous way. Also experiment with the following strategies.

SWITCH CULTURAL LENSES

Diversity skills begin with learning about yourself and understanding the lenses through which you see the world. One way to do this is to intentionally switch lenses—to consciously perceive familiar events in a new way.

For example, think of a situation in your life that involved an emotionally charged conflict among several people. Now mentally put yourself inside the skin of another person in that conflict. Ask yourself, "How would I see this situation if I were that person? Or if I were a person of the opposite gender? Or if I were a member of a different racial or ethnic group? Or if I were older or younger?"

Do this consistently and you'll discover that we live in a world of multiple realities. There are many different ways to interpret any event—and just as many ways to respond, given our individual differences.

REFLECT ON EXPERIENCES OF PRIVILEGE AND PREJUDICE

Someone might tell you that he's more likely to be promoted at work because he's white and male—*and* that he's been called "white trash" because he lives in a trailer park.

See whether you can recall incidents such as these from your own life. Think of times when you were favored due to your gender, race, or age. Also think of times when you were excluded or ridiculed based on one of those same characteristics. In doing this, you'll discover ways to identify with a wider range of people.

To complete this process, turn your self-discoveries into possibilities for new behaviors. For example, if you're a younger student, you may tend to join study groups with people who are about your age. If so, then plan to invite an older student to your group's next meeting. When choosing whether to join a campus organization, take into account the diversity of its membership. And before you make a statement about anyone who differs significantly from you, ask yourself, "Is what I'm about to say accurate, or is it based on a belief that I've held for years and never examined?"

LOOK FOR COMMON GROUND

Students in higher education often find that they worry about many of the same things—including tuition bills, the quality of dormitory food, and the shortage of on-campus parking spaces. More important, our fundamental goals as human beings—such as health, physical safety, and economic security—are desires that cross culture lines.

The key is to honor the differences among people while remembering what we have in common. Diversity is not just about our differences—it's about our similarities. On a biological level, less than 1 percent of the human genome accounts for visible characteristics such as skin color. In terms of our genetic blueprint, we are more than 99 percent the same.[1]

LOOK FOR INDIVIDUALS, NOT GROUP REPRESENTATIVES

Sometimes the way we speak glosses over differences among individuals and reinforces stereotypes. For example, a student worried about her grade in math expresses concern over "all those Asian students who are skewing the class curve." Or a white music major assumes that her African American classmate knows a lot about jazz or hip-hop music. We can avoid such errors by seeing people as individuals—not spokespersons for an entire group.

BE WILLING TO ACCEPT FEEDBACK

Members of another culture might let you know that some of your words or actions had a meaning other than what you intended. Perhaps a comment that seems harmless to you is offensive to them. And they may tell you directly about it.

8

Avoid responding to such feedback with comments such as "Don't get me wrong," "You're taking this way too seriously," or "You're too sensitive."

Instead, listen without resistance. Open yourself to what others have to say. Remember to distinguish between the *intention* of your behavior from its actual impact on other people. Then take the feedback you receive and ask how you can use it to communicate more effectively in the future.

If you are new at responding to diversity, then expect to make some mistakes along the way. As long as you approach people in a spirit of tolerance, your words and actions can always be changed.

SPEAK UP AGAINST DISCRIMINATION

You might find yourself in the presence of someone who tells a racist joke, makes a homophobic comment, or utters an ethnic slur. When this happens, you have a right to state what you observe, share what you think, and communicate how you feel.

Depending on the circumstance, you might say:

- "That's a stereotype, and we don't have to accept it."

- "Other people are going to take offense at that. Let's tell jokes that don't put people down."

- "I realize that you don't mean to offend anybody, but I feel hurt and angry by what you just said."

- "As members of the majority culture around here, we can easily forget how comments like that affect other people."

Also keep in mind that someone from a specific ethnic or cultural background can also be the source of negative comments about that culture. Speak up against discriminatory comments from any source.

This kind of speaking may be the most difficult communicating you ever do. And if you *don't* do it, you give the impression that you agree with biased speech.

In response to your candid comments, many people will apologize and express their willingness to change. Even if they don't, you can still know that you practiced integrity by aligning your words with your values.

LEARN ABOUT OTHER CULTURES

People from different cultures read differently, write differently, think differently, eat differently, and learn differently than you. If you know this from the beginning, you can be more effective with your classmates, coworkers, and neighbors.

One key to understanding styles is to look for several possible interpretations of any behavior. For example, consider the hand signal that signifies *okay* to many Americans—thumb and index finger forming a circle. In France, that signal denotes the number zero. In Japan, it is a symbol for money. And in Brazil, it could be considered an obscene gesture.[2]

This example could be extended to cover many areas—posture, eye contact, physical contact, facial expressions, and more. The various ways of interpreting these behaviors are neither right nor wrong. They simply represent differing styles in making meaning out of what we see.

You might find yourself fascinated by the styles that make up a particular culture. Consider learning as much about that culture as possible. Immerse yourself in it. Read novels, see plays, go to concerts, listen to music, look at art, take courses, learn the language.

DISTINGUISH BETWEEN INDIVIDUALIST AND COLLECTIVIST CULTURES

Part of your learning is to look for differences between individualist and collectivist cultures.

Individualist cultures flourish in the United States, Canada, and Western Europe. If your family has deep roots in one of these areas, you were probably raised to value personal fulfillment and personal success. You received recognition or rewards when you stood out from your peers—for example, by earning the highest grades in your class, scoring the most points during a basketball season, or making another individual achievement.

In contrast, collectivist cultures value cooperation over competition. Group progress is more important than individual success. Credit for an achievement is widely shared. If you were raised in such a culture, you probably place a high value on your family and were taught to respect your elders. Collectivist cultures dominate Asia, Africa, and Latin America.

In short, individualist cultures emphasize "I," whereas collectivist cultures emphasize "we." Forgetting about the differences between them can strain a friendship or wreck an international business deal.

If you were raised in an individualist culture:

- *Remember that someone from a collectivist culture may place a high value on "saving face."* This involves more than simply avoiding embarrassment. The person may not want to be singled out from other members of a group even for a positive achievement. If you have a direct request for this person or want to share something that could be taken as a personal criticism, save it for a private conversation.

- *Respect titles and last names.* Although Americans often like to use first names immediately after meeting someone, in some cultures this practice is acceptable only among family members. Especially in work settings, use last names and job titles during your first meetings. Allow time for informal relationships to develop.

- *Put messages in context.* For members of collectivist cultures, words convey only part of an intended message. Notice gestures and other nonverbal communication as well.

If you were raised in a collectivist culture, you can creatively "reverse" the above list. For instance, remember that direct questions from an American student or coworker are usually meant not to offend but only to clarify an idea. Don't be surprised if you are called by a nickname, if no one asks about your family, or if you are rewarded for a personal achievement. And in social situations, remember that indirect cues might not get another person's attention. Practice asking clearly and directly for what you want.

 You're One Click Away . . .
from more ways to thrive in a diverse world.

JOURNAL ENTRY 19

Practice the art of saying no

All your study plans can go down the drain when a friend says, "Time to parrr-ty!" Sometimes, succeeding in school means replying with a graceful no. Saying no helps you to prevent an overloaded schedule that compromises your health, your relationships, and your grade point average.

Discovery Statement

We find it hard to say no when we make certain assumptions—when we assume that others will think we're rude or that we'll lose friends if we turn down a request.

But think about it: You are in charge of your time only when you have the option to say *no*. Without this option, you are at the mercy of anyone who interrupts you. These will not be relationships based on equality. People who care about you will respect your wishes.

Recall a situation when you wanted to say no to someone but did not. Were you making assumptions about how the other person would react? If so, describe what you were thinking.

I discovered that I . . .

_____
_____
_____
_____
_____
_____
_____
_____
_____
_____
_____

Intention Statement

Next, consider some strategies for giving someone a *no* that's both polite and firm. For instance, you can wait for the request. People who worry about saying no often give in to a request before it's actually been made. Wait until you hear a question: "Would you go to a party with me?"

You can also remind yourself that one no leads to another yes. Saying no to a movie allows you to say yes to getting a paper outlined or a textbook chapter read. Then you can give an unqualified yes to the next social activity.

Describe any strategies that you plan to use the next time you find it difficult to say no.

I intend to . . .

_____
_____
_____
_____
_____
_____

Action Statement

You might find it easier to act on your intention when you don't have to grasp for words. Choose some key phrases in advance. For example: "That doesn't work for me today." "Thanks for asking; my schedule for today is full." Or, "I'll go along next time when my day is clear."

To effectively deliver my next *no*, I will say . . .

_____
_____
_____
_____
_____
_____
_____
_____

 You're One Click Away . . .
from more ways to say no gracefully.

8

12 tools for deep listening

People love a good listener. The most popular salespeople, managers, coworkers, teachers, parents, and friends are the best listeners.

To listen well, begin from a clear intention. *Choose* to listen well. Then you can use the following 12 techniques to take your listening to deeper levels.

1. BE QUIET

Silence is more than staying quiet while someone is speaking. Allowing several seconds to pass before you begin to talk gives the speaker time to catch her breath and gather her thoughts. If the message being sent is complete, this short break gives you time to form your response and helps you avoid the biggest barrier to listening—listening with your answer running. If you make up a response before the person is finished, you might miss the end of the message, which is often the main point.

2. DISPLAY OPENNESS

You can display openness through your facial expression and body position. Uncross your arms and legs. Sit up straight. Face the other person and remove any physical barriers between you, such as a pile of books.

3. SEND ACKNOWLEDGMENTS

Let the speaker know periodically that you are still there. Words and nonverbal gestures of acknowledgment convey to the speaker that you are interested and that you are receiving her message. Examples are "Uh huh," "Okay," "Yes," and head nods. These acknowledgments do not imply your agreement. They just indicate that you are listening.

4. RELEASE DISTRACTIONS

Even when your intention is to listen, you might find your mind wandering. Thoughts about what *you* want to say or something you want to do later might claim your attention.

There's a simple solution: Notice your wandering mind without judgment. Then bring your attention back to the act of listening.

There are times when you might not want to listen. You might be fully distracted by your own concerns. Be honest. Don't pretend to listen. You can say, "What you're telling me is important, but I'm not able to listen well right now. Can we set aside another time to talk about this?" Sometimes it's okay not to listen.

5. SUSPEND JUDGMENTS

Listening and agreeing are two different activities. As listeners, our goal is to fully receive another person's message. This does not mean that we're obligated to agree with the message. Once you're confident that you accurately understand a speaker's point of view, you are free to agree or disagree with it. One key to effective listening is understanding *before* evaluating.

6. LISTEN FOR REQUESTS AND INTENTIONS

An effective way to listen to complaints is to look for the request hidden in them. "This class is a waste of my time" can be heard as "Please tell me what I'll gain if I participate actively in class." "The instructor talks too fast" might be asking "What strategies can I use to take notes when the instructor covers material rapidly?"

We can even transform complaints into intentions. Take this complaint: "The parking lot by the dorms is so dark at night that I'm afraid to go to my car." This complaint can lead to "I intend to talk to someone who can see that a light gets installed in the parking lot."

Viewing complaints as requests and intentions gives us more choices. We can stop responding with defensiveness ("What does he know anyway?"), resignation ("It's always been this way and always will be"), or indifference ("It's not my job"). We can choose whether to grant the request or help people translate their complaint into an action plan.

7. ALLOW EMOTION

In the presence of full listening, some people will share things that they feel deeply about. They might cry, shake, or sob. If you feel uncomfortable when this happens, see whether you can accept the discomfort for a little while longer. Emotional release can bring relief and trigger unexpected insights.

8. NOTICE VERBAL AND NONVERBAL MESSAGES

You might point out that the speaker's body language seems to be the exact opposite of her words. For example: "I noticed you said you are excited, but to me you look bored."

Keep in mind that the same nonverbal behavior can have various meanings across cultures. Someone who looks bored might simply be listening in a different way.

9. FEED BACK MEANING

Summarize the essence of that person's message: "Let me see whether I understood what you said . . ." or "What I'm hearing you say is. . . ." Often, the other person will say, "No, that's not what I meant. What I said was. . . ."

There will be no doubt when you get it right. The sender will say, "Yeah, that's it," and either continue with another message or stop sending when she knows you understand.

When you feed back meaning, be concise. This is not a time to stop the other person by talking on and on about what you think you heard.

10. BE CAREFUL WITH QUESTIONS AND ADVICE

Questions are directive. They can take conversations in a new direction, which may *not* be where the speaker wants to go. Ask questions only to clarify the speaker's message. Later, when it's your turn to speak, you can introduce any topic that you want.

Also be cautious about advice. Unsolicited advice can be taken as condescending or even insulting. Skilled listeners recognize that people are different, and they do not assume that they know what's best for someone else.

11. ASK FOR MORE

Full listening with unconditional acceptance is a rare gift. Many people have never experienced it. They are used to being greeted with resistance, so they habitually stop short of saying what they truly think and feel. Help them change this habit by routinely asking, "Is there anything more you want to say about that?" This sends the speaker a message that you truly value what she has to say.

12. STAY OPEN TO THE ADVENTURE OF LISTENING

Receiving what another person has to say is an act of courage. Listening fully—truly opening yourself to the way another person sees the world—means taking risks. Your opinions may be challenged. You may be less certain or less comfortable than you were before.

Along with the risks come rewards. Listening in an unguarded way can take your relationships to a new depth and level of honesty. This kind of listening can open up new possibilities for thinking, feeling, and behavior. And when you practice full listening, other people are more likely to listen when it's your turn to speak.

You're One Click Away . . .
from more strategies for deep listening.

7 steps to effective complaints

Sometimes relationship building involves making a complaint. Whining, blaming, pouting, screaming, and yelling insults usually don't get results. Here are some guidelines for complaining effectively:

1. Go to the source.
Start with the person who is most directly involved with the problem.

2. Present the facts without blaming anyone.
Your complaint will carry more weight if you document the facts. Keep track of names and dates. Note which actions were promised and which results actually occurred.

3. Go up the ladder to people with more responsibility.
If you don't get satisfaction at the first level, go to that person's direct supervisor. Requesting a supervisor's name will often get results. Write a letter to the company president.

4. Ask for commitments.
When you find someone who is willing to solve your problem, get him to say exactly what he is going to do and when.

5. Use available support.
There are dozens of groups as well as government agencies willing to get involved in resolving complaints. Contact consumer groups or the Better Business Bureau. Trade associations can sometimes help. Ask city council members, county commissioners, state legislators, and senators and representatives. All of them want your vote, so they are usually eager to help.

6. Take legal action, if necessary.
Small claims court is relatively inexpensive, and you don't have to hire a lawyer. These courts can handle cases involving small amounts of money (usually up to a few thousand dollars). Legal aid offices can sometimes answer questions.

7. Don't give up.
Assume that others are on your team. Many people are out there to help you. State what you intend to do and ask for their partnership.

8

Managing
conflict

Conflict management is one of the most practical skills you'll ever learn. Here are suggestions that can help. Think of ways to use them in a conflict that you face right now.

SET THE STAGE FOR A SOLUTION

Conflict heightens the differences between people. When this happens, it's easy to forget how much we still agree with each other.

As a first step in managing conflict, back up to common ground. List all of the points on which you are *not* in conflict. For example: "I know that we disagree about how much to spend on a new car, but we do agree that the old one needs to be replaced." Once you've got this perspective, you can build on it with the following strategies.

Commit to the relationship. The thorniest conflicts usually arise between people who genuinely care for each other. Begin by affirming your commitment to the other person: "I care about you, and I want this relationship to last. So I'm willing to do whatever it takes to resolve this problem." Also ask the other person for a similar commitment.

Allow strong feelings. Permitting conflict can also mean permitting emotion. Being upset is all right. Feeling angry is often appropriate. Crying is okay. Allowing other people to see the strength of our feelings can help resolve the conflict. This suggestion can be especially useful during times when differences are so extreme that reaching common ground seems possible.

Expressing the full range of your feelings can transform the conflict. Often what's on the far side of anger is love. When we express and release resentment, we might discover compassion in its place.

Notice your need to be "right." Some people approach conflict as a situation where only one person wins. That person has the "right" point of view. Everyone else loses.

When this happens, step back. See whether you can approach the situation in a neutral way. Define the conflict as a problem to be solved, not as a contest to be won. Explore the possibility that you might be mistaken. There might be more than one acceptable solution. The other person might simply have a different learning style than yours. Let go of being "right," and aim for being effective at resolving conflict instead.

Sometimes this means apologizing. Conflict can arise from our own errors. Others might move quickly to end the conflict when we acknowledge this fact and ask for forgiveness.

Slow down the communication. In times of great conflict, people often talk all at once. Words fly like speeding bullets, and no one listens. Chances for resolving the conflict take a nosedive.

When everyone is talking at once, choose either to listen or to talk—not both at the same time. Just send your message. Or just receive the other person's message. Usually, this technique slows down the pace and allows everyone to become more levelheaded.

To slow down the communication even more, take a break. Depending on the level of conflict, this might mean anything from a few minutes to a few days.

A related suggestion is to do something nonthreatening together. Share an activity with the people involved that's not a source of conflict.

USE "I" MESSAGES

When conflict occurs, we often make statements about another person. We say such things as these:

"You are rude."

"You make me mad."

"You must be crazy."

"You don't love me anymore."

These are "You" messages. Usually they result in defensiveness. The responses might be:

"I am not rude."

"I don't care."

"No, you are crazy."

"No, *you* don't love *me!*"

"You" messages are hard to listen to. They label, judge, blame, and assume things that might or might not be true. They demand rebuttal.

The next time you're in conflict with someone, consider replacing "You" messages with "I" messages:

"You are rude" might become "I feel upset."

"You make me mad" could be "I feel angry."

"You must be crazy" can be "I don't understand."

"You don't love me anymore" could become "I'm afraid we're drifting apart."

"I" messages don't judge, blame, criticize, or insult. They don't invite the other person to counterattack. "I" messages are also more accurate. They stick to the facts and report our own thoughts and feelings.

Suppose a friend asks you to pick her up at the airport. You drive 20 miles and wait for the plane. No friend. You decide your friend missed her plane, so you wait three hours for the next flight. No friend. Perplexed and worried, you drive home. The next day, you see your friend downtown.

"What happened?" you ask.

"Oh, I caught an earlier flight."

"You are a rude person," you reply.

Instead, look for and talk about the facts—the observable behavior. Everyone will agree that your friend asked you to pick her up, that she did take an earlier flight, and that you did not receive a call from her. But the idea that she is rude is not a fact—it's a judgment. Perhaps she had an emergency and was unable to call.

When you see your friend, choose an "I" message instead: "I waited and waited at the airport. I was worried about you. I didn't get a call. I feel angry and hurt. I don't want to waste my time. Next time, you can call me when your flight arrives, and I'll be happy to pick you up."

An "I" message can include any or all of the following five elements:

1. Observations. Describe the facts—the indisputable, observable realities. Talk about what you, or anyone else, can see, hear, smell, taste, or touch. Avoid judgments, interpretations, or opinions. Instead of saying, "You're a slob," say, "Last night's lasagna pan was still on the stove this morning."

2. Feelings. Describe your own feelings. It is easier to listen to "I feel frustrated" than to "You never help me." Stating how you feel about another's actions can be valuable feedback for that person.

3. Wants. You are far more likely to get what you want if you say what you want. If someone doesn't know what you want, she doesn't have a chance to help you get it. Ask clearly. Also avoid demanding or using the word *need*. Most people like to feel helpful, not obligated. Instead of saying, "Do the dishes when it's your turn, or else!" say, "I want to divide the housework fairly."

4. Thoughts. Communicate your thoughts, and use caution. Beginning your statement with the word "I" doesn't make it an "I" message. "I think you are a slob" is a "You" judgment in disguise. Instead, say, "I'd have more time to study if I didn't have to clean up so often."

5. Intentions. The last part of an "I" message is a statement about what you intend to do. Have a plan that doesn't depend on the other person. For example, instead of "From now on we're going to split the dishwashing evenly," you could say, "I intend to do my share of the housework and leave the rest."

STATE THE PROBLEM

Now you can move into the actual content of the conflict. Using "I" messages, state the problem. Tell people what you observe, feel, think, want, and intend to do. Allow the other people in a particular conflict to do the same.

Each person might have a different perception of the problem. That's fine. Let the conflict come into clear focus. It's hard to fix something unless people agree on what's broken.

Remember that the way you state the problem largely determines the solution. Defining the problem in a new way can open up a world of possibilities. For example, "I need a new roommate" is a problem statement that dictates one solution. "We could use some agreements about who cleans the apartment" opens up more options, such as resolving a conflict about who will wash the dishes tonight.

If you want to defuse tension or defensiveness, set aside your opinions for a moment. Take the time to understand the other points of view. Sum up those viewpoints in words that the other parties can accept. When people feel that they've been heard, they're often more willing to listen.

In times of conflict, we often say one thing and mean another. So before responding to what the other person says, use active listening. Check to see whether you have correctly received that person's message by saying, "What I'm hearing you say is … Did I get it correctly?"

FOCUS ON SOLUTIONS

After stating the problem, dream up as many solutions as you can. Be outrageous. Don't hold back. Quantity—not quality—is the key. If you get stuck, restate the problem and continue brainstorming.

Next, evaluate the solutions you brainstormed. Discard the unacceptable ones. Talk about which solutions will work and how difficult they will be to implement. You might hit upon a totally new solution.

Choose one solution that is most acceptable to everyone involved, and implement it. Agree on who is going to do what by when. Then keep your agreements.

Finally, evaluate the effectiveness of your solution. If it works, pat yourselves on the back. If not, make changes or implement a new solution.

Remember to focus on the future. Instead of rehashing the past, talk about new possibilities. Think about what you can do to prevent problems in the future. State how you intend to change, and ask others for their contributions to the solution. ∎

8

You're One Click Away . . .
from discovering more ways to manage conflict.

JOURNAL ENTRY 20

Write an "I" message

The purpose of this exercise is to help you experiment with "I" messages. Practice in the space below, but also start practicing this with the next person you communicate with, whether it's a teacher, roommate, friend, parent, or child. Watch how making this small shift in language can make a big change in your relationships.

Discovery Statement

Pick something about a teacher, friend, or family member that irritates you. Then pretend that you are talking to the person who is associated with this irritation. In the space below, write down what you would say to this person as a "You" message.

I discovered that I would say . . .

_____

_____

_____

_____

_____

_____

_____

_____

_____

_____

_____

_____

_____

_____

_____

_____

_____

Intention Statement

Now consider the possibility of sending a different message. How interested are you in actually using "I" messages with the person described above?

There are several possible levels of commitment. For example, you might choose to deliver a few "I" messages to this person and then see how well they work. Or you might commit to using "I" messages on a permanent basis with this person—and with other key people in your life. Describe your current level of commitment to using "I" messages in the space below.

I intend to . . .

_____

_____

_____

_____

_____

Action Statement

Give some thought to exactly what you'll say if you do use this technique. Take the "You" message above and rewrite it as an "I" message. Include at least the first three elements suggested in "Managing conflict" on page 116.

I will say . . .

_____

_____

_____

_____

_____

_____

_____

_____

_____

 You're One Click Away . . .
from more ways to deliver an effective "I" message.

Developing
EMOTIONAL INTELLIGENCE

In his book *Working with Emotional Intelligence*, Daniel Goleman defines emotional intelligence as a cluster of traits:

- *Self-awareness*—recognizing your full range of emotions and knowing your strengths and limitations.
- *Self-regulation*—responding skillfully to strong emotions, practicing honesty and integrity, and staying open to new ideas.
- *Motivation*—persisting to achieve goals and meet standards of excellence.
- *Empathy*—sensing other people's emotions and taking an active interest in their concerns.
- *Skill in relationships*—listening fully, speaking persuasively, resolving conflict, and leading people through times of change.

Goleman concludes that "IQ washes out when it comes to predicting who among a talented pool of candidates *within* an intellectually demanding profession will become the strongest leader." At that point, emotional intelligence starts to become more important. [3]

If you're emotionally intelligent, you're probably described as someone with good "people skills." You're aware of your feelings. You act in thoughtful ways, show concern for others, resolve conflict, and make responsible decisions.

Your emotional intelligence skills will serve you in school and in the workplace, especially when you collaborate on project teams. You can deepen your skills with the following strategies.

RECOGNIZE THREE ELEMENTS OF EMOTION

Even the strongest emotion consists of just three elements: physical sensations, thoughts, and action. Usually they happen so fast that you can barely distinguish them. Separating them out is a first step toward emotional intelligence.

Imagine that you suddenly perceive a threat—such as a supervisor who's screaming at you. Immediately your heart starts beating in double-time and your stomach muscles clench (physical sensations). Then thoughts race through your head: *This is a disaster. She hates me. And everyone's watching.* Finally, you take action, which could mean staring at her, yelling back, or running away.

NAME YOUR EMOTIONS

Naming your emotions is a first step to going beyond the "fight or flight" reaction to any emotion. Naming gives you power. The second that you attach a word to an emotion, you start to gain perspective. People with emotional intelligence have a rich vocabulary to describe a wide range of emotions. For example, do an Internet search with the key words *feeling list*. Read through the lists you find for examples of ways that you can name your feelings in the future.

ACCEPT YOUR EMOTIONS

Another step toward emotional intelligence is accepting your emotions—*all* of them. This can be challenging if you've been taught that some emotions are "good," whereas others are "bad." Experiment with another viewpoint: You do not choose your emotional reactions. However, you can choose what you *do* in response to any emotion.

EXPRESS YOUR EMOTIONS

One possible response to any emotion is expressing it. The key is to speak without blaming others for the way you feel. The basic tool for doing so is using "I" messages, as described on page 116.

RESPOND RATHER THAN REACT

The heart of emotional intelligence is moving from mindless reaction to mindful action. See whether you can introduce an intentional gap between sensations and thoughts on the one hand and your next action on the other hand. To do this more often:

- *Run a "mood meter."* Check in with your moods several times each day. On a 3 × 5 card, note the time of day and your emotional state at that point. Rate your mood on a scale of 1 (relaxed and positive) to 10 (very angry, very sad, or very afraid).
- *Write Discovery Statements.* In your journal, write about situations in daily life that trigger strong emotions. Describe these events—and your usual responses to them—in detail.
- *Write Intention Statements.* After seeing patterns in your emotions, you can consciously choose to behave in new ways. Instead of yelling back at the angry supervisor, for example, make it your intention to simply remain silent and breathe deeply until he finishes. Then say, "I'll wait to respond until we've both had a chance to cool down."

MAKE DECISIONS WITH EMOTIONAL INTELLIGENCE

When considering a possible choice, ask yourself, "How am I likely to feel if I do this?" You can use "gut feelings" to tell when an action might violate your values or hurt someone.

Think of emotions as energy. Anger, sadness, and fear send currents of sensation through your whole body. Ask yourself how you can channel that energy into constructive action. ∎

You're One Click Away . . .
from learning more ways online to develop emotional intelligence.

8

Creating high-performance teams

Most work in organizations get done by teams. Collaboration and cooperative learning are key. Yet not all teams are created equal. Some produce long-term, positive change. Other teams produce bland reports that make a direct trip to the recycling bin. Use the following suggestions to prevent the problems that take teams down.

CHOOSE TEAM MEMBERS WHO ARE WILLING TO LEARN

Set the stage for success by selecting team members based on the cycle of learning as described in Chapter 1. Remember David Kolb's idea that people learn from experience through four kinds of activity that occur in a repeating cycle. Teams learn in the same way. This means choosing members who will operate in these ways:

- Get fully involved with the team and commit to its purpose (concrete experience).

- Talk about the team's experiences and stay open to new ideas (reflective observation).

- Think critically about which agreements and actions will achieve the team's purpose (abstract conceptualization).

- Make decisions and take action (active experimentation).

Not everyone you know will have all these skills, so invite team members with a variety of learning styles.

CREATE A PROJECT PLAN

After choosing team members, get the big picture of your project:

- Clarify your purpose—the specific outcome you will produce along with the benefits that outcome will create.

- Next, set dates for producing that outcome and each of the milestones along the way.

- Follow up with a list of actions that your team will take to meet the milestones as well as who will be responsible for completing each action.

Be sure to put all your agreements on these points in writing and share them with every team member.

ENCOURAGE NEW IDEAS

In an empowered team, all ideas are welcome, problems are freely admitted, and any item is open for discussion. In other words, people who want a team to succeed will treat ideas as tools. Instead of automatically looking for what's wrong with a proposal, they search for potential applications. Even a proposal that seems outlandish at first might become workable with a few modifications.

During meetings, allow members to fully express any idea before thinking critically about it. To make this happen more often:

- *Put your opinions on hold*. If you're leading a meeting, pose a question and ask other people to contribute answers. Then look for the potential value in any idea. Avoid nonverbal language that signals a negative reaction, such as frowning or rolling your eyes.

- *Divide large teams into working groups*. People might be more willing to ask questions and volunteer answers in a smaller group.

- *Assign a "devil's advocate."* Give one person free permission to ask tough questions and poke holes in any proposal.

- *Invite a guest expert*. A fresh perspective from someone outside the group can stimulate fresh questions and spark insights.

- *Set up a suggestion box*. Let team members submit questions and ideas anonymously, in writing.

EVEN OUT THE WORKLOAD

One potential trap for teams is that one person ends up doing most of the work. This person might feel resentful and complain. If you find yourself in this situation, transform your complaint into a request. Instead of scolding team members for being lazy, request help. Ask team members to take over tasks that you've been doing. Delegate specific jobs.

SHARE THE LEADERSHIP ROLE

Teams often begin by choosing a leader with a vision, charisma, and expertise. As your team matures, however, consider letting other members take turns in a leadership role. This strategy can work especially well in groups where people have a wide range of opinions. Sharing the leadership role is one way to encourage a diversity of viewpoints and help people expand their learning styles.

SUSTAIN TEAM FOCUS WITH TWO KEY QUESTIONS

When a team tries to tackle too many problems or achieve too many goals, the members can easily get distracted. They can forget the team's purpose and lose their enthusiasm for the whole project. Often you can restore your team's focus and energy level by asking: "What is the single most important goal that our team can meet?" and "What is the single most important thing we can do now to meet that goal?"

CELEBRATE AND RECAP

When your project is finished, take time to celebrate with your team members. Talk about what you learned and how to apply those lessons in the future. Also celebrate your growing skills in creative thinking, critical thinking, communication, and collaboration. Working in teams helps you to develop all these qualities of a master student. ■

You're One Click Away . . .
from finding more strategies for constructive collaboration.

CRITICAL THINKING EXERCISE 8

Try on a new interpretation

The purpose of this exercise is to see the difference between behaviors and interpretations. Understanding this difference can help you think more accurately about what other people say and do. In turn, this thinking skill can help you prevent and resolve conflict.

A *behavior* is a physical action that we can directly observe. When we describe behaviors, we're stating facts. In contrast, an *interpretation* is a statement of opinion about what a behavior means.

The following chart lists two behaviors and two different ways to interpret each behavior.

Behavior	Interpretation #1	Interpretation #2
Someone enters a classroom 10 minutes after a lecture starts.	"She's too irresponsible to get to a lecture on time."	"She's normally on time; maybe her car broke down at the last minute."
Someone gets up during a conversation and runs out of the room.	"He ran out of the room because he was so angry with me."	"maybe he left the room suddenly because he got a text message about an emergency."

In both cases, Interpretation #1 places blame and invites an argument. Interpretation #2 avoids blame and invites further conversation rather than argument. Interpretation #1 increases conflict, while Interpretation #2 decreases conflict.

With this distinction in mind, think of a recent situation when you were in conflict with someone. In the chart below, brainstorm a list of any behaviors that were involved in this conflict. List each behavior on a separate line. Then think of two ways to interpret each behavior. Finally, place a plus sign (+) next to any interpretation that could increase conflict. Then place a minus sign (−) next to any interpretation that could decrease conflict.

Behavior	Interpretation #1	Interpretation #2

8

 You're One Click Away . . .
from more examples of the differences between observations and interpretations.

8 CHAPTER SKILLS *Snapshot*

Take a minute to reflect on your responses to the Relationships section of the Discovery Wheel on page 9. Reflect on the progress you've made, and clarify your intentions to develop further mastery. Complete the following sentences.

DISCOVERY

My score on the Relationships section of the Discovery Wheel was . . .

The technique that has made the biggest difference in my skill at listening is . . .

When I feel angry with people, the way I usually express it is to . . .

When I'm effective at managing conflict, I remember to . . .

INTENTION

By the time I finish this course, I visualize giving myself a score of ___ on the Relationships section of the Discovery Wheel.

I'll know that I've reached a new level of mastery with my "people skills" when . . .

More specifically, my goal is to . . .

ACTION

To achieve the goal I just described, the most important thing I can do next is to . . .

Choosing Greater Health

Use this **Master Student Map** to ask yourself

WHY THIS CHAPTER MATTERS...

- Succeeding in higher education calls for a baseline of physical and emotional well-being.

WHAT IS INCLUDED...

HOW YOU CAN USE THIS CHAPTER...

- Maintain my physical and mental energy.
- Manage stress.
- Make decisions about alcohol and other drugs in a way that supports my success.

WHAT IF...

- I could meet the demands of daily life with energy and optimism to spare?

JOURNAL ENTRY 21

Discover what you want from this chapter

This chapter allows you to look closely at your health. Aim to change your behavior in specific ways that make a dramatic, positive difference in your life. Begin now by quickly previewing this chapter and completing the following sentences.

What concerns me more than anything else about my health right now is . . .

_____

_____

_____

Three suggestions from this chapter that could help me deal with this health concern are ...

_____

_____

_____

Note: You can expand on your responses to this Journal Entry—and keep them private—by writing on a separate piece of paper.

_____

_____

_____

POWER process

Surrender

Life can be magnificent and satisfying. It can also be devastating. Sometimes there is too much pain or confusion. Problems can be too big and too numerous. Life can bring us to our knees in a pitiful, helpless, and hopeless state. A broken relationship, a sudden diagnosis of cancer, a dependence on drugs, or a stress-filled job can leave us feeling overwhelmed—powerless.

In these troubling situations, the first thing we can do is to admit that we don't have the resources to handle the problem. No matter how hard we try and no matter what skills we bring to bear, some problems remain out of our control. When this is the case, we can tell the truth: "It's too big and too mean. I can't handle it." In that moment, we take a step toward greater health.

Desperately struggling to control a problem can easily result in the problem controlling us. Surrender is letting go of being the master in order to avoid becoming the slave.

Many traditions make note of this idea. Western religions speak of surrendering to God. Hindus say surrender to the Self. Members of Alcoholics Anonymous talk about turning their lives over to a Higher Power. Agnostics might suggest surrendering to their intellect, their intuition, or their conscience.

In any case, surrender means being receptive. Once we admit that we're at the end of our rope, we open ourselves up to help. We learn that we don't have to go it alone. We find out that other people have faced similar problems and survived. We give up our old habits of thinking and behaving as if we have to be in control of everything. We stop acting as general manager of the universe. We surrender. And that creates a space for something new in our lives.

Surrender is not "giving up." It is not a suggestion to quit and do nothing about your problems. Giving up is fatalistic and accomplishes nothing. You have many skills and resources. Use them. You can apply all of your energy to handling a situation and still surrender at the same time. You can surrender to weight gain even as you step up your exercise program. You can surrender to a toothache even as you go to the dentist. You can surrender to the past while adopting new habits for a healthy future.

Surrender includes doing whatever you can in a positive, trusting spirit. Let go, keep going, and know when a source of help lies beyond you.

You're One Click Away . . .
from accessing Power Process Media online and finding out more about how to "surrender."

Hannamariah/Shutterstock.com

Wake up TO HEALTH

Some people see health as just a matter of common sense. These people might see little value in reading a health chapter. After all, they already know how to take care of themselves.

Yet *knowing* and *doing* are two different things. Health information does not always translate into healthy habits.

We expect to experience health challenges as we age. Even youth, though, is no guarantee of good health. Over the last 3 decades, obesity among young adults has tripled. Twenty-nine percent of young men smoke. And 70 percent of deaths among adults ages 18 to 29 result from unintentional injuries, accidents, homicide, and suicide.[1]

As a student, your success in school is directly tied to your health. Lack of sleep and exercise have been associated with lower grade point averages among undergraduate students. So have alcohol use, tobacco use, gambling, and chronic health conditions.[2] And any health habit that undermines your success in school can also undermine your success in later life.

On the other hand, we can adopt habits that sustain our well-being. One study found that people lengthened their lives an average of 14 years by adopting just four habits: staying tobacco-free, eating more fruits and vegetables, exercising regularly, and drinking alcohol in moderation if at all.[3]

Health also hinges on a habit of exercising some tissue that lies between your ears—the organ called your brain. One path to greater health starts not with new food or a new form of exercise, but with new ideas.

Olena Pivnenko/Shutterstock.com

Consider the power of beliefs. Some of them create barriers to higher levels of health: "Your health is programmed by your heredity." "Some people are just low on energy." "Healthy food doesn't taste very good." "Over the long run, people just don't change their habits." Be willing to test these ideas and change them when it serves you.

People often misunderstand what the word *health* means. Remember that this word is similar in origin to *whole, hale, hardy,* and even *holy.* Implied in these words are qualities that most of us associate with healthy people: alertness, vitality, vigor. Healthy people meet the demands of daily life with energy to spare. Illness or stress might slow them down for a while, but then they bounce back. They know how to relax, create loving relationships, and find satisfaction in their work.

To open up your inquiry into health—and to open up new possibilities for your life—consider three ideas.

First, health is a continuum. On one end of that continuum is a death that comes too early. On the other end is a long life filled with satisfying work and fulfilling relationships. Many of us exist between those extremes at a point we might call average. Most of the time we're not sick. And most of the time we're not truly thriving either.

Second, health changes. Health is not a fixed state. In fact, health fluctuates from year to year, day to day, and moment to moment. Those changes can occur largely by chance. Or they can occur more often by choice, as we take conscious control of our thinking and behavior.

Third, even when faced with health challenges, we have choices. We can choose attitudes and habits that promote a higher quality of life. For example, people with diabetes can often manage the disease by exercising more and changing their diet.

Health is one of those rich, multilayered concepts that we can never define completely. In the end, your definition of *health* comes from your own experience. The proof lies not on these pages but in your life—in the level of health that you create, starting now.

You have choices. You can remain unaware of habits that have major consequences for your health. Or you can become aware of current habits (discovery), choose new habits (intention), and take appropriate action.

Health is a choice you make every moment, with each thought and behavior. Wake up to this possibility by experimenting with the suggestions in this chapter. ■

9

Take a fearless look at your health

Take a few minutes right now to take a detailed look at your health. If you generally look and feel healthy, then understanding your body better can help you be aware of what you're doing well. If you are not content with your current level of health, you can discover some ways to adjust your personal habits and increase your sense of well-being.

As with the Discovery Wheel exercise, the usefulness of this exercise is determined by your honesty and courage.

PART ONE

To begin, draw a simple outline of your body on a separate piece of paper. You might have positive and negative feelings about various internal and external parts of your body. Label the parts and include a short description of the attributes you like or dislike—for example, straight teeth, fat thighs, clear lungs, double chin, straight posture.

PART TWO

The body you just drew reflects your past health practices. To discover how well you take care of your body, complete the following sentences. Again, if you're concerned about privacy, then do this writing on a separate sheet of paper.

Eating

1. What I know about the way I eat is . . .

2. What I would most like to change about my diet is . . .

3. My eating habits lead me to be . . .

Exercise

1. The way I usually exercise is . . .

2. The last time I did 20 minutes or more of heart/lung (aerobic) exercise was . . .

3. As a result of my physical conditioning, I feel . . .

4. And I look . . .

5. It would be easier for me to work out regularly if I . . .

6. The most important benefit for me in exercising more is . . .

Drug use

1. My history of cigarette smoking is . . .

2. An objective observer would say that my use of alcohol is . . .

3. In the last 10 days, the number of alcoholic drinks I have had is . . .

4. I would describe my use of coffee, colas, and other caffeinated drinks as . . .

5. I have used the following illegal drugs in the past week:

6. I take the following prescription drugs:

7. When it comes to drugs, what I am sometimes concerned about is . . .

Relationships

1. Someone who knows me fairly well would say that my emotional health is . . .

_____

_____

2. The way I look and feel has affected my relationships by . . .

_____

_____

3. My use of drugs or alcohol has been an issue with . . .

_____

_____

4. The best thing I could do for myself and my relationships would be to . . .

_____

_____

Sleep

1. The average number of hours I sleep each night is . . .

_____

_____

2. On weekends I normally sleep . . .

_____

_____

3. I have trouble sleeping when . . .

_____

4. Last night, the quality of my sleep was . . .

_____

5. Overall, the quality of my sleep is usually . . .

_____

Following up

1. In doing this exercise, I discovered that my top three concerns about my health are . . .

_____

_____

_____

2. I could make a big difference in my health by changing some of my habits. Specifically, I intend to . . .

_____

_____

_____

3. I will act on my intention today by . . .

_____

_____

Protect yourself from sexually transmitted infection

9

Make careful choices about sex. Abstain from sex, or have sex exclusively with one person who is free of infection and has no other sex partners. These are the only ways to be absolutely safe from STIs.

Make careful choices about drug use.
People are more likely to have unsafe sex when drunk or high. Also remember that sharing needles or other paraphernalia with drug users can spread STIs.

Talk to your partner. Before you have sex with someone, talk about the risk of STIs. If you are infected, tell your partner.

Talk to your doctor. See your family doctor or someone at the student health center about STIs. Some methods of contraception, such as using condoms, can also prevent STIs. Also ask about vaccinations for hepatitis B and HPV infection, symptoms of STIs, and when to get screened for STIs.

You're One Click Away . . .
from more ways to prevent STIs and unwanted pregnancy.

CHOOSE YOUR FUEL

Food is your primary fuel for body and mind. And even though you've been eating all your life, the demands of higher education are bound to affect the amount of time that you spend on planning and preparing meals.

There have been hundreds of books written about nutrition. One says don't drink milk. Another says buy a cow: The calcium provided by milk is an essential nutrient we need daily.

Although such debate seems confusing, take comfort. There is actually wide agreement about how to fuel yourself for health. One reliable source of nutrition information is the U.S. Department of Agriculture.[4] Its latest guidelines include these suggestions:

- Make half your plate fruits and vegetables.
- Switch to skim or 1 percent milk.
- Make at least half your grains whole.
- Vary your protein food choices.
- Choose foods and drinks with little or no added sugars.
- Look out for salt (sodium) in foods you buy—it all adds up.
- Eat fewer foods that are high in solid fats.
- Enjoy your food, but eat less.
- Cook more often at home, where you are in control of what's in your food.
- When eating out, choose lower-calorie menu options.
- If you drink alcoholic beverages, do so sensibly—limit to 1 drink a day for women or to 2 drinks a day for men.

Michael Pollan, a writer for the *New York Times Magazine,* spent several years sorting out the scientific literature on nutrition.[5] He

boiled the key guidelines down to seven words in three statements:

- *Eat food.* In other words, choose whole, fresh foods over processed products with a lot of ingredients.
- *Mostly plants.* Fruits, vegetables, and grains are loaded with chemicals that help to prevent disease. Plant-based foods, on the whole, are also lower in calories than foods from animals (meat and dairy products).
- *Not too much.* If you want to manage your weight, then control how much you eat. Notice portion sizes. Pass on snacks, seconds, and desserts—or indulge just occasionally.

Finally, forget diets. *How* you eat can matter more than *what* you eat. If you want to eat less, then eat slowly. Savor each bite. Stop when you're satisfied instead of when you feel full. Use meal times as a chance to relax, reduce stress, and connect with people. ∎

You're One Click Away . . .
from more healthy ways to fuel your body.

Prevent and treat eating disorders

Eating disorders affect many students. These disorders involve serious disturbances in eating behavior. Examples are overeating or extreme reduction of food intake, as well as irrational concern about body shape or weight. Women are much more likely to develop these disorders than are men, though cases are on the rise among males.

Bulimia involves cycles of excessive eating and forced purges. A person with this disorder might gorge on a pizza, doughnuts, and ice cream and then force herself to vomit. Or she might compensate for overeating with excessive use of laxatives, enemas, or diuretics.

Anorexia nervosa is a potentially fatal illness marked by self-starvation. People with anorexia may practice extended fasting or eat only one kind of food for weeks at a time.

These disorders are not due to a failure of willpower. They are real illnesses in which harmful patterns of eating take on a life of their own.

Eating disorders can lead to many complications, including life-threatening heart conditions and kidney failure. Many people with eating disorders also struggle with depression, substance abuse, and anxiety. They need immediate treatment to stabilize their health. This is usually followed by continuing medical care, counseling, and medication to promote a full recovery.

If you're worried you might have an eating disorder, visit a doctor, campus health service, or local public health clinic. If you see signs of an eating disorder in someone else, express your concern with "I" messages, as explained in Chapter 8: Creating Positive Relationships.

For more information, contact the National Eating Disorders Association at 1-800-931-2237 or online at www.nationaleatingdisorders.org.

© iStockphoto.com/jgroup

Choose to EXERCISE

© iStockphoto.com/Anterovium

Exercise promotes weight control and reduces the symptoms of depression. It also helps to prevent heart attack, diabetes, and several forms of cancer.[6] In addition, exercise refreshes your body and your mind. If you're stuck on a math problem or blocked on writing a paper, take an exercise break. Use the following simple ways to include more physical activity in your life.

Stay active throughout the day. Park a little farther from work or school. Walk some extra blocks. Take the stairs instead of the elevator. For an extra workout, climb two stairs at a time. An hour of daily activity is ideal, but do whatever you can.

Adapt to your campus environment. Look for exercise facilities on campus. Search for classes in aerobics, swimming, volleyball, basketball, golf, tennis, and other sports. Intramural sports are another option.

Do what you enjoy. Stay active over the long term with aerobic activities that you enjoy, such as martial arts, kickboxing, yoga, dancing, or rock climbing. Check your school catalog for classes. Find several activities that you enjoy, and rotate them throughout the year. Your main form of activity during winter might be ballroom dancing, riding an exercise bike, or skiing. In summer, you could switch to outdoor sports. Whenever possible, choose weight-bearing activities such as walking, running, or stair climbing.

Get active early. Work out first thing in the morning. Then it's done for the day. Make it part of your daily routine, just like brushing your teeth.

Exercise with other people. Making exercise a social affair can add a fun factor and raise your level of commitment.

Before beginning any vigorous exercise program, consult a health care professional. This is critical if you are overweight, over age 60, in poor condition, or a heavy smoker, or if you have a history of health problems. ■

You're One Click Away . . .
from more ways to make exercise a regular part of your life.

7 ways to stay healthy

in (almost) no time

The best intentions to stay healthy can go out the window when you have only 20 minutes to eat between classes or when you don't get home from classes until 10 p.m. The more hurried you become, the more important it becomes to take care of yourself. Following are 7 little things you can do to experience maximum health benefits in minimum time:

1. When you're in a hurry, eat vegetarian.
There's no meat to thaw or cook. In the time it takes to cook a pot of pasta, you can cut and steam some fresh vegetables.

2. For a quick, nutritious meal, choose cereal.
Buy whole grain cereal and add skim milk.

3. Make healthier choices from vending machines.
Instead of soda, choose bottled water. Also choose packages of nuts or whole grain crackers instead of candy.

4. Eat more fruit.
It's still the world's most portable, nutritious food. For a meal that takes almost no time to prepare, combine fresh fruit with some nuts and whole grain crackers.

5. Switch to whole grain bread.
Choosing whole grain over wheat takes no extra time from your schedule. And the whole grain comes packed with more nutrients than white bread.

6. Park farther away from your destination.
You'll build some exercise time into your day without having to join a gym.

7. Whenever possible, walk.
Walk between classes or while taking a study break. Instead of meeting a friend for a restaurant meal or a movie, go for a walk instead.

9

CHOOSE EMOTIONAL HEALTH

A little tension before a test, a presentation, or a date is normal. That feeling can keep you alert and boost your energy. The problem comes when tension is persistent and extreme. That's when average levels of stress turn into *distress.*

You can take simple and immediate steps toward freedom from distress. Start with your overall health. Your thoughts and emotions can get scrambled if you go too long feeling hungry or tired. Use the suggestions in this chapter for eating and exercise. Also get plenty of sleep.

The suggestions in "Relax—it's just a test" on page 76 can help you manage *any* form of distress. Start with those strategies; then experiment with the following ideas for more freedom from distress.

Make contact with the present moment. If you feel anxious, see whether you can focus your attention on a specific sight, sound, or other sensation that's happening in the present moment. In a classroom, for example, take a few seconds to listen to the sounds of squeaking chairs, the scratching of pencils, the muted coughs. Focus all of your attention on one point—anything other than the flow of thoughts through your head. This is one way to use the "Power Process: Be here now" as a simple and quick stress-buster.

Use guided imagery. This technique can work especially well after making contact with the present moment. For example, you might imagine yourself at a beach. Hear the surf rolling in and the seagulls calling to each other. Feel the sun on your face and the hot sand between your toes. Smell the sea breeze. Taste the salty mist from the surf. Notice the ships on the horizon and the rolling sand dunes. Use all of your senses to create a vivid imaginary trip.

Don't believe everything you think. Stress results not from events in our lives but from the way we *think* about those events. One thought that sets us up for misery is *People should always behave in exactly the way I expect.* Another one is *Events should always turn out exactly as I expect.*

A more sane option is to dispute such irrational beliefs and replace them with more rational ones: *I can control my own behavior, but not the behavior of others.* And *Some events are beyond my control.* Changing our beliefs can reduce our stress significantly.

Another way to deal with stressful thoughts is to release them altogether. Simply notice your thoughts as they arise and pass. Instead of reacting to them, observe them. Over time, you might notice that your stream of thinking slows down. You might also enter a state of relaxation that also yields life-changing insights.

Solve problems. Although you can't "fix" an unpleasant feeling in the same way that you can fix a machine, you can choose to change a situation associated with that feeling. There might be a problem that needs a solution. Use distress as your motivation to take action.

Stay active. A related strategy is to do something—*anything* that's constructive, even if it's not a solution to a specific problem.

The basic principle is that you can separate emotions from actions. It is appropriate to feel miserable when you do. It's normal to cry and express your feelings. It is also possible to go to class, study, work, eat, and feel miserable at the same time. Unless you have a diagnosable problem with your emotional health, continue normal activities until the misery passes.

Share what you're thinking and feeling. There are times when negative thoughts and emotions persist even when you take appropriate action. Tell a family member or friend about your feelings. This is a powerful way to gain perspective. The simple act of describing a problem can sometimes reveal a solution or give you a fresh perspective.

Ask for help. Student health centers are not just for treating colds, allergies, and flu symptoms. Counselors expect to help students deal with adjustment to campus, changes in mood, academic problems, and drug use disorders.

Remember a basic guideline about *when* to seek help: whenever problems with your thinking, moods, or behaviors consistently interfere with your ability to sleep, eat, go to class, work, or sustain relationships.

Your tuition helps to pay for health services. It's smart to use them. ■

You're One Click Away . . .
from more ways to manage distress.

ASKING FOR HELP

The world responds to people who ask. If you're not consistently getting what you want in life, then consider the power of asking for help.

"Ask and you shall receive" is a gem of wisdom from many spiritual traditions. Yet acting on this simple idea can be challenging.

Some people see asking for help as a sign of weakness. Actually, it's a sign of strength. Focus on the potential rewards. When you're willing to receive and others are willing to give, resources become available. Circumstances fall into place. Dreams that once seemed too big become goals that you can actually achieve. You benefit, and so do other people.

Remember that asking for help pays someone a compliment. It means that you value what people have to offer. Many will be happy to respond. The key is asking with skill.

ASK WITH CLARITY

Before asking for help, think about your request. Take time to prepare, and consider putting it in writing before you ask in person.

The way you ask has a great influence on the answers you get. For example, "I need help with money" is a big statement. People might not know how to respond. Be more specific: "Do you know any sources of financial aid that I might have missed?" Or: "My expenses exceed my income by $200 each month. I don't want to work more hours while I'm in school. How can I fill the gap?"

ASK WITH SINCERITY

People can tell when a request comes straight from your heart. Although clarity is important, remember that you're asking for help—not making a speech. Keep it simple and direct. Just tell the truth about your current situation, what you want, and the gap between the two. It's okay to be less than perfect.

ASK WIDELY

Consider the variety of people who can offer help. They include parents, friends, classmates, coworkers, mentors, and sponsors. People such as counselors, advisors, and librarians are *paid* to help you.

Also be willing to ask for help with tough issues in any area of life—sex, health, money, career decisions, and more. If you consistently ask for help only in one area, you limit your potential.

To get the most value from this suggestion, direct your request to an appropriate person. For example, you wouldn't ask your instructors for advice about sex. However, you can share any concern with a professional counselor.

ASK WITH AN OPEN MIND

When you ask for help, see whether you can truly open up. If an idea seems strange or unworkable, put your objections on hold for the moment. If you feel threatened or defensive, just notice the feeling. Then return to listening. Discomfort can be a sign that you're about to make a valuable discovery. If people only confirm what you already think and feel, you miss the chance to learn.

ASK WITH RESPONSIBILITY

If you want people to offer help, then avoid statements such as "You know that suggestion you gave me last time? Wow, that really bombed!"

When you act on an idea and it doesn't work, the reason may have nothing to do with the other person. Perhaps you misunderstood or forgot a key point. Ask again for clarity. In any case, the choice about what to do—and the responsibility for the consequences—is still yours.

ASK WITH AN OPENING FOR MORE IDEAS

Approaching people with a specific, limited request can work wonders. So can asking in a way that takes the conversation to a new place. You can do this with creative questions: "Do you have any other ideas for me?" "Would it help if I approached this problem from a different angle?" "Could I be asking a better question?"

ASK AGAIN

People who make a living by selling things know the power of a repeated request. Some people habitually respond to a first request with "no." They might not get to "yes" until the second or third request.

Some cultures place a value on competition, success, and "making it on your own." In this environment, asking for help is not always valued. Sometimes people say no because they're surprised or not sure how to respond. Give them more time and another chance to come around. ∎

9

Alcohol and other drugs:
The truth

The truth is that using alcohol, tobacco, caffeine, cocaine, heroin, and other drugs can be fun. The payoffs might include relaxation, self-confidence, excitement, or the ability to pull an all-nighter.

In addition to the payoffs, there are costs. And sometimes these are much greater than the payoff.

Lectures about drug use and abuse can be pointless. We don't take care of our bodies because someone says we should. We might take care of ourselves when we see that the costs of using alcohol and other drugs *outweigh* the benefits.

It's your body. You get to choose.

Some people will choose to stop using a drug when the consequences get serious enough. Other people don't stop. They continue their self-defeating behaviors, no matter what the consequences. Their top priority in life is finding and using drugs. At that point, the problem is commonly called addiction. The technical term for addiction is *alcohol use disorder* or *substance use disorder*. Fortunately, help is available.

As you choose you relationship with alcohol and other drugs, consider the following suggestions.

Use responsibly. Show people that you can have a good time without drugs. If you do choose to drink, consume alcohol with food. Pace yourself. Take time between drinks.

Avoid promotions that encourage excess drinking. "Ladies Drink Free" nights are especially dangerous. Women are affected more quickly by alcohol, making them targets for rape. Also stay out of games that encourage people to guzzle. And avoid people who make fun of you for choosing not to drink.

Pay attention. Whenever you use alcohol or another drug, do so with awareness. Then pay attention to the consequences. Act with deliberate decision rather than out of habit or under pressure from others.

Admit problems. People with active addictions are a varied group—rich and poor, young and old, successful and unsuccessful. Often these people do have one thing in common: They are masters of denial. They deny that they are unhappy. They deny that they have hurt anyone. They are convinced that they can quit any time they want. They sometimes become so good at hiding the problem from themselves that they die.

Take responsibility for recovery. Nobody plans to become addicted. If you have pneumonia, you seek treatment and recover without shame. Approach addiction in the same way. You can take responsibility for your recovery without blame or shame.

Get help. Two broad options exist. One is the growing self-help movement. The other is formal treatment. People who seek help often combine the two.

Many self-help groups are modeled after Alcoholics Anonymous (AA)—one of the oldest and most successful programs in this category. Groups based on AA principles exist for many other problems as well.

Some people feel uncomfortable with the AA approach. Other resources exist for them, including private therapy and group therapy. Also investigate organizations such as Women for Sobriety, the Secular Organizations for Sobriety, and Rational Recovery.

Use whatever works for you. ■

You're One Click Away . . .
from more ways to choose your relationship to alcohol and other drugs.

© Patrick Strattner/Jupiter Images

CRITICAL THINKING EXERCISE 9

Addiction—how do I know?

People who have problems with drugs and alcohol can hide this fact from themselves and from others. And any of us can find it hard to admit that a friend or loved one has a problem.

The purpose of this exercise is to give you an objective way to look at your relationship with drugs or alcohol. There are signals that indicate when drug or alcohol use calls for getting treatment. Answer the following questions quickly and honestly with yes, no, or n/a (not applicable). If you are concerned about someone else, rephrase each question using his/her name.

_____ Are you uncomfortable discussing drug abuse?

_____ Are you worried about your own drug or alcohol use?

_____ Are any of your friends worried about your drug or alcohol use?

_____ Have you ever hidden from a friend, spouse, employer, or coworker the fact that you were drinking?

_____ Do you sometimes use alcohol or drugs to escape lows rather than to produce highs?

_____ Have you ever gotten angry when confronted about your use?

_____ Do you brag about how much you consume?

_____ Do you think about or do drugs when you are alone?

_____ Do you store up alcohol, drugs, cigarettes, or caffeine (in coffee or soft drinks) to be sure you won't run out?

_____ Does having a party almost always include alcohol or drugs?

_____ Do you try to control your drinking so that it won't be a problem? ("I drink only beer.")

_____ Do you often explain to other people why you are drinking? ("It's my birthday." "It's a hot day.")

_____ Have you changed friends to accommodate your drinking or drug use?

_____ Has your behavior changed in the last several months? (Grades down? Lack of motivation?)

_____ Do you drink or use drugs to relieve tension?

_____ Do you have medical problems that could be related to drinking or drugs?

_____ Have you ever decided to quit drugs or alcohol and then changed your mind?

_____ Have you had any fights, accidents, or similar incidents related to drinking or drugs in the last year?

_____ Has your use ever caused a problem at home?

_____ Do you envy people who go overboard with alcohol or drugs?

_____ Have you ever told yourself you can quit at any time?

_____ Have you ever been in trouble with the police after or while you were drinking?

_____ Have you ever missed school or work because you had a hangover?

_____ Have you blacked out during or after drinking?

_____ Do you wish that people would mind their own business when it comes to your use of alcohol or drugs?

_____ Is the cost of alcohol or other drugs taxing your budget or resulting in financial stress?

_____ Do you need increasing amounts of the drug to produce the desired effect?

_____ When you stop taking the drug, do you experience withdrawal?

_____ Do you spend a great deal of time obtaining and using alcohol or other drugs?

_____ Have you used alcohol or another drug when it was physically dangerous to do so (such as when driving a car or working with machines)?

_____ Have you been arrested or had other legal problems resulting from the use of a substance?

Now count the number of times you answered yes. If the total is more than one, then consider talking with a professional. This does not necessarily mean that you are addicted. It does point out that alcohol or other drugs could be adversely affecting your life. Talk to someone with training in recovery from chemical dependency. If you filled out this questionnaire about another person and you answered yes two or more times, then your friend might need help. Seek out a counselor and a support group such as Alcoholics Anonymous.

9

CHAPTER 9 SKILLS *Snapshot*

Now that you've reflected on the ideas in this chapter and experimented with some new strategies, revisit your responses to the Health section of the Discovery Wheel exercise on page 9. Also think about ways to develop more mastery in this area of your life. Complete the following sentences:

DISCOVERY

My score on the Health section of the Discovery Wheel was . . .

To monitor my current level of health, I look for specific changes in . . .

After reading and doing this chapter, my top three health concerns are . . .

INTENTION

In response to those health concerns, I intend to . . .

ACTION

The most important intention for me to act on next is . . .

At the end of this course, I would like my Health score on the Discovery Wheel to be . . .

Choosing Your Major & Planning Your Career

Use this **Master Student Map** to ask yourself

WHY THIS CHAPTER MATTERS...

- Your courses come alive when you connect them with a focus for your education—and a direction for the rest of your life.

WHAT IS INCLUDED...

HOW YOU CAN USE THIS CHAPTER...

- Get a comprehensive picture of my current skills.
- Choose my major.
- Create a career plan and set goals for life beyond graduation.

WHAT IF...

- I could begin creating the life of my dreams —starting today?

JOURNAL ENTRY 23

Discover what you want from this chapter

Review the "Power Process: Discover what you want" on page 2. Then complete the following sentences with the first thoughts that come to mind:

I discovered that what I want most from life is ...

_____

_____

_____

To get what I want from my life, the most important habits I can develop are ...

_____

_____

_____

Three articles in this chapter that can help me adopt those habits are ...

_____

_____

_____

© Ruslan Nantsov/Shutterstock.com

POWER process Be it

$\textbf{U}$se this Power Process to enhance all of the techniques in this book.

Consider that most of our choices in life fall into three categories. We can do the following:

- Increase our material wealth (what we have).
- Improve our skills (what we do).
- Develop our "being" (who we are).

Many people devote their entire lifetime to the first two categories. They act as if they are "human havings" instead of human beings. For them, the quality of life hinges on what they have. They devote most of their waking hours to getting more—more clothes, more cars, more relationships, more degrees, more trophies. "Human havings" define themselves by looking at the circumstances in their lives—what they have.

Some people escape this materialist trap by adding another dimension to their identities. In addition to living as "human havings," they also live as "human doings." They thrive on working hard and doing everything well. They define themselves by how efficiently they do their jobs, how effectively they raise their children, and how actively they participate in clubs and organizations. Their thoughts are constantly about methods, techniques, and skills.

In addition to focusing on what we have and what we do, we can also focus on our being. That last word describes how we *see* ourselves.

All of the techniques in this book can be worthless if you operate with the idea that you are an ineffective student. You might do almost everything this book suggests and still never achieve the success in school that you desire.

Instead, picture yourself as a master student right now. Through higher education, you are simply gaining knowledge and skills that reflect and reinforce this view of yourself. Change the way you see yourself. Then watch your actions and results shift as if by magic.

Remember that "Be it" is not positive thinking or mental cheerleading. This Power Process works well when you take a First Step—when you tell the truth about your current abilities. The very act of accepting who you are and what you can do right now unleashes a powerful force for personal change.

If you can first visualize where you want to be, if you can go there in your imagination, if you can *be* it today, then you set yourself up to succeed.

If you want it, be it.

You're One Click Away . . .
from from accessing Power Process Media online and finding out more about how to "be it.."

iStockphoto.com/Rubén Hidalgo

Give up the myth of "someday"

© igor.stevanovic/Shutterstock.com

If you're using this book fully—actively reading the contents, writing the Journal Entries, doing the exercises, and putting the suggestions to work—then you are having quite a journey. You're gaining experience in setting goals, taking charge of your habits, and getting what you want in life.

That sounds like a tall order—like something that can only be accomplished in the distant future. Actually, it's all about the present moment. The main factor in creating your future is what you do today.

This is easy to forget. And it doesn't help when other people tell you that your life will *really* start someday in the future—when you graduate . . . or get married . . . or have kids . . . or get promoted . . . or retire.

Agreeing with this advice can condemn us to perpetual waiting. Using this logic, we could wait our whole life to start living.

There's a mistaken belief about planning that adds to the problem. This is the assumption that life works only when you get all the way through your to-do list. Happiness, fulfillment, and satisfaction can only come someday in the future—when you finally achieve your next goal, or maybe the next one, or maybe even the one after that.

That doesn't sound like much fun.

However, there is another option: Give up the myth of "someday." This means taking a new attitude toward the future.

In fact, one of the best ways to get what you want in the future is to realize that you do not have a future. The only time you have is right now.

The problem with this idea is that some students might think, "No future, huh? Terrific! Party time!"

Giving up the myth of "someday," however, is not the same as living only for today and forgetting about tomorrow. Nor is it a call to abandon goals.

The point is this: Goals are useful tools when we use them to direct our actions right now. Goals allow us to live fully in the present. The idea is to make commitments for the future that change your actions *today*. Set a goal that might take years to accomplish—and then enjoy every step along the way.

You can start now. Use this chapter to choose your major, plan your career, find your place in the new economy, and otherwise create a vision for your life that makes a difference in the present moment.

As you do, consider the possibility that you can live the life of your dreams. If you're willing to master new ways to learn, the possibilities are endless. Your responses to any of the ideas in this book can lead you to think new thoughts, say new things, and do what you never believed you could.

Just start doing it today. ■

You're One Click Away . . .
from more suggestions for choosing what's next in your life.

Values ... the invisible link to success

Values are the things in life that you want for their own sake. Even though they are invisible, values shape your attitudes, direct your goals, and guide your moment-by-moment choices. Your values define who you are and who you want to be. Success is about defining your values and aligning your actions with them.

This book is based on a specific set of values. You live these values when you demonstrate:

- *Focused attention*—living fully and mindfully in the present moment.
- *Self-responsibility*—seeing your own thinking and behavior as the major factor in your success.
- *Integrity*—making and keeping agreements and staying true to your word.
- *Risk taking*—stretching yourself to accomplish larger goals, even if you fail occasionally.
- *Contribution*—taking action to reduce human suffering and promote the happiness of other people.

Take this list as a starting point in defining your own set of personal values. Gain inspiration from the creeds, scriptures, philosophies, myths, and sacred stories of our ancestors. Also consider ideas that are closer to home. For example, the creed of your local church, mosque, or temple might eloquently describe your values. Another way to define your values is to describe the qualities of people you admire.

In any case, translate your values into behavior. Although defining your values is powerful, it doesn't guarantee any results. To achieve your goals, take actions that align with your values.

You're One Click Away . . .
from more information about defining your values and aligning your actions.

1C

Discovering the skilled person
you already are

When meeting with an academic advisor, you may be tempted to say, "I've just been taking courses. I don't have any marketable skills yet."

Think again.

Few words are as widely misunderstood as *skill*. Defining it carefully can have an immediate and positive impact on your career planning.

IDENTIFY TWO KINDS OF SKILLS

One dictionary defines *skill* as "the ability to do something well, usually gained by training or experience." Some skills—such as the ability to repair fiber-optic cables or do brain surgery—are acquired through formal schooling, on-the-job training, or both. These abilities are called *technical skills*. People with such skills have mastered a specialized body of knowledge needed to do a specific kind of work.

However, there is another category of skills that we develop through experiences both inside and outside the classroom. These are *transferable skills*. Transferable skills are abilities that help people thrive in any job—no matter what technical skills they have. You start developing these skills even before you take your first job.

Perhaps you've heard someone described this way: "She's really smart and knows what she's doing, but she's got lousy people skills." People skills—such as *listening* and *negotiating*—are prime examples of transferable skills.

© Dudarev Mikhail/Shutterstock.com

SUCCEED IN MANY SITUATIONS

Transferable skills are often invisible to us. The problem begins when we assume that a given skill can be used in only one context, such as being in school or working at a particular job. Thinking in this way places an artificial limit on our possibilities.

As an alternative, think about the things you routinely do to succeed in school. Analyze your activities to isolate specific skills. Then brainstorm a list of jobs where you could use the same skills.

Consider the task of writing a research paper. This calls for the following skills:

- *Planning*, including setting goals for completing your outline, first draft, second draft, and final draft
- *Managing time* to meet your writing goals
- *Interviewing* people who know a lot about the topic of your paper
- *Researching* using the Internet and campus library to discover key facts and ideas to include in your paper

- *Writing* to present those facts and ideas in an original way
- *Editing* your drafts for clarity and correctness

Now consider the kinds of jobs that draw on these skills.

For example, you could transfer your skill at writing papers to a possible career in journalism, technical writing, or advertising copywriting.

You could use your editing skills to work in the field of publishing as a magazine or book editor.

Interviewing and research skills could help you enter the field of market research. And the abilities to plan, manage time, and meet deadlines will help you succeed in all the jobs mentioned so far.

Use the same kind of analysis to think about transferring skills from one job to another. Say that you work part-time as an administrative assistant at a computer dealer that sells a variety of hardware and software. You take phone calls from potential customers, help current customers solve problems using their computers, and attend meetings where your coworkers plan ways to market new products. You are developing skills at *selling, serving customers*, and *working on teams*. These skills could help you land a job as a sales representative for a computer manufacturer or software developer.

The basic idea is to take a cue from the word *transferable*. Almost any skill you use to succeed in one situation can *transfer* to success in another situation. The concept of transferable skills creates a powerful link between higher education and the work world. Skills are the core elements of any job. While taking any course, list the specific skills you are developing and how you can transfer them to the work world. Almost everything you do in school can be applied to your career—if you consistently pursue this line of thought.

Getting past the "I-don't-have-any-skills" syndrome means that you can approach career planning job hunting with more confidence. As you uncover these hidden assets, your list of qualifications will grow as if by magic. You won't be padding your résumé. You'll simply be using action words to tell the full truth about what you can do. ■

You're One Click Away . . .
from learning more about transferable skills online.

50 transferable skills

There are literally hundreds of transferable skills. To learn more, check out O*Net OnLine, a Web site from the federal government at www.onetonline.org. There you'll find tools for discovering your skills and matching them to specific occupations. Additional information on careers and job hunting is available through CareerOneStop at www.careeronestop.org.

SELF-DISCOVERY AND SELF-MANAGEMENT SKILLS

1. Assessing your current knowledge and skills
2. Seeking out opportunities to acquire new knowledge and skills
3. Choosing and applying learning strategies
4. Showing flexibility by adopting new attitudes and behaviors

For more information about self-discovery skills, review the Introduction to this book and Chapter 1.

TIME MANAGEMENT SKILLS

5. Scheduling due dates for projects and goals
6. Choosing technology and applying it to goal-related tasks
7. Choosing materials and facilities needed to meet goals
8. Designing other processes, procedures, or systems to meet goals
9. Working independently to meet projects and goals on schedule
10. Planning projects for teams
11. Managing multiple projects at the same time
12. Monitoring progress toward goals

For more information about these skills, see this chapter and review Chapter 2.

MONEY SKILLS

13. Monitoring income and expenses
14. Raising funds
15. Decreasing expenses
16. Estimating costs and preparing budgets

For more information about money skills, review Chapter 2.

READING SKILLS

17. Reading for key ideas and major themes
18. Reading for detail
19. Reading to synthesize information from several sources
20. Reading to find strategies for solving problems or meeting goals

For more information about reading skills, review Chapter 3.

NOTE-TAKING SKILLS

21. Taking notes on material presented verbally, in print, or online
22. Creating graphs and other visuals to summarize and clarify
23. Organizing information in digital and paper forms
24. Researching information online or in the library
25. Gathering data through research or primary sources

For more information about note-taking skills, review Chapter 4.

TEST-TAKING AND RELATED SKILLS

26. Using test results and other assessments to improve performance
27. Working cooperatively in study and project groups
28. Managing stress
29. Applying scientific findings and methods to solve problems
30. Using math to do computations and solve problems

For more information about test-taking skills, review Chapter 5.

TECHNOLOGY SKILLS

31. Using basic office software.
32. Searching for information efficiently.
33. Using technology to capture, refine, and share ideas and information.
34. Engaging with social networks to achieve goals.
35. Maintaining online security and troubleshooting technology problems.

For more information about technology skills, review Chapter 6.

THINKING SKILLS

36. Thinking to create new ideas, products, or services

37. Thinking to evaluate and improve ideas, products, or services

38. Evaluating material presented verbally, in print, or online

39. Choosing appropriate strategies for making decisions

40. Stating problems accurately and generating solutions

41. Choosing and implementing solutions

For more information about thinking skills, review Chapter 7.

COMMUNICATION SKILLS

42. Coaching, consulting, and counseling

43. Giving people feedback about the quality of their performance

44. Interpreting and responding to nonverbal messages

45. Interviewing people

46. Leading meetings and project teams

47. Listening fully (without judgment or distraction)

48. Preventing and resolving conflicts

49. Speaking to diverse audiences

50. Writing and editing

For more information about communication skills, review Chapters 7 and 8.

 You're One Click Away . . .
from more examples of transferable skills.

JOURNAL ENTRY 24

Inventory your skills

This exercise is about discovering your skills. Before you begin, gather 100 blank 3 × 5 cards. Allow about one hour to complete the following steps.

Step 1

Recall your activities during the past week or month. To refresh your memory, review your responses to "Journal Entry 7" on page 28. Write down as many activities as you can, listing each one on a separate card. Include work-related activities, school activities, and hobbies.

Write down any rewards you've received or recognition of your achievements. Examples include scholarship or athletic awards and recognitions for volunteer work.

Spend 20 minutes on this step, listing all of the activities, rewards, and recognitions you can recall.

Step 2

Next, look over your activity cards. Then take another 20 minutes to list any specialized knowledge or procedures needed to complete those activities or gain those awards and recognitions. These are your *technical skills*. For example, tutoring a French class requires a working knowledge of that language. (See "Discovering the skilled person you already are" on page 138 for more on technical skills.) You might be able to list several technical skills for any one activity, recognition, or reward.

Write each technical skill on a separate card, and label it "technical skill."

Step 3

Go over your activity cards one more time. Now look for examples of *transferable skills*—those that could be applied to a variety of jobs. For instance, giving a speech or working as a salesperson in a computer store requires the ability to persuade people. You can use this ability in just about any career you choose. Write each on a separate card labeled "transferable skill."

You now have a detailed picture of your current skills. Take a few minutes to reflect on the experience of creating that picture. Complete the following sentences:

While listing my skills, I was surprised to discover that . . .

_____

_____

New skills that I intend to develop include . . .

_____

_____

To develop those skills, I will take specific steps, including . . .

_____

_____

Keep your lists of technical and transferable skills on hand when planning your career, choosing your major, writing your résumé, and preparing for job interviews. As you gain new skills, be sure to add them to your lists.

 You're One Click Away . . .
from more ways to identify your skills.

Four ways to choose YOUR MAJOR

1 DISCOVER OPTIONS

Follow the fun. Perhaps you look forward to attending one of your classes and even like completing the assignments. This is one clue to a choice of major. Also see whether you can find lasting patterns in the subjects and extracurricular activities that you've enjoyed over the years. Look for a major that allows you to continue and expand on these experiences.

Consider your abilities. In choosing a major, ability counts as much as interest. In addition to considering what you enjoy, think about times and places when you excelled. List the courses that you aced, the work assignments that you mastered, and the hobbies that led to rewards or recognition. Let your choice of a major reflect a discovery of your passions *and* strengths.

Link to long-term goals. Your choice of a major can fall into place once you determine what you want in life. Before you choose a major, back up to a bigger picture. List your core values, such as contributing to society, achieving financial security and professional recognition, enjoying good health, or making time for fun. Also write down specific goals that you want to accomplish 5 years, 10 years, or even 50 years from today.

Gather information. Check your school's catalog or Web site for a list of available majors. Here is a gold mine of information. Take a quick glance, and highlight all the majors that interest you. Then talk to students who have declared them. Also read descriptions of courses required for these majors. Do you get excited about the chance to enroll in them? Pay attention to your "gut feelings."

Also chat with instructors who teach courses in specific majors. Ask for copies of their class syllabi. Go the bookstore and browse the required texts. Based on all this information, write a list of prospective majors. Discuss them with an academic advisor and someone at your school's career-planning center.

Consider a complementary minor. You can add flexibility to your academic program by choosing a minor to complement or contrast with your major. An effective choice of a minor can expand your skills and career options.

Think critically about the link between your major and your career. You might be able to pursue a rewarding career by choosing among *several* different majors. After graduation, many people are employed in jobs with little relationship to their major. And you might choose a career in the future that is unrelated to any currently available major.

2 MAKE A TRIAL CHOICE

Pretend that you have to choose a major today. Based on the options for a major that you've already discovered, write down the first three ideas that come to mind. Consider that list for a few days, and then just choose one.

3 EVALUATE YOUR TRIAL CHOICE

When you've made a trial choice of major, take on the role of a scientist. Treat your choice as a hypothesis, and then design a series of experiments to evaluate and test it. For example:

- Schedule office meetings with instructors who teach courses in the major.
- Discuss your trial choice with an academic advisor or career counselor.
- Enroll in a course related to your possible major.
- Find a volunteer experience, internship, part-time job, or service-learning experience related to the major.
- Interview students who have declared the same major.
- Interview people who work in a field related to the major and "shadow" them—that is, spend time with those people during their workday.
- Think about whether you can complete your major given the amount of time and money that you plan to invest in higher education.
- Consider whether declaring this major would require a transfer to another program or even another school.

4 CHOOSE AGAIN

Keep your choice of a major in perspective. There is probably no single "correct" choice. Odds are that you'll change your major at least once—and that you'll change careers several times during your life.

As you sort through your options, help is always available from administrators, instructors, advisors, and peers. Look at choosing a major as the start of a continuing path that involves discovery, choice, and passionate action. ■

You're One Click Away . . .
from finding more strategies for choosing a major.

Declare your major today

Pretend that you are required to choose a major today. Of course, your choice is not permanent. You can change it in the future. The purpose of this exercise is simply to begin a process that will lead to declaring an official major.

1. To begin, review your responses to "Journal Entry 24: Inventory your skills" on page 140.

2. Next, look at your school's catalog (print or online) for a list of majors. Print out this list or make a copy of it.

Based on knowledge of your skills and your ideas about your future career, cross out all of the majors that do not interest you. You will probably eliminate well over half the list.

From the remaining majors on the list, circle those that you're willing to consider.

Now, scan the majors that you circled and look for those that interest you the most. See whether you can narrow your choices down to five. List those majors here.

_____

_____

_____

_____

_____

_____

_____

_____

_____

_____

_____

Write an asterisk next to the major that interests you most right now. *This is your trial choice of major.*

Don't stop there. Now, move into action. Review the article "Four ways to choose your major" on page 141. Then list the suggestions from that article that you will definitely use. List those suggestions below, including at least one action that you will take within the next 24 hours.

I will . . .

_____

_____

_____

_____

_____

_____

_____

_____

_____

_____

_____

_____

_____

_____

_____

Create your
career

There's an old saying: "If you enjoy what you do, you'll never work another day in your life." A satisfying and lucrative career is often the goal of education. If you clearly define your career goals and your strategy for reaching them, then you can plan your education effectively.

Career planning involves continuous exploration. There are dozens of effective paths to take. Begin now with the following ideas.

YOU ALREADY KNOW A LOT ABOUT YOUR CAREER PLAN

When people go to school to gain skills, they often start discovering things that they don't know. Career planning is different. You can begin by realizing how much you know right now.

In fact, you've already made many decisions about your career. This is true for young people who say, "I don't have any idea what

I want to be when I grow up." It's also true for midlife career changers.

Consider the student who can't decide whether she wants to be a cost accountant or a tax accountant and then jumps to the conclusion that she is totally lost when it comes to career planning. Or take the student who doesn't know whether he wants to be a veterinary assistant or a nurse.

These people forget that they already know a lot about their career choices.

The person who is debating tax accounting versus cost accounting already knows that she doesn't want to be a doctor, playwright, or taxicab driver. She also knows that she likes working with numbers and balancing books.

The person who is choosing between veterinary assistance and nursing has already ruled out becoming a lawyer, computer programmer, or teacher. He just doesn't know yet whether he has the right bedside manner for horses or for people.

Such people have already narrowed their list of career choices to a number of jobs in the same field—jobs that draw on the same core skills. In general, they already know what they want to be when they grow up.

Demonstrate this for yourself. Find a long list of occupations. (One source is *The Dictionary of Occupational Titles,* a government publication available at many libraries and online.) Using a stack of 3×5 cards, write down randomly selected job titles, one title per card. Then sort through the cards and divide them into two piles. Label one pile "Careers I've Definitely Ruled Out for Now." Label the other pile "Careers I'm Willing to Consider."

You might go through a stack of 100 such cards and end up with 95 in the "definitely ruled out" pile and five in the "willing to consider" pile. This demonstrates that you already have many ideas about the career you want.

YOUR CAREER IS A CHOICE, NOT A DISCOVERY

Many people approach career planning as if they were panning for gold. They keep sifting through dirt, clearing away dust, and throwing out rocks. They are hoping to strike it rich and discover the perfect career.

Other people believe that they'll wake up one morning, see the heavens part, and suddenly know what they're supposed to do. Many of them are still waiting for that magical day to dawn.

We can approach career planning in a different way. Instead of seeing a career as something we discover, we can see it as something we choose. We don't find the right career. We create it.

There's a big difference between these two approaches. Thinking that there's only one "correct" choice for your career can lead to a lot of anxiety: "Did I discover the right one?" "What if I made a mistake?"

Viewing your career as your creation helps you relax. Instead of anguishing over finding the right career, you can stay open to possibilities. You can choose one career today, knowing that you can choose again later.

Suppose that you've narrowed your list of possible careers to five, and you're still unsure. Then just choose one. Any one. Many people will have five careers in a lifetime anyway. You might be able to pursue all five of your careers, and you can do any one of them first. The important thing is to choose.

One caution is in order. Choosing your career is not something to do in an information vacuum. Rather, choose after you've done a lot of research. That includes research into yourself—your skills and interests—and a thorough knowledge of what careers are available.

YOU'VE GOT A WORLD OF CHOICES

Our society offers a limitless array of careers. You no longer have to confine yourself to a handful of traditional categories, such as business, education, government, or manufacturing. People are constantly creating new products and services to meet new demands. The number of job titles is expanding so rapidly that we can barely keep track of them.

For instance, there are people who work as *ritual consultants,* helping people to plan weddings, anniversaries, graduations, and other ceremonies. *Auto brokers* visit dealers, shop around, and buy a car for you. *Professional organizers* walk into your home or office and advise you on managing workflow and organizing your space. *Pet psychologists* help you raise a happy and healthy animal. *Life coaches* assist you in setting and achieving goals.

In addition to choosing the *content* of your career, you have many options for the *context* in which you work. You can work full-time. You can work part-time. You can commute to a cubicle in a major corporation. Or you can work at home and take the one-minute commute from your bedroom to your desk. You can join a thriving business—or create one of your own.

PLAN BY NAMING NAMES

One key to making your career plan real and to ensuring that you can act on it is naming. Go back over your plan to see whether you can include specific names whenever they're called for.

Name your job. Take the skills you enjoy using and find out which jobs use them. What are those jobs called? List them. Note that one job might have different names.

Name your company. Name the agency or organization you want to work for. If you want to be self-employed or start your own business, then name the product or service you'd sell.

Name your contacts. Take the list of organizations you just compiled. Which people in these organizations are responsible for hiring? List those people and contact them directly. If you choose self-employment, list the names of possible customers or clients.

Name more contacts. Expand your list of contacts by brainstorming with your family and friends. Come up with a list of names—anyone who can help you with career planning and job hunting. Write each of these names on a 3 × 5 card or Rolodex card. Or use a contact manager on a computer.

Name your location. Ask whether your career choices are consistent with your preferences about where to live and work. For example, someone who wants to make a living as a studio musician might consider living in a large city such as New York or Toronto. This contrasts with the freelance graphic artist who conducts his business mainly by phone and e-mail. He might be able to live anywhere and still pursue his career.

Name your career goal for others to hear. Develop a "pitch"—a short statement of your career goal that you can easily share with your contacts. For example: "After I graduate, I plan to work in the travel business. I'm looking for an internship in an international travel agency for next summer. Do you know of any agencies that take interns?" Consider everyone you meet a potential member of your job network, and be prepared to talk about what you do.

Note: Career planning services at your school can help with all of the above tasks. Make an appointment to see someone at that office right away.

TEST YOUR CHOICE—AND BE WILLING TO CHANGE

On the basis of all the thinking you've done, make a trial career choice. Then look for experiences that can help you evaluate that choice. Here are some examples of actions you can take:

- Contact people who are actually doing the job you're researching and ask them a lot of questions about what it's like (an *information interview*).

- Choose an internship or volunteer position in a field that interests you.

- Get a part-time or summer job in your career field.

- If you enjoy such experiences, then you've probably made a wise career choice. The people you met might be sources of recommendations, referrals, and employment in the future. If you did *not* enjoy your experiences, then celebrate what you learned about yourself. Now you're free to refine your initial career choice or go in a new direction.

Remember that career plans are made to be changed and refined as you gain new information about yourself and the world. If your present career no longer feels right, you can choose again—no matter what stage of life you're in. The process is the same, whether you're choosing your first career or your fifth.

You're One Click Away . . .
from more career planning strategies.

Plan your career now

Write your career plan. Now. That's right—*now*. Get started with the process of career planning, even if you're not sure where to begin.

Your response to this exercise could be just a rough draft of your plan, which you can revise and rewrite many times. The point is to start a conversation about your career choice—and to get your ideas in writing.

The format of your plan is up to you. You could include many details, such as the next job title you'd like to have, the courses required for your major, and other training that you want to complete. You could list the names of companies to research and people that could hire you. You could also include target dates to complete each of these tasks.

Another option is to represent your plan visually. Consider using charts, timelines, maps, or drawings. You can generate these by hand or with computer software.

To prime your thinking, complete the following sentences. Use the space below and continue on additional paper as needed.

The skills I most enjoy using include . . .

_____

_____

_____

_____

Careers that require these skills include . . .

_____

_____

_____

_____

_____

_____

Of those careers, the one that interests me most right now is . . .

_____

_____

_____

_____

_____

_____

The educational and work experiences that would help me prepare for this career include . . .

_____

_____

_____

_____

_____

_____

_____

The immediate steps I will take to pursue this career are . . .

_____

_____

_____

_____

_____

_____

_____

Tap the hidden job market

One of the most useful job skills you can ever develop is the ability to discover job openings *before they* are advertised. (Most never are.) The more you can tap the hidden job market, the less you need to fear getting fired, laid off, or stuck in a job that no longer serves you.

DISCOVER YOUR NETWORK

Networking is one of the most powerful ways to tap the hidden job market. Mastering this skill can do more for your career over the long-term than endlessly revising your résumé or trying to craft the perfect cover letter.

You might not believe that you have a network. If so, then just notice that thought and gently let it go. *Everyone* has a network. The key is to discover it and develop it.

Begin by listing contacts—any person who can help you find a job. Contacts can include roommates, classmates, teachers, friends, relatives, and their friends. Also list former employers and current employers.

In addition, go to your school's alumni office and see whether you can get contact information for past graduates—especially people who are working in your career field. This is a rich source of contacts that many students ignore.

Start your contact list now. Record each person's name, phone number, and e-mail address on a separate 3×5 card or Rolodex card. Another option is to keep your list on a computer, using word processing, database, contact management software, or an app on your smartphone.

CONTACT PEOPLE IN YOUR NETWORK

Next, send a short e-mail to a person on your list—someone who's doing the kind of work that you'd love to do. Invite that person to coffee or lunch. If that's not feasible, then ask for a time to make a phone call. Explain that you'd like to have a 20-minute conversation to learn more about what this person does for a living. Whenever possible, make this contact after getting an introduction from someone that both of you know. The key point is that you're asking for an *information interview* rather than a job interview.

Before you meet with your contacts in person or over the phone, create a short list of questions to ask. Plan to ask them how they chose their career and found their job. Ask about what they enjoy, what they find challenging, and what trends are shaping their work. In particular, ask about how people find jobs in their field, and if there is anyone else you could meet with for more information.

During the actual interview, listen closely to what people say. Take notes and highlight any follow-up actions that you'd like to take. Keep the focus of the conversation on the other person rather than you. Stick to your agreed time limit for the conversation—unless it's clear that both of you want to continue. When you're done, say thank you.

After the interview, send a thank-you note. Refer to a specific topic or point from your conversation. If the person made a suggestion and you acted on it, then be sure to mention this.

EXPAND YOUR NETWORK

Through your job research and information interviews, you'll learn about many people in your career field. Some of them might be people who fall outside your current network. You can reach out to them anyway.

Tap the power of the Internet. Get the name of the person that you'd like to meet and key it into your favorite search engine. Scan the search results to find out whether this person has a Web site, blog, or both. Also look for their presence on social networks such as Facebook, Twitter, and LinkedIn. With this information you do many things to connect. For example:

- Comment on a blog post that the person wrote.

- Join Twitter and post an update about this person or "retweet" one of their updates.

- Create your own Web site, add a blog, and write a post about this person.

- Send a short e-mail—or handwritten note—that expresses your appreciation for their work.

In any case, do not ask anything of people at this stage. Your goal is simply to show up on their personal "radar." Over time, they might initiate a contact with you. When that happens, celebrate. You've tapped the hidden job market. ■

CRITICAL THINKING EXERCISE 10

Examine beliefs about careers and jobs

Belief #1: *The best way to plan a career is to enter a field that's in demand.*

This statement sounds reasonable. However, you might find it practical to choose a career that's not in demand right now. Even in careers that are highly competitive, job openings often exist for qualified people who are passionate about the field. Also, jobs that are "hot" right now might be "cool" by the time you complete your education. In a constantly changing job market, your own interests and values could guide you as reliably as current trends.

Belief #2: *The best way to find a job is through "want ads" and online job listings.*

There's a problem with these job-hunting strategies: *Many job openings are not advertised.* According to Richard Bolles, author of *What Color Is Your Parachute? A Practical Manual for Job-Hunters and Career-Changers*, employers turn to help wanted listings, résumés, and employment agencies only as a last resort. When jobs open up, they prefer instead to hire people they know— or people who walk through the door and prove that they're excellent candidates for available jobs.[1]

Now, based on the above examples, do some critical thinking of your own. Evaluate each of the following beliefs, stating whether you agree with it. Also provide some reasons for your agreement or disagreement.

Belief #3: *Writing a career plan now is a waste of time. I'll just have to change it later.*

_____

_____

_____

_____

_____

_____

Belief #4: *Writing a résumé is a waste of time until you're actually ready to hunt for a job.*

_____

_____

_____

_____

_____

_____

_____

_____

_____

_____

_____

_____

_____

_____

_____

_____

_____

_____

 You're One Click Away . . .
from strategies for successful job hunting, including résumé writing and job interviewing.

The Discovery Wheel
reloaded

The purpose of this book is to give you the opportunity to adopt habits that promote success. This exercise gives you a chance to see what behaviors you have changed on your journey toward becoming a master student. Answer each question quickly and honestly. Record your results on the Discovery Wheel that follows, and then compare it with the one you completed in the Introduction to this book.

As you complete this self-evaluation, keep in mind that *your scores might be lower here than on your earlier Discovery Wheel.* That's okay. Lower scores might result from increased self-awareness, honesty, and other valuable assets.

As you did with the earlier Discovery Wheel, read the following statements and give yourself points for each one. Use the point system described below. Then add up your point total for each category and shade the Discovery Wheel on page 149 to the appropriate level.

5 points
This statement is always or almost always true of me.

4 points
This statement is often true of me.

3 points
This statement is true of me about half the time.

2 points
This statement is seldom true of me.

1 points
This statement is never or almost never true of me.

1. _____ I can clearly state my overall purpose in life.
2. _____ I can explain how school relates to what I plan to do after I graduate.
3. _____ I capture key insights in writing and clarify exactly how I intend to act on them.
4. _____ I am skilled at making transitions.
5. _____ I seek out and use resources to support my success.

_____ Total score (1) *Purpose*

1. _____ I enjoy learning.
2. _____ I make a habit of assessing my personal strengths and areas for improvement.
3. _____ I monitor my understanding of a topic and change learning strategies if I get confused.
4. _____ I use my knowledge of various learning styles to support my success in school.
5. _____ I am open to different points of view on almost any topic.

_____ Total score (2) *Learning Styles*

1. _____ I can clearly describe what I want to experience in major areas of my life, including career, relationships, financial well-being, and health.
2. _____ I set goals and periodically review them.
3. _____ I plan each day and often accomplish what I plan.
4. _____ I will have enough money to complete my education.
5. _____ I monitor my income, keep track of my expenses, and live within my means.

_____ Total score (3) *Time and Money*

1. _____ I ask myself questions about the material that I am reading.
2. _____ I preview and review reading assignments.
3. _____ I relate what I read to my life.
4. _____ I select strategies to fit the type of material I'm reading.
5. _____ When I don't understand what I'm reading, I note my questions and find answers.

_____ Total score (4) *Reading*

1. _____ When I am in class, I focus my attention.
2. _____ I take notes in class.
3. _____ I can explain various methods for taking notes, and I choose those that work best for me.
4. _____ I distinguish key points from supporting examples.
5. _____ I put important concepts into my own words.

_____ Total score (5) *Notes*

1. _____ The way that I talk about my value as a person is independent of my grades.
2. _____ I often succeed at predicting test questions.
3. _____ I review for tests throughout the term.
4. _____ I manage my time during tests.
5. _____ I use techniques to remember key facts and ideas.

_____ Total score (6) *Memory and Tests*

1. _____ I am in charge of how I manage my time and attention when I use technology.
2. _____ I use technology in ways that directly support my success in school.
3. _____ I think critically about information that I find online.
4. _____ I use social networks to build constructive relationships with people.
5. _____ I use technology to collaborate effectively with other people on projects.

_____ Total score (7) *Technology*

6. _____ I use brainstorming to generate solutions to problems.
7. _____ I can detect common errors in logic and gaps in evidence.
8. _____ When researching, I find relevant facts and properly credit their sources.
9. _____ I edit my writing for clarity, accuracy, and coherence.
10. _____ I prepare and deliver effective presentations.

_____ Total score (8) *Thinking and Communicating*

1. _____ Other people tell me that I am a good listener.
2. _____ I communicate my upsets without blaming others.
3. _____ I build rewarding relationships with people from other backgrounds.
4. _____ I effectively resolve conflict.
5. _____ I participate effectively in teams and take on leadership roles.

_____ Total score (9) *Relationships*

1. _____ I have enough energy to study, attend classes, and enjoy other areas of my life.
2. _____ The way I eat supports my long-term health.
3. _____ I exercise regularly.
4. _____ I can cope effectively with stress.
5. _____ I am in control of any alcohol or other drugs I put into my body.

_____ Total score (10) *Health*

1. _____ I have a detailed list of my skills.
2. _____ I have a written career plan and update it regularly.
3. _____ I use the career-planning services offered by my school.
4. _____ I participate in internships, extracurricular activities, information interviews, and on-the-job experiences to test and refine my career plan.
5. _____ I have declared a major related to my interests, skills, and core values.

_____ Total score (11) *Major and Career*

Using the total score from each category, shade in each section of the blank Discovery Wheel. If you want, use different colors. For example, you could use green for areas you want to work on.

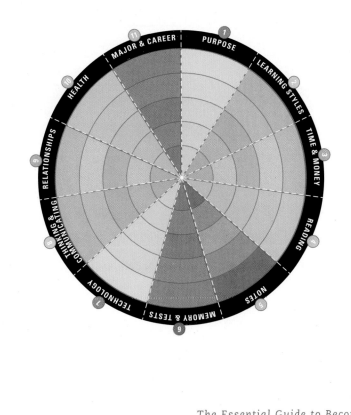

REFLECT ON YOUR DISCOVERY WHEEL

Take this opportunity to review both of the Discovery Wheels you completed in this book. Write your scores from each section of the Discovery Wheel from the Introduction in the chart below. Then add your scores for each section of the Discovery Wheel that you just completed.

	Introduction	Chapter 10
Purpose		
Learning Styles		
Time and Money		
Reading		
Notes		
Memory and Tests		
Technology		
Thinking and Communicating		
Relationships		
Health		
Major and Career		

Finally, summarize your insights from doing the Discovery Wheels. Then declare how you will use these insights to promote your continued success.

Comparing the Discovery Wheel in this chapter with the Discovery Wheel in the Introduction, I discovered that I . . .

_____

_____

_____

_____

_____

_____

_____

_____

_____

_____

_____

In the next six months, I intend to review the following articles from this book for additional suggestions I could use:

_____

_____

_____

_____

_____

_____

_____

_____

_____

_____

_____

_____

_____

_____

_____

_____

_____

_____

_____

_____

You're One Click Away . . .
from an online version of this exercise.

Create your future with a lifeline

On a large sheet of paper, draw a horizontal line. This line will represent your entire lifetime.

Now add key events in your life to this line in chronological order. Focus on key events that have already occurred in your life. Examples are your birth date, your first day at school, the date of your graduation from high school, and the date that you enrolled in higher education. Plot each of these events on a separate point on your lifeline. Label each point with a date.

Now extend your lifeline into the future. Write down key events and outcomes that you *want* to occur in the future. Think about the events you'd like to experience 1 year, 3 years, 5 years, and 10 or more years from now. Examples might include graduation from school, career milestones, major trips you'd like to take, and retirement. Again, plot these events as points on your lifeline, and add a projected date for each one.

As you create this map of your possible future, work quickly in the spirit of a brainstorm. Choose events that align with your core values. Also remember that this plan for your life can be revised at any time.

Afterward, take a few minutes to reflect on your lifeline. Complete the following sentences:

Discovery

In creating my lifeline, I discovered that the key things I want to create in my future include . . .

_____

_____

_____

_____

_____

_____

_____

_____

Intention

The next key event on my lifeline that I definitely intend to create is . . .

_____

_____

_____

_____

_____

_____

_____

_____

_____

Action

The actions that I will take to create this event include . . .

_____

_____

_____

_____

_____

_____

_____

_____

_____

_____

Note: You can write Discovery, Intention, and Action Statements for any event or outcome listed on your lifeline.

 You're One Click Away . . .
from more ways to identify your skills.

10 SKILLS *Snapshot*

I f you fully participated with this chapter, you've got a lot of answers to the opening question: What's next? Reflect on these answers in light of your responses to the Major & Career section of the Discovery Wheel in this chapter on page 149.

DISCOVERY

My score on the Major & Career section on the Discovery Wheel was . . .

Three transferable skills that I've already developed are . . .

In making a trial choice of major, I discovered that . . .

When thinking and talking about my career plan, I feel . . .

INTENTION

Three new transferable skills that I want to develop are . . .

What I want most as a result of completing the requirements for my major is to . . .

What I want most from any career I choose is . . .

What I want most from my education is . . .

ACTION

The three most important things I can do in the next 6 months to achieve my career and educational goals are to . . .

Endnotes

INTRODUCTION

1. Excerpts from *Creating Your Future*. Copyright © 1998 by David B. Ellis. Adapted by permission of Houghton Mifflin Company. All rights reserved.
2. Charles Duhigg, *The Power of Habit* (New York: Random House, 2012).

CHAPTER 1

1. David A. Kolb, *Experiential Learning: Experience as the Source of Learning and Development* (Englewood Cliffs, NJ: Prentice-Hall, 1984).

CHAPTER 2

1. Jane B. Burka and Lenora R. Yuen, *Procrastination: Why You Do It, What to Do About It*, Reading, MA, Addison-Wesley, 1983.

CHAPTER 3

1. Jeffrey D. Karpicke and Janell R. Blunt, "Retrieval Practice Produces More Learning than Elaborative Studying with Concept Mapping," *Science* 20 (January 2011), accessed January 21, 2011, from www.sciencemag.org/content/early/2011/01/19/science.1199327.abstract.
2. O. Pineño and R. R. Miller, "Primacy and Recency Effects in Extinction and Latent Inhibition: A Selective Review with Implications for Models of Learning," *Behavioural Processes* 69 (2005): 223–235.

CHAPTER 4

1. Gayle A. Brazeau, "Handouts in the Classroom: Is Note Taking a Lost Skill?" *American Journal of Pharmaceutical Education* 70, no. 2 (April 15, 2006): 38.
2. Walter Pauk and Ross J. Q. Owens, *How to Study in College*, 11th ed. (Boston: Cengage Learning, 2014).
3. Joseph Novak and D. Bob Gowin, *Learning How to Learn* (New York: Cambridge University Press, 1984).

CHAPTER 5

1. Theodore Cheney, *Getting the Words Right: How to Revise, Edit and Rewrite*, Cincinnati, OH, Writer's Digest, 1983.
2. Alzheimer's Association, "Brain Health," 2012, accessed June 18, 2012, from http://www.alz.org/brainhealth/overview.asp.
3. This article incorporates detailed suggestions from reviewer Frank Baker.

CHAPTER 6

1. Nicholas Carr, "Is Google Making Us Stupid?" *The Atlantic*, July 2008, accessed June 25, 2012, from http://www.theatlantic.com/magazine/archive/2008/07/is-google-making-us-stupid/6868/.
2. From Raimes/Jerskey. *Universal Keys for Writers*, 2e. pg. 709-712. Copyright (c) 2008 Heinle/Arts & Sciences, a part of Cengage Learning, Inc. Reproduced by permission. www.cengage.com/permissions

CHAPTER 7

1. L. W. Anderson and D. R. Krathwohl, *A Taxonomy For Learning, Teaching, and Assessing: A Revision Of Bloom's Taxonomy of Educational Objectives* (New York: Addison Wesley Longman, 2001).
2. Quoted in Arthur L. Costa and Bena Kallick, "Habit Is a Cable . . . : Quotations to Extend and Illuminate Habits of Mind," accessed June 26, 2012, from http://www.habits-of-mind.net.
3. M. T. Motley, *Overcoming Your Fear of Public Speaking: A Proven Method* (New York: Houghton Mifflin, 1998).

CHAPTER 8

1. Maia Szalavitz, "Race and the Genome," Howard University Human Genome Center, March 2, 2001, accessed February 6, 2011, from www.genomecenter.howard.edu/article.htm.
2. Vincent A. Miller, *Guidebook for International Trainers in Business and Industry* (New York: Van Nostrand Reinhold, 1979), 46–55.
3. Daniel Goleman, *Emotional Intelligence: Why It Can Matter More Than IQ* (New York: Bantam, 1995), xiv–xv.

CHAPTER 9

1. Centers for Disease Control and Prevention, "Health Habits of Adults Aged 18-29 Highlighted in Report on Nation's Health," February 18, 2009, accessed June 26, 2012, from www.cdc.gov/media/pressrel/2009/r090218.htm.
2. University of Minnesota, "Health and Academic Performance: Minnesota Undergraduate Students," accessed April 10, 2010, from www.bhs.umn.edu/ reports/HealthAcademicPerformanceReport_2007.pdf, 2007.
3. Kay-Tee Khaw, Nicholas Wareham, Sheila Bingham, Ailsa Welch, Robert Luben, and Nicholas Day, "Combined Impact of Health Behaviours and Mortality in Men and Women: The EPIC-Norfolk Prospective Population Study," *PLoS Medicine* 5, no. 1, 2008, accessed June 26, 2012, from www.plosmedicine.org/article/info:doi/10.1371/journal.pmed.0050012.
4. U.S. Department of Agriculture, "Dietary Guidelines Consumer Brochure," accessed June 26, 2012, from http://www.choosemyplate.gov/print-materials-ordering/dietary-guidelines.html.
5. Michael Pollan, "Unhappy Meals," *New York Times*, January 28, 2007, accessed June 26, 2012, from http://www.nytimes.com/2007/01/28/magazine/28nutritionism.t.html.
6. Harvard Medical School, *HEALTHbeat: 20 No-Sweat Ways to Get More Exercise*, Boston, Harvard Health Publications, October 14, 2008.

CHAPTER 10

1. Richard N. Bolles, *What Color Is Your Parachute? A Practical Manual for Job-Hunters and Career-Changers* (Berkeley, CA: Ten Speed, updated annually).

Index

Additional Reading

Adler, Mortimer, and Charles Van Doren, *How to Read a Book: The Classic Guide to Intelligent Reading* (New York: Touchstone, 1972).

Allen, David, *Getting Things Done: The Art of Stress-Free Productivity* (New York: Penguin, 2001).

Belsky, Scott, *Making Ideas Happen: Overcoming the Obstacles Between Vision and Reality* (New York: Portfolio, 2010).

Bolles, Richard N., *What Color Is Your Parachute? A Practical Manual for Job-Hunters and Career-Changers* (Berkeley, CA: Ten Speed, updated annually).

Boston Women's Health Book Collective, *Our Bodies, Ourselves: A New Edition for a New Era* (New York: Touchstone, 2005).

Buzan, Tony, *How to Mind Map: Make the Most of Your Mind and Learn to Create, Organize and Plan* (New York: Thorsons/Element, 2003).

Chaffee, John, *Thinking Critically*, 10th ed. (Boston: Cengage, 2012).

Colvin, George, *Talent is Overrated: What Really Separates World-Class Performers from Everybody Else* (New York: Portfolio, 2008).

Coplin, Bill, *10 Things Employers Want You to Learn in College* (Berkeley, CA: Ten Speed, 2003).

Covey, Stephen R., *The Seven Habits of Highly Effective People: Powerful Lessons in Personal Change* (New York: Simon & Schuster, 1989).

Davis, Deborah, *The Adult Learner's Companion*, 2nd ed. (Boston: Cengage, 2012).

Downing, Skip, *On Course: Strategies for Creating Success in College and in Life*, 6th ed. (Boston: Cengage, 2011).

Elgin, Duane, *Voluntary Simplicity* (New York: Morrow, 1993).

Ellis, Dave, *Becoming a Master Student*, 13th ed. (Boston: Cengage, 2011).

Ellis, Dave, *Falling Awake: Creating the Life of Your Dreams* (Rapid City, SD: Breakthrough Enterprises, 2000).

Facione, Peter, *Critical Thinking: What It Is and Why It Counts* (Millbrae, CA: California Academic Press, 1996).

Fletcher, Anne, *Sober for Good* (Boston: Houghton Mifflin, 2001).

From Master Student to Master Employee, 3rd ed. (Boston: Cengage, 2011).

Gawain, Shakti, *Creative Visualization* (New York: New World Library, 1998).

Glasser, William, *Take Effective Control of Your Life* (New York: HarperCollins, 1984).

Godin, Seth, *Linchpin: Are You Indispensable?* (New York: Portfolio, 2010).

Golas, Thaddeus, *The Lazy Man's Guide to Enlightenment* (New York: Bantam, 1993).

Greene, Susan D., and Melanie C. L. Martel, *The Ultimate Job Hunter's Guidebook*, 5th ed. (Boston: Cengage, 2008).

Hallowell, Edward M., *Crazy Busy: Overstretched, Overbooked, and About to Snap!* (New York: Ballantine, 2006).

Keyes, Ken, Jr., *Handbook to Higher Consciousness* (Berkeley, CA: Living Love, 1974).

Kolb, David A., *Experiential Learning: Experience as the Source of Learning and Development* (Englewood Cliffs: Prentice-Hall, 1984).

Levy, Frank, and Richard J. Murname, *The New Division of Labor: How Computers Are Creating the Next Job Market* (Princeton, NJ: Princeton University Press, 2004).

Newport, Cal, *How to Win at College* (New York: Random House, 2005).

Nolting, Paul D., *Math Study Skills Workbook*, 4th ed. (Boston: Cengage, 2011).

Pirsig, Robert, *Zen and the Art of Motorcycle Maintenance* (New York: Perennial Classics, 2000).

Raimes, Anne and Maria Jerskey, *Universal Keys for Writers*, 2nd ed. (Boston: Cengage, 2008).

Ram Dass, *Be Here Now* (Santa Fe, NM: Hanuman Foundation, 1971).

Robinson, Adam, *What Smart Students Know: Maximum Grades, Optimum Learning, Minimum Time* (New York: Crown, 1993).

Ruggiero, Vincent Ryan, *Becoming a Critical Thinker*, 6th ed. (Boston: Cengage, 2009).

Schacter, Daniel L., *Searching for Memory: The Brain, the Mind, and the Past* (New York: HarperCollins, 1997).

Toft, Doug, ed., *Master Student Guide to Academic Success* (Boston: Cengage, 2005).

Trapani, Gina, *Lifehacker: 88 Tech Tricks to Turbocharge Your Day* (Indianapolis, IN: Wiley, 2007).

Ueland, Brenda, *If You Want to Write: A Book About Art, Independence and Spirit* (St. Paul, MN: Graywolf, 1987).

U.S. Department of Education, *Funding Education Beyond High School: The Guide to Federal Student Aid*. Published yearly, available at http://studentaid.ed.gov/students/publications/student_guide/index.html.

Watkins, Ryan, and Michael Corry, *E-learning Companion: A Student's Guide to Online Success*, 3rd ed. (Boston: Cengage, 2011).

Wurman, Saul Richard, *Information Anxiety 2* (Indianapolis: QUE, 2001).

Master Student Index Cards

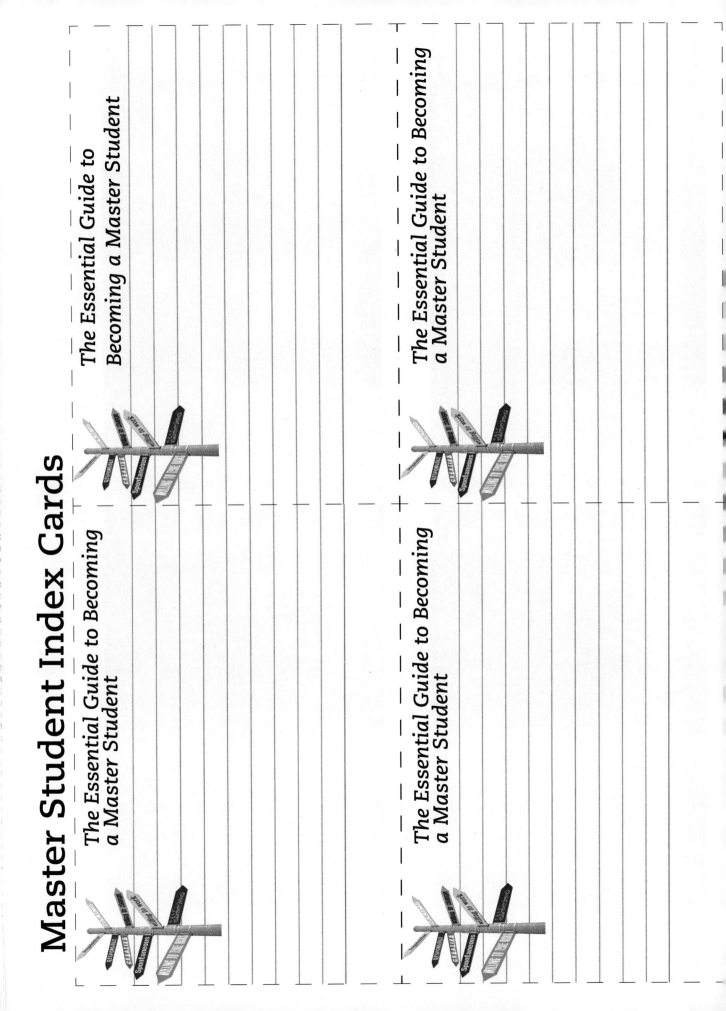

The Essential Guide to Becoming a Master Student

The Essential Guide to Becoming a Master Student

The Essential Guide to Becoming a Master Student

The Essential Guide to Becoming a Master Student

The Essential Guide to Becoming
a Master Student

The Essential Guide to Becoming
a Master Student

The Essential Guide to Becoming
a Master Student

The Essential Guide to Becoming
a Master Student

Master Student Index Cards

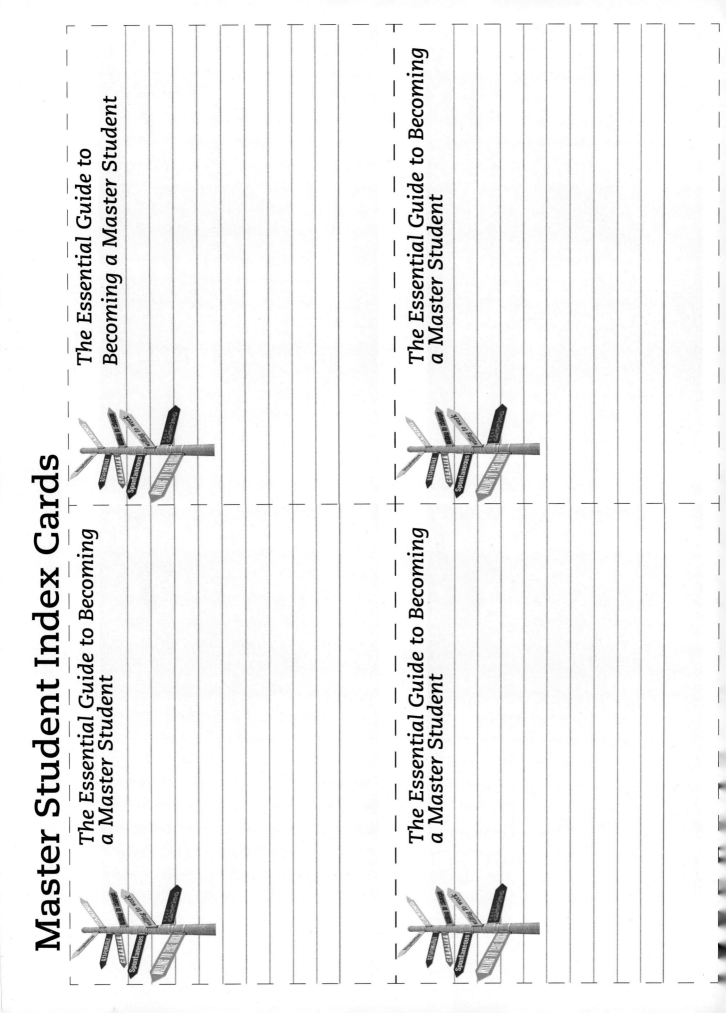

The Essential Guide to Becoming a Master Student

The Essential Guide to Becoming a Master Student

The Essential Guide to Becoming a Master Student

The Essential Guide to Becoming a Master Student

The Essential Guide to Becoming
a Master Student

The Essential Guide to Becoming
a Master Student

The Essential Guide to Becoming
a Master Student

The Essential Guide to Becoming
a Master Student

Appendix

To access the Wizard, go to: <u>www.VaWizard.org</u>.

Start by selecting the login link at the top right of the page. Community college students and personnel already have accounts in the Wizard and may <u>Login</u> to accounts using their MyVCCS account credentials.

The Wizard contains a number of powerful tools aimed at helping users find careers, find education that leads to careers, pay for college and much more. Explore all of the Wizard's functions by selecting from the main subjects on the navigation bar (pictured below) which appears at the top of each webpage.

A tool available in the Wizard for community college students is the Career and Course Planner. VCCS students can access the Planner by selecting the link at the top of the page that says "Career and Course Planner." **(Note: You must be logged in with your VCCS credentials to utilize this resource).**

Once a student selects the Career and Course Planner link, they will see the screen to the right. There is a short description of the Career and Course Planner, and the student can select Start/Continue.

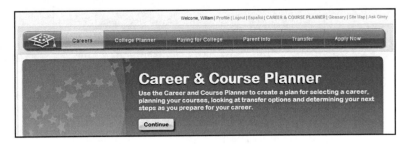

Once the student is in the Career and Course Planner, the first screen they will see is the Intake screen. This will populate student information from SIS on the right hand side of the screen, and display their first semester of enrollment, with a drop down menu to allow the student to select their anticipated graduation date. Once completed, the student can click save to move to the next step.

The next section of the Career and Course Planner focuses on the careers a student is interested in pursuing. Any careers that have been saved to the student's Wizard profile are automatically imported into the Career and Course Planner. Additionally, if the student would like to add more courses, they can do so using the drop down menus in this section.

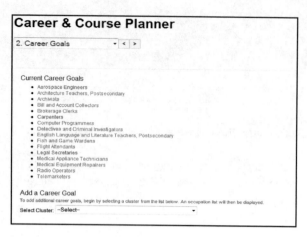

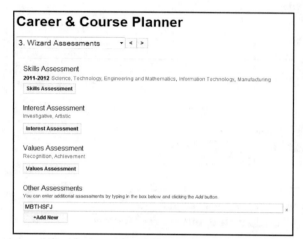

The third section of the Career and Course Planner imports the Career Assessments available in the Wizard. Once students have completed any of the assessments in the Wizard, the results will import into their Career and Course Plan. If the student has not completed the assessments, they can click on the gray boxes and be taken to that assessment page in the Wizard.

The Career and Course Planner now asks a student about whether or not they intend to transfer to another institution. If no transfer is intended, the student can move on to the next section. However, if a student is considering a transfer option, they should complete the postsecondary goals, colleges and universities of interest and the transfer planner checklist.

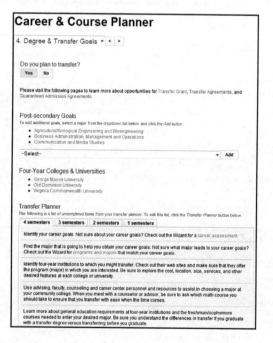

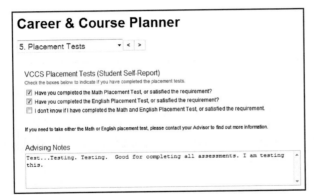

In the next step, students are prompted to answer whether or not they have completed the VCCS placement tests for Mathematics and English. There is also a third option if students are unsure whether they have satisfied that requirement. **This data is student self-reported, and is not directly pulled from their student academic record.**

Students have the ability to identify the courses they plan to take at the community college. By clicking on the gray link that says "Launch Peoplesoft Academic Advising," they will be taken into the Self Service section of Peoplesoft. In this screen, students can plan their future courses by semester in order to develop a "road map" leading toward completion of their program of study.

If a student is unsure of the semester in which they will take a course, they can list courses that are required in their program, and leave the semester as unassigned. The courses can be updated at any time, as a student's plans adapt and change. **Students can plan future courses in advance based on the future semesters their college has scheduled in Peoplesoft.**

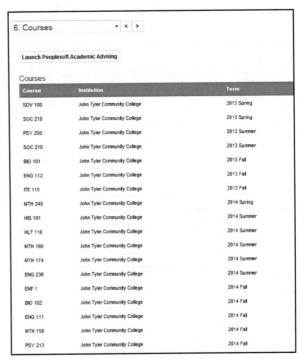

Under the Experiences section of the Planner, students have the ability to enter any organizations, leadership positions, internships, community service hours, or other relevant experience.

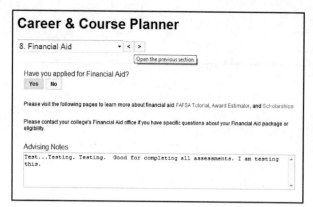

It is important for students to complete the financial aid process in order to make themselves eligible for federal, state and college financial aid resources. In this section of the Career and Course Plan, students are asked whether or not they have completed the Financial Aid process at their institution. If they select no, Financial Aid resources found within the Wizard will be made available to the student.

Students have the option to export their completed Career and Course Plan as a PDF document, allowing them to save it externally, print a copy, or upload it to Blackboard for a course assignment. Students also have the option to email a PDF copy of their Planner to anyone they would like, including instructors, counselors, family, or friends.

Below, please find a sample completed Career and Course Planner. Students have the ability to use this planner throughout their enrollment with the VCCS. It can be used as a course requirement in SDV courses, as a component of academic advising, or in general career counseling conversations.

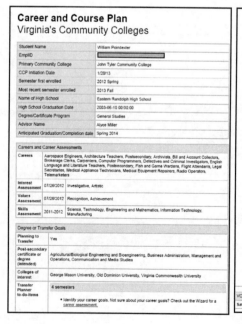

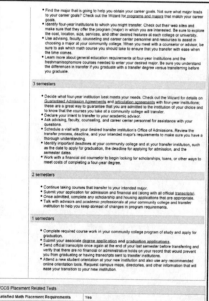

Case Study in Critical Thinking

THE LATE PAPER

Professor Freud announced in her syllabus for Psychology 101 that final term papers had to be in her hands by noon on December 18. No student, she emphasized, would pass the course without a completed term paper turned in on time. As the semester drew to a close, **Kim** had an "A" average in Professor Freud's psychology class, and she began researching her term paper with excitement.

Arnold, Kim's husband, felt threatened that he had only a high school diploma while his wife was getting close to her college degree. Arnold worked the evening shift at a bakery, and his coworker **Philip** began teasing that Kim would soon dump Arnold for a college guy. That's when Arnold started accusing Kim of having an affair and demanding she drop out of college. She told Arnold he was being ridiculous. In fact, she said, a young man in her history class had asked her out, but she had refused. Instead of feeling better, Arnold became even more angry. With Philip continuing to provoke him, Arnold became sure Kim was having an affair, and he began telling her every day that she was stupid and would never get a degree.

Despite the tension at home, Kim finished her psychology term paper the day before it was due. Since Arnold had hidden the car keys and Professor Freud refused to accept assignments sent by email, Kim decided to take the bus to the college and turn in her psychology paper a day early. While she was waiting for the bus, **Cindy**, one of Kim's psychology classmates, drove up and invited Kim to join her and some other students for an end-of-semester celebration. Kim told Cindy she was on her way to turn in her term paper, and Cindy promised she'd make sure Kim got it in on time. "I deserve some fun," Kim decided, and hopped into the car. The celebration went long into the night. Kim kept asking Cindy to take her home, but Cindy always replied, "Don't be such a bore. Have another drink." When Cindy finally took Kim home, it was 4:30 in the morning. She sighed with relief when she found that Arnold had already fallen asleep.

When Kim woke up, it was 11:30 a.m., just 30 minutes before her term paper was due. She could make it to the college in time by car, so she shook Arnold and begged him to drive her. He just snapped, "Oh sure, you stay out all night with your college friends. Then, I'm supposed to get up on my day off and drive you all over town. Forget it." "At least give me the keys," she said, but Arnold merely rolled over and went back to sleep. Panicked, Kim called Professor Freud's office and told **Mary**, the administrative assistant, that she was having car trouble. "Don't worry," Mary assured Kim, "I'm sure Professor Freud won't care if your paper's a little late. Just be sure to have it here before she leaves at 1:00." Relieved, Kim decided not to wake Arnold again; instead, she took the bus.

At 12:15, Kim walked into Professor Freud's office with her term paper. Professor Freud said, "Sorry, Kim, you're 15 minutes late." She refused to accept Kim's term paper and gave Kim an "F" for the course.

Listed below are the characters in this story. Rank them in order of their *responsibility for Kim's failing grade in Psychology 101*. Give a different score to each character. Be prepared to explain your choices.

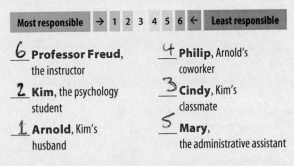

Most responsible → 1 2 3 4 5 6 ← Least responsible

6 **Professor Freud,** the instructor

2 **Kim,** the psychology student

1 **Arnold,** Kim's husband

4 **Philip,** Arnold's coworker

3 **Cindy,** Kim's classmate

5 **Mary,** the administrative assistant

▶ **DIVING DEEPER** Is there someone not mentioned in the story who may also bear responsibility for Kim's failing grade?

Case Study in Critical Thinking

POPSON'S DILEMMA

Fresh from graduate school, Assistant Professor Popson was midway through his first semester of college teaching when he began to get discouraged. Long gone were the excitement and promise of the first day of class. Now, only about two-thirds of his students were attending, and some of them were barely holding on. When Popson asked a question during class, the same few students answered every time. The rest stared off in bored silence. One student always wore a knit cap with a slender cord slithering from under it to an iPod in his shirt pocket. With 10 or even 15 minutes remaining in a class period, students would start stuffing notebooks noisily into their backpacks or book bags. Only one student had visited him during office hours, despite Popson's numerous invitations. And when he announced one day that he was canceling the next class to attend a professional conference, a group in the back of the room pumped their fists in the air and hooted with glee. It pained Popson to have aroused so little academic motivation in his students, and he began asking experienced professors what he should do.

Professor Assante said, "Research says that about 70 percent of students enroll in college because they see the degree as their ticket to a good job and fat paycheck. And they're right. College grads earn nearly a million dollars more in their lives than high school grads. Show them how your course will help them graduate and prosper in the work world. After that, most of them will be model students."

Professor Buckley said, "Everyone wants the freedom to make choices affecting their lives, so have your students design personal learning contracts. Let each one choose assignments from a list of options you provide. Let them add their own choices if they want. Even have them pick the dates they'll turn in their assignments. Give them coupons that allow them to miss any three classes without penalty. Do everything you can to give them choices and put them in charge of their own

education. Once they see they're in control of their learning and you're here to help them, their motivation will soar."

Professor Chang said, "Deep down, everyone wants to make a difference. I just read a survey by the Higher Education Research Institute showing that two-thirds of first-year students believe it's essential or very important to help others. Find out what your students want to do to make a contribution. Tell them how your course will help them achieve those dreams. Even better, engage them in a service learning project. When they see how your course can help them live a life with real purpose, they'll be much more interested in what you're teaching."

Professor Donnelly said, "Let's be realistic. The best motivator for students is grades. It's the old carrot and stick. Start every class with a quiz and they'll get there on time. Take points off for absences and they'll attend regularly. Give extra points for getting assignments in on time. Reward every positive action with points and take off points when they screw up. When they realize they can get a good grade in your class by doing what's right, even the guy with the iPod will get involved."

Professor Egret said, "Most people work harder and learn better when they feel they're part of a team with a common goal, so help your students feel part of a community of learners. Give them interesting topics to talk about in pairs and small groups. Give them team assignments and group projects. Teach them how to work well in groups so everyone contributes their fair share. When your students start feeling like they belong and start caring about one another, you'll see their academic motivation go way up."

Professor Fanning said, "Your unmotivated students probably don't expect to pass your course, so they quit trying. Here's my suggestion: Assign a modest challenge at which they can all succeed if they do it. And every student *has* to do it. No exceptions. Afterward, give students specific feedback on what they did well and what they can do to improve. Then give them a slightly more challenging assignment and repeat the cycle again and again. Help them *expect* to be successful by *being* successful. At some point they're going to say, 'Hey, I can do this!' and then you'll see a whole different attitude."

Professor Gonzales said, "Learning should be active and fun. I'm not talking about a party; I'm talking engaging students in educational experiences that teach deep and important lessons about your subject. Your students should be thinking, 'I can't wait to get to class to see what we're going to do and learn today!' You can use debates, videos, field trips, group projects, case studies, learning games, simulations, role plays, guest speakers, visualizations . . . the possibilities are endless. When learning is engaging and enjoyable, motivation problems disappear."

Professor Harvey said, "I've been teaching for 30 years, and if there's one thing I've learned, it's this: You can't motivate someone else. Maybe you've heard the old saying, 'When the student is ready, the teacher will arrive.' You're just wasting your energy trying to make someone learn before they're ready. Maybe they'll be back in your class in five or ten years and

they'll be motivated. But for now, just do the best you can for the students who *are* ready."

Listed below are the eight professors in this story. Based on your experience, rank the quality of their advice on the scale below. Give a different score to each professor. Be prepared to explain your choices.

| Best advice | ← 1 2 3 4 5 6 7 8 → | Worst advice |

___ **Professor Assante**   ___ **Professor Egret**

___ **Professor Buckley**   ___ **Professor Fanning**

___ **Professor Chang**   ___ **Professor Gonzales**

___ **Professor Donnelly**   ___ **Professor Harvey**

▶ **DIVING DEEPER** Is there an approach not mentioned by one of the eight professors that would be even more motivating for you?

LEARNING
BY SEEING, HEARING, AND MOVING: the VAK system

Alternatively, you can approach the topic of learning styles with a simple and powerful system—one that focuses on just three ways of perceiving through your senses:

- Seeing, or visual learning
- Hearing, or auditory learning
- Movement, or kinesthetic learning

To recall this system, remember the letters **VAK**, which stand for **visual**, **auditory**, and **kinesthetic**. The theory is that each of us prefers to learn through one of these senses. And we can enrich our learning with activities that draw on the other channels.

To reflect on your VAK preferences, answer the following questions. Each question has three possible answers. Circle the answer that best describes how you would respond in the stated situation. This is not a formal inventory—just a way to prompt some self-discovery.

When you have problems spelling a word, you prefer to:
1. Look it up in the dictionary.
2. Say the word out loud several times before you write it down.
3. Write out the word with several different spellings and then choose one.

You enjoy courses the most when you get to:
1. View slides, overhead displays, videos, and readings with plenty of charts, tables, and illustrations.
2. Ask questions, engage in small-group discussions, and listen to guest speakers.
3. Take field trips, participate in lab sessions, or apply the course content while working as a volunteer or intern.

When giving someone directions on how to drive to a destination, you prefer to:
1. Pull out a piece of paper and sketch a map.
2. Give verbal instructions.
3. Say, "I'm driving to a place near there, so just follow me."

When planning an extended vacation to a new destination, you prefer to:
1. Read colorful, illustrated brochures or articles about that place.
2. Talk directly to someone who's been there.
3. Spend a day or two at that destination on a work-related trip before taking a vacation there.

You've made a commitment to learn to play the guitar. The first thing you do is:
1. Go to a library or music store and find an instruction book with plenty of diagrams and chord charts.
2. Pull out your favorite CDs, listen closely to the guitar solos, and see whether you can play along with them.
3. Buy or borrow a guitar, pluck the strings, and ask someone to show you how to play a few chords.

You've saved up enough money to lease a car. When choosing from among several new models, the most important factor in your decision is:
1. Reading information about the car from sources like *Consumer Reports*.
2. The information you get by talking to people who own the cars you're considering.
3. The overall impression you get by taking each car on a test drive.

You've just bought a new computer system. When setting up the system, the first thing you do is:
1. Skim through the printed instructions that come with the equipment.
2. Call someone with a similar system and ask her for directions.
3. Assemble the components as best as you can, see whether everything works, and consult the instructions only as a last resort.

You get a scholarship to study abroad next semester, which starts in just three months. You will travel to a country where French is the most widely spoken language. To learn as much French as you can before you depart, you:
1. Buy a video-based language course that's recorded on a DVD.
2. Set up tutoring sessions with a friend who's fluent in French.
3. Sign up for a short immersion course in an environment in which you speak only French, starting with the first class.

Now take a few minutes to reflect on the meaning of your responses. All of the answers numbered "1" are examples of visual learning. The "2's" refer to auditory learning, and the "3's" illustrate kinesthetic learning. Finding a consistent pattern in your answers indicates that you prefer learning through one sense channel more than the others. Or you might find that your preferences are fairly balanced.

Listed here are suggestions for learning through each sense channel. Experiment with these examples, and create more techniques of your own. Use the suggestions to build on your current preferences and develop new options for learning.

TO ENHANCE VISUAL LEARNING:
- Preview reading assignments by looking for elements that are highlighted visually—bold headlines, charts, graphs, illustrations, and photographs.
- When taking notes in class, leave plenty of room to add your own charts, diagrams, tables, and other visuals later.
- Whenever an instructor writes information on a blackboard or overhead display, copy it exactly in your notes.
- Transfer your handwritten notes to your computer. Use word-processing software that allows you to format your notes in lists, add headings in different fonts, and create visuals in color.
- Before you begin an exam, quickly sketch a diagram on scratch paper. Use this diagram to summarize the key formulas or facts you want to remember.
- During tests, see whether you can visualize pages from your handwritten notes or images from your computer-based notes.

TO ENHANCE AUDITORY LEARNING:
- Reinforce memory of your notes and readings by talking about them. When studying, stop often to recite key points and examples in your own words.

- After reciting several summaries of key points and examples, record your favorite version or write it out.
- Read difficult passages in your textbooks slowly and out loud.
- Join study groups, and create short presentations about course topics.
- Visit your instructors during office hours to ask questions.

TO ENHANCE KINESTHETIC LEARNING:

- Look for ways to translate course content into three-dimensional models that you can build. While studying biology, for example, create a model of a human cell using different colors of clay.

- Supplement lectures with trips to museums, field observations, lab sessions, tutorials, and other hands-on activities.
- Recite key concepts from your courses while you walk or exercise.
- Intentionally set up situations in which you can learn by trial and error.
- Create a practice test, and write out the answers in the room where you will actually take the exam.

One variation of the VAK system has been called VARK.[4] The *R* describes a preference for learning by reading and writing. People with this preference might benefit from translating charts and diagrams into statements, taking notes in lists, and converting those lists into possible items on a multiple-choice test. ■

Master Students
IN ACTION

You're One Click Away...
from a video about Master Students in Action.

"*At the beginning of the term, I would have said that I learned best by doing (hands-on). But now that I have grown and expanded the boundaries of my mind's learning capabilities, I learn best with a mixture of all three (watching, listening, and doing). This is because I have come to realize that all three types of learning are connected through a balance; leading one to discover the "perfect" method of learning.*"

—Deondré Lucas, Valencia
Community College

Choosing your purpose

S uccess is a choice—your choice. To *get* what you want, it helps to *know* what you want. That is the purpose of this two-part Journal Entry. You can begin choosing success by completing this Journal Entry right now. If you choose to do it later, then plan a date, time, and place and then block out the time on your calendar.

1

Date: _____ Time: _____ Place: _____

Part 1

Select a time and place when you know you will not be disturbed for at least 20 minutes. (The library is a good place to do this exercise.) Relax for two or three minutes, clearing your mind. Next, complete the following sentences—and then keep writing. When you run out of things to write, stick with it just a bit longer. Be willing to experience a little discomfort. Keep writing. What you discover might be well worth the extra effort.

What I want from my education is . . . _____

_____

When I complete my education, I want to be able to . . . _____

_____

I also want . . . _____

_____

_____

_____

Part 2

After completing Part 1, take a short break. Reward yourself by doing something that you enjoy. Then come back to this Journal Entry.

Now, review the list you just created of things that you want from your education. See whether you can summarize them in one sentence. Start this sentence with "My purpose for being in school is. . . ." Allow yourself to write many drafts of this mission statement, and review it periodically as you continue your education. With each draft, see whether you can capture the essence of what you want from higher education and from your life. State it in a vivid way—in a short sentence that you can easily memorize, one that sparks your enthusiasm and makes you want to get up in the morning.

You might find it difficult to express your purpose statement in one sentence. If so, write a paragraph or more. Then look for the sentence that seems most charged with energy for you. Following are some sample purpose statements:

- My purpose for being in school is to gain skills that I can use to contribute to others.

- My purpose for being in school is to live an abundant life that is filled with happiness, health, love, and wealth.

- My purpose for being in school is to enjoy myself by making lasting friendships and following the lead of my interests.

Write at least one draft of your purpose statement here:

_____

_____

_____

_____